Contents

Lamb, Date, + Walnut Stew 10
North African Osso Buco 10
Roasted Red Pepper + Eggplant Dip 11
Quinoa Tabbouleh 12
Pressure Cooker Hummus 13
Chinese Pork Belly 13
Mango Dal 14
Easy Filipino Chicken Adobo 15
Chicken Curry 15
Chickpea Curry 16
Arroz con Pollo 17
Coconut Chicken Curry 18
Spicy Mahi-Mahi w/ Honey + Orange 19
Pork Fried Rice 19
Hawaiian Pork 20
Spicy Barbacoa 21
Beef + Tortilla Casserole 22
Flank Steak w/ Sweet Potato Gravy 23
Beef Brisket w/ Veggies 23
Sweet-Spicy Meatloaf 24
Pressure Cooker Pot Roast 25
Teriyaki Short Ribs 26
Beefy Lasagna 26
Corned Beef + Cabbage in Spiced Cider 27
Top Round w/ Bacon, Bourbon, + Potatoes 28
Corn Pudding 29
Beets w/ Goat Cheese 29
Brown-Butter Fingerling Potatoes 30
.... 31
.... 31
.... 32

- Whole-Wheat Mac 'n Cheese 33
- Classic Potato Salad 34
- Broccoli Pesto 34
- Cranberry Sauce 35
- Italian-Style Meat Sauce 35
- Homemade BBQ Sauce 36
- Goat Cheese Mashed Potatoes 37
- Butternut Squash 38
- Brown-Sugar Carrots 38
- Quick Baked Potatoes 39
- Buttery Orange Brussels Sprouts 39
- Red Beans 40
- Simple Spaghetti Squash 41
- Cheesy Potatoes 41
- Steamed Crab Legs w/ Garlic Butter 42
- Tuna Noodles 42
- White Fish w/ Beer and Potatoes 43
- Spicy Lemon Salmon 44
- One-Pot Shrimp Scampi 44
- Seafood Gumbo 45
- Scallop Chowder 45
- Shrimp + Corn Stew 46
- Clam Rolls 47
- Lobster Casserole 48
- Vegan Strawberries + Cream Oats 49
- Buckwheat Porridge w/ Rice Milk 49
- Vegan Yogurt 50
- No-Dairy Mashed Potatoes 50
- Minestrone Soup 51
- Three-Bean Chili 51
- Vegan Feijoada 52
- Spicy-Sweet Braised Cabbage 53
- Chipotle-Pumpkin Soup 54
- Sweet Potato + Kidney Bean Stew 54

Vegan Taco Mix	55
Spaghetti Squash Lasagna w/ Cashew Cheese Sauce	56
Black-Eyed Peas + Kale Bowl	57
Sweet Potato Peanut Butter Soup	58
Vegan Chocolate Cheesecake	59
Chocolate-Chip Zucchini Bread w/ Walnuts	60
Chocolate-Chip Cheesecake w/ Brownie Crust	60
Graham-Cracker Crust Lemon Cheesecake	62
Greek Yogurt Cheesecake	62
Ricotta + Ginger Cheesecake	63
Sea-Salt Dulce de Leche	64
Orange-Chocolate Bread Pudding	64
Mini Pumpkin Puddings	65
Blueberry-Peach Cobbler	66
Apple Dumplings	67
Creamy Rice Pudding w/ Golden Raisins	67
Red-Wine Baked Apples	68
Cinnamon-Crumble Stuffed Peaches	69
Individual Brownie Cakes	69
Homemade Yogurt	70
Sweet 'n Easy Peachy-Cream Oatmeal	71
Cheesy Egg Bake	71
Berry Breakfast Cake	72
Mushroom-Thyme Steel Cut Oats	73
Vanilla Latte Oatmeal	74
Tomato-Spinach Quiche	74
Homemade Bacon Hash Browns	75
Breakfast Burritos	76
Coconut Steel-Cut Oatmeal	76
Huevos Rancheros	77
Stone-Ground Cheesy Grits	77
Cranberry-Apple Chicken w/ Cabbage	78
Chicken Pot "Pie"	79
Chipotle Chicken w/ Rice and Black Beans	80

- Pressure Cooker Chicken Lo Mein ... 80
- Easy Teriyaki Chicken ... 81
- Honey-Sesame Chicken ... 82
- Chicken Alfredo w/ Broccoli ... 83
- Chicken, Black Bean, and Rice Bowl ... 84
- Chicken and Cornbread Stuffing ... 85
- Homemade Chicken + Gravy ... 85
- Easy Orange Chicken ... 86
- Pulled Turkey w/ BBQ Mustard Sauce ... 87
- Smoked Turkey + Black Bean Soup ... 88
- Cranberry-Spiced Beef Roast ... 89
- Maple-Balsamic Beef ... 89
- Teriyaki-Garlic Flank Steak ... 90
- Beef Stroganoff ... 91
- Freezer Pulled Pepper Steak ... 92
- Ground Beef, Potato, and Kale Soup ... 92
- Smoky-Maple Brisket ... 93
- Classic Spaghetti and Meatballs ... 94
- Pressure Cooker Jambalaya ... 94
- Coney Island-Style Chili ... 95
- Cuban-Style Braised Beef ... 96
- Stuffed Flank Steak ... 97
- Pineapple-Pork Stew ... 97
- Apple-Cherry Pork Loin ... 98
- Honey Pork Chops w/ Ginger ... 99
- Jerk-Style Pork Roast ... 100
- Pork Chops w/ Hong-Kong Tomato Sauce ... 100
- Citrus-Garlic Shredded Pork ... 101
- Bacon-Wrapped Ribeye Steak ... 102
- Asian Pork Chops ... 103
- Apricot-BBQ Pork Roast ... 104
- Pork-Rib Stew ... 104
- Pork Shoulder w/ Dr. Pepper BBQ Sauce ... 105
- Pork Medallions with Cremini Mushrooms ... 106

Easy Baby-Back Ribs	107
Pasta w/ Sausage + Bacon	107
Sausage + Peppers	108
Simple Lemon-Dill Cod w/ Broccoli	109
Southern Shrimp Boil	109
5-Minute Alaskan Cod	110
Cajun-Style Shrimp w/ Broth	110
Shrimp + Spinach Risotto	111
Roasted Rosemary-Shrimp Risotto	112
Lobster Tails	113
Orange-Ginger White Fish	113
Creole-Style Cod	114
Pressure Cooker Cod w/ Mango Salsa	115
Creamy-Tomato Haddock w/ Potatoes, Kale, and Carrots	116
Cod Fillets w/ Almonds and Peas	116
Halibut w/ Dijon-Mustard Sauce	117
Tapioca Parfait w/ Berries	118
Butternut-Squash Apple Butter	119
Black Bean Chili	119
Easy Chickpea Curry	120
Lasagna Soup	121
Coconut-Milk Corn Chowder	122
White Vegetable Stew	123
Curried Pear and Squash Soup	123
Rainbow Soup	124
Lemon Polenta w/ Chickpeas and Asparagus	125
Vegan Brazilian Potato Salad	126
Easy Seitan (Vegan Meat Substitute)	126
Pressure Cooker Garlic Broth	127
Sweet 'n Sour Mango Chicken	128
Red Chicken Soup	129
Chicken Drumstick Soup	130
Mexi-Meatloaf	130
Beef + Broccoli Soup	131

Beef + Plantain Curry	132
Easy Beef Stew	133
Bone Broth	133
Creamy Cabbage w/ Bacon	134
Crunchy Corn Niblets	134
Pressure Cooker Cornbread	135
Apple Crisp	135
Two-Ingredient Chocolate Fondue	136
Cranberry Bread Pudding w/ Bourbon Sauce	137
Crème brûlée	138
Orange Marble Cheesecake	138
Cinnamon-Poached Pears w/ Warm Chocolate Sauce	139
Samoa Cheesecake	140
Sugar-Pumpkin Pie Filling	141
Mango Cake	142
Chocolate-Chocolate Cheesecake	143
Key Lime Pie	144
Cheesy Egg Bake	145
Creamy Eggs with Prosciutto	145
Coconut Milk Steel-Cut Oats	146
Freeze-Dried Strawberry Oats	147
Homemade Vanilla Yogurt	147
Peach + Cream Oatmeal	148
Blackberry-Coconut Breakfast Quinoa	148
Freezer Egg-and-Sausage Burritos	149
Huevos Rancheros	150
Honey-Chili Chicken Wings	150
Cranberry Chicken	151
BBQ Chicken Sandwiches	151
Lemon-Coconut Chicken	152
White Balsamic-Braised Game Hens	152
Cream-of-Mushroom Cheddar Chicken	153
Chicken + Cornbread Stuffing	154
Honey-Balsamic Chicken Drumsticks	154

French Onion Pork Chops 155

Easiest Southern Pork-Sausage Gravy 155

Blueberry-Coconut Pork Roast 156

Shredded BBQ Pork 157

Pork Tenderloin with Apples + Onion 157

Brown-Sugar Baked Ham 158

Jamaican-Jerk Pork Roast 159

Sweet Sausage + Peppers 159

Simple Pork Belly 160

Basic Beef Picadillo 160

Beef Ribs 161

Shredded Pepper Steak 161

Top Round Beef Roast with Bourbon Potatoes 162

Easiest Pot Roast 163

Italian Beef 163

Easy Teriyaki Beef 164

Sprouted Rice + Quinoa 164

Broccoli Cheese Rice 165

Pineapple Brown Rice 165

Turkey Verde Rice 166

Pasta with Meat Sauce 166

Chicken Alfredo Pasta 167

Simple Salmon + Broccoli 168

Lemon-Thyme Halibut 168

Halibut-Salsa Packets with Artichoke Hearts 169

Easy Alaskan Cod with Cherry Tomatoes 169

Crab Legs with Garlic-Butter Sauce 170

Spicy Sockeye Salmon 170

Lemon-Ginger Cod with Mixed Frozen Veggies 171

Salmon Steaks 172

Lobster Tails 172

Balsamic Mushrooms 173

Bacon Ranch Potatoes 173

Smashed Sweet Potato with Ginger Butter 174

Spaghetti Squash with Apple Juice Glaze	174
Butternut Squash with Sage-Infused Butter	175
Prosciutto-Wrapped Asparagus	176
Carrots with Bacon + Butter	176
Corn with Cilantro Butter	177
Sweet Potato Puree	177
Balsamic Brussels Sprouts with Bacon	178
Whole White Beets + Beet Greens	179
Zucchini-Ricotta Bites	179
Cranapple (Cranberry + Apple) Sauce	180
Garlic Roasted Potatoes	180
2-Minute Steamed Asparagus	181
Stewed Tomatoes + Green Beans	182
Cheesy Stone-Ground Grits	182
Green Beans + Mushrooms	183
Vegan Apple Spice Oats	183
Blueberry-Buckwheat Porridge	184
Vegan Italian Tofu Scramble	184
Lentil + Potato Soup	185
Spiced-Carrot Chilled Soup	185
Spiced Cauliflower Rice	186
Vegan Alfredo Sauce	187
Vegan Holiday Roast	187
Vegan Mashed Potatoes	188
Mexican Casserole	188
Easy Seitan (Vegan Meat Substitute)	189
Tapioca with Fresh Berries	189
Cranberry-Almond Quinoa	190
Sweet Thai Coconut Rice	190
Coconut-Cream Chocolate Fondue	191
Potato Soup	191
White Chicken Chili	192
Chicken Congee	193
Hearty Chicken Stew	193

Beef + Broccoli Soup	194
Split Asparagus Soup	194
Apple Dumpling Cobbler	195
Tapioca Pudding	196
Peach Simple Syrup	196
Lemon-Ruby Pears	197
Pear Sauce	198
Fresh Raspberry Jam	198
Granola-Stuffed Peaches	199
Apple Cider	199
Orange-Glazed Poached Pears	200
Pumpkin Butter	201
Chai Rice Pudding	201
Peach Cobbler	202
Almond Fudge Drop Candy	202
Homemade Vanilla Yogurt	203
Steel-Cut Oats	203
Easy Soft-Boiled Egg Breakfast	204
Maple-Syrup Quinoa	204
French Toast Bake	205
Cheesy Sausage Frittata	205
Creamy Strawberry Oatmeal	206
Creamy Banana Oatmeal	206
Ham, Apple, and Grits Casserole	207
Savory Breakfast Porridge	208
Blueberry Croissant Pudding	209
Sticky Sesame Chicken	209

Lamb, Date, + Walnut Stew

Serves: 4
Time: 50 minutes

Ingredients:
- 2 ½ pounds boneless leg of lamb
- 1 thinly-sliced red onion
- 1 cup pitted dried dates, cut in half
- ½ cup chicken broth
- ½ cup walnuts
- ½ cup unsweetened apple juice
- 2 tablespoons olive oil
- ½ tablespoon ground cinnamon
- 1 teaspoon ground ginger
- ½ teaspoon salt
- ¼ teaspoon grated nutmeg
- ¼ teaspoon allspice

Directions:
1. Mix ginger, cinnamon, allspice, nutmeg, and salt in a bowl.
2. Coat the lamb in the spices.
3. Turn your pressure cooker to "Sauté" and heat the olive oil.
4. When shiny, add the onion and soften for 5 minutes.
5. Add the meat into the pot and brown.
6. Toss in the dates, walnuts, apple juice, and broth, and deglaze.
7. Close and lock the lid.
8. Press "Manual," and then 38 minutes on "high pressure."
9. When the timer goes off, hit "Cancel" and let the pressure go down naturally.
10. Open the lid and stir.
11. Serve!

Nutritional Info (¼ recipe):
Total calories: 897 Protein: 76 Carbs: 23 Fiber: 1 Fat: 57

North African Osso Buco

Serves: 4
Time: 1 hour, 20 minutes (+ four hours marinade time)

Ingredients:
- 4 pounds of veal shank (four separate shanks)
- 1 big onion, sliced very thin
- 1 cup white wine
- 14-ounce can of diced tomatoes
- 1 medium-sized lemon, cut into quarters

- 2 tablespoons minced garlic
- 2 tablespoons butter
- 2 tablespoons olive oil
- 2 tablespoons grated lemon zest
- One, 4-inch cinnamon stick
- ½ teaspoon ground ginger
- ½ teaspoon salt
- ½ teaspoon ground allspice
- ½ teaspoon ground cardamom
- ½ teaspoon ground turmeric
- ½ teaspoon grated nutmeg

Directions:
1. In a bowl, mix oil, garlic, salt, and olive oil.
2. Rub all over the meat.
3. Plate meat, cover with plastic wrap, and store in fridge for at least 4 hours.
4. In your pressure cooker, melt the butter on "Sauté."
5. Add veal in batches and brown for about 8 minutes.
6. Add the onion and soften for 4 minutes.
7. Toss in the ginger, cardamom, allspice, turmeric, and nutmeg.
8. Cook until the spices become fragrant.
9. Pour in the wine and deglaze, letting it come to a boil.
10. Return the meat to the pot, along with the tomatoes.
11. Toss in the cinnamon stick and quartered lemon.
12. Secure the lid.
13. Hit "Manual," and then select "high pressure" for 50 minutes.
14. When time is up, hit "Cancel" and wait for a natural-pressure release.
15. Open the pot.
16. Pick out the cinnamon stick before serving.

Nutritional Info (¼ recipe): Total calories - 444 Protein - 73 Carbs - 11 Fiber - 2.8 Fat - 10

Roasted Red Pepper + Eggplant Dip

Serves: 6-8
Time: 20 minutes

Ingredients:
- 2 pounds eggplant cut into 1-inch chunks
- 4 minced garlic cloves
- ¼ chopped roasted red peppers
- 5 tablespoons olive oil
- 1 cup water
- 5 tablespoons lemon juice
- 1 tablespoon tahini
- 1 tablespoon cumin

- 1 teaspoon salt
- Black pepper

Directions:
1. Turn your pressure cooker to "Sauté."
2. Pour in 3 tablespoons of olive oil.
3. Add half of the eggplant and brown on one side for about 4 minutes.
4. Take out the eggplant and pour in another tablespoon of oil.
5. Add garlic and the rest of the unbrowned eggplant.
6. Cook 1 minute before adding the browned eggplant back into the pot, along with water and salt.
7. Close and lock the lid.
8. Press "Manual" and 3 minutes on "high pressure."
9. When the timer goes off, hit "Cancel" and quick-release.
10. Add red peppers, stir, and let them warm up.
11. After 5 minutes, drain the cooking liquid.
12. Add the lemon juice, 1 tablespoon of oil, tahini, black pepper, and cumin.
13. Using a blender or food processor, puree till creamy.
14. Serve with pita or chips.

Nutritional Info: Total calories - 165 Protein - 3 Carbs - 12 Fiber - 6 Fat - 2

Quinoa Tabbouleh

Serves: 4-6
Time: 20 minutes

Ingredients:
- 1 ⅔ cups water
- 1 cup rinsed and drained quinoa
- 1 chopped tomato
- 1 chopped cucumber
- Juice of 1 lemon
- 1 minced garlic clove
- ½ cup chopped mint
- 2 tablespoons olive oil
- Salt + pepper

Directions:
1. Pour water, quinoa, 1 tablespoon of oil, and salt into the pressure cooker.
2. Close the lid.
3. Press "Manual" and 1 minute on "high pressure."
4. When time is up, hit "Cancel" and wait for pressure to release naturally.
5. Move the quinoa to a bowl to cool.
6. Mix in the cucumber, tomato, garlic, mint, lemon juice, and 1 tablespoon of oil.
7. Season to taste with salt and pepper.
8. Serve!

Nutritional Info: Total calories - 256 Protein - 8 Carbs - 35 Fiber - 4 Fat – 1

Pressure Cooker Hummus

Serves: 8-10
Time: 1 hour, 10 minutes

- 4 cups water
- 8 ounces rinsed and dried chickpeas
- 3 minced garlic cloves
- 6 tablespoons olive oil
- ⅓ cup tahini
- ¼ cup lemon juice
- 1 ½ teaspoons salt
- ½ teaspoon smoked paprika

Directions:
1. Add water, chickpeas, and 2 tablespoons of olive oil to the pressure cooker.
2. Close and lock the lid.
3. Hit "Manual" and select "high pressure" for 45 minutes.
4. When time is up, hit "Cancel" and wait for the pressure to decrease naturally.
5. The chickpeas should be soft, but not mushy.
6. Drain the chickpeas, saving one cup of cooking liquid.
7. Put the chickpeas in a food processor and puree with 4 tablespoons of olive oil, salt, garlic, lemon juice, paprika, and ¼ cup of cooking liquid.
8. Add additional liquid to get the texture you want.
9. The hummus will last up to five days covered in the fridge.

Nutritional Info: Total calories - 264 Protein - 8 Carbs - 20 Fiber - 6 Fat - 3

Chinese Pork Belly

Serves: 4
Time: About 40 minutes

Ingredients:
- 2 pounds of pork belly sliced into 5-inch pieces
- 2 cups water
- ½ cup soy sauce
- 6 sliced garlic cloves
- 5 slices fresh ginger
- 4 star anise
- 3 tablespoons Chinese cooking wine
- 2 teaspoons cane sugar
- 1 teaspoon ground white pepper

Directions:
1. Turn on your pressure cooker to "sauté" and add a little oil.
2. When shiny, sear the pork belly slices on both sides, which should take about 2 minutes per side.

3. Throw in the garlic and ginger.
4. Cook and stir for another 5 minutes.
5. Add in the rest of the ingredients and lock the pressure cooker.
6. Select "Manual," and then cook for 30 minutes.
7. Press "Cancel" and quick-release the pressure when the timer goes off.
8. The pork belly should be extremely tender.
9. Serve with rice and veggies.

Nutritional Info (¼ recipe): Total calories - 365 Protein - 24.5 Carbs - 7 Fiber - 0 Fat – 30

Mango Dal

Serves: 4-6
Time: About 50 minutes

Ingredients:
- 4 cups chicken broth
- 1 cup chana dal
- 2 peeled and diced mangoes
- 4 minced garlic cloves
- ½ cup chopped cilantro
- 1 minced onion
- 1 tablespoon minced ginger
- 1 tablespoon coconut oil
- Juice from ½ lime
- 1 teaspoon ground cumin
- 1 teaspoon sea salt
- 1 teaspoon ground coriander
- 1 teaspoon ground turmeric
- ⅛ teaspoon cayenne pepper

Directions:
1. Rinse the dal in a colander.
2. Turn the pressure cooker to "sauté" and heat coconut oil.
3. Add the cumin and cook for about 30 seconds.
4. Toss in the onion and cook for 5 minutes, until soft.
5. Next, add the coriander, ginger, cayenne, garlic, and salt.
6. Pour in the broth and add the dal and turmeric.
7. Keep the pot on "sauté" and bring the contents to a boil.
8. It should boil for about 10 minutes. If it gets foamy, skim it off with a large spoon.
9. Add the mangoes.
10. Secure the lid and hit "Beans/Chili," and then 20 minutes.
11. When time is up, hit "Cancel" and wait for the pressure to reduce naturally.
12. Add the lime juice and cilantro.
13. Serve with rice.

Nutritional Info (¼ recipe): Total calories - 486 Protein - 21 Carbs - 91 Fiber - 11 Fat - 3

Easy Filipino Chicken Adobo

Serves: 5-6
Time: About 15 minutes

Ingredients:
- 4-5 pounds of chicken thighs
- 4 crushed garlic cloves
- 3 bay leaves
- ½ cup soy sauce
- ½ cup white vinegar
- 1 teaspoon black peppercorns

Directions:
1. Throw everything in the pressure cooker and secure the lid.
2. Hit "Poultry" and adjust to 15 minutes.
3. When ready, quick-release.
4. Serve with Nishiki white rice.

Nutritional Info (⅕ recipe): Total calories - 526 Protein - 90 Carbs - 9 Fiber - 0 Fat - 14

Chicken Curry

Serves: 6
Time: 15 minutes + 1 hour marinade

Ingredients:
- 6 boneless chicken breasts
- 2 tablespoons olive oil
- 1 chopped tomato
- 1 yellow onion
- 2 teaspoons garam masala powder
- 1 teaspoon grated ginger
- 1 teaspoon chili powder
- 1 teaspoon coriander seeds
- Salt
- Juice of 1 lemon
- 2 teaspoons ginger powder
- 2 teaspoons coriander powder
- 2 teaspoons garlic powder
- 1 ¼ teaspoons chili powder
- ½ teaspoon turmeric
- Salt

Directions:
1. Mix the ingredients in the second list and rub over the chicken.

2. Place in a bag and chill in the fridge for an hour.
3. When ready, heat oil in the pressure cooker on "sauté."
4. Toss in the coriander seeds and heat them till a few pop open.
5. Add the chopped onion and cook till they become clear.
6. Add in the garam masala, coriander powder, chili powder, garlic, and ginger.
7. After a few minutes, add chopped tomatoes until they soften.
8. Take out the chicken and sauté to brown them a little.
9. Close the pot lid.
10. Choose "Poultry" and adjust to 8 minutes on "high pressure."
11. When ready, quick-release the pressure.
12. Serve with the tomatoes and onions, and rice.

Nutritional Info (⅙ recipe): Total calories - 234 Protein - 19.9 Carbs - 9.7 Fiber - 3 Fat - 12.7

Chickpea Curry

Serves: 3-4
Time: About 35 minutes + overnight soak

Ingredients:
- 2 cups dry chickpeas
- 1 can diced tomatoes
- 1 big, diced onion
- 4-6 tablespoons olive oil
- 2 tablespoons chholey masala
- 2-4 tablespoons lemon juice
- 1 tablespoon garlic paste
- 1 tablespoon ginger paste
- 1 teaspoon turmeric
- ½ teaspoon garam masala
- Coriander leaves
- Salt

Directions:
1. Soak the chickpeas in water in a bowl on the counter overnight.
2. The next day, pour 2 cups of water into your pressure cooker and hit "sauté."
3. When the water is boiling, add chickpeas.
4. Boil for 10 minutes.
5. When time is up, pour the peas and water into another bowl.
6. Heat oil in the pot.
7. Add garam masala and diced onion.
8. When clear, add turmeric.
9. Toss in ginger and garlic paste, and stir.
10. Add tomatoes and cook for a few minutes.
11. Add chholey masala.
12. Pour in chickpeas with their water.

13. Sprinkle in a little salt.
14. Close and secure the lid.
15. Hit "Manual" and then adjust to 20 minutes on "high pressure."
16. When the timer beeps, hit "Cancel" and wait for the pressure to reduce naturally.
17. Add coriander leaves and lemon juice before serving.

Nutritional Info (¼ recipe): Total calories - 177 Protein - 5.9 Carbs - 29 Fiber - 6.2 Fat -5

Arroz con Pollo

Serves: 6-8
Time: About 40 minutes (+ one hour soak time)

Ingredients:
- 12 boneless, skinless chicken thighs
- 3 chopped garlic cloves
- ¼ cup olive oil
- 3 tablespoons minced oregano
- 2 tablespoons lime juice
- 1 tablespoon salt
- 2 teaspoons cumin
- ½ teaspoon black pepper
- 3 garlic cloves
- ½ seeded and chopped green bell pepper
- ½ chopped yellow onion
- 1 bunch of cilantro
- ½ teaspoon salt
- ¼ teaspoon black pepper
- 5 cups chicken stock
- 3 cups long-grain brown rice
- 28-ounces of fire-roasted, diced tomatoes (with liquid)
- 1 ½ cups Spanish olives
- 1 seeded and diced bell pepper
- 2 tablespoons olive brine
- 2 tablespoons coconut oil
- 1 tablespoon minced oregano
- 1 teaspoon ground cumin
- ¼ teaspoon salt

Directions:
1. Mix the ingredients in the first list and coat the chicken with it. This should marinate for at least 1 hour.
2. To **Make** the sofrito, mix the ingredients in the second list in a food processor till smooth.
3. Turn your pressure cooker to "sauté" and melt the coconut oil.
4. Take out the chicken and brown, 5 minutes on each side.
5. Plate.

6. Toss in the onion, red bell pepper, cumin, and oregano (from the last ingredient list) into the pot and sauté till tender.
7. Stir in the sofrito and cook for 3 minutes.
8. Add the diced tomatoes, salt, and stock, and let everything simmer for 2 minutes.
9. Add the olives, olive brine, and rice.
10. Lastly, return the chicken to the cooker.
11. Lock the lid.
12. Hit "Meat/Stew" and adjust time to 15 minutes.
13. When the beeper goes off, hit "Cancel" and wait for the pressure to come down on its own.
14. Serve!

Nutritional Info (⅙ recipe): Total calories - 257 Protein - 13 Carbs - 28 Fiber - 1 Fat - 10

Coconut Chicken Curry

Serves: 6
Time: About 45-50 minutes

Ingredients:
- 6 peeled and halved shallots
- 4 whole cloves
- 4 little dried red chilies
- 3 green cardamom pods
- ¾ cup grated, unsweetened coconut
- 1-inch cinnamon stick
- 2 teaspoons black peppercorns
- 2 teaspoons fennel seeds
- 2 teaspoons coriander seeds
- 1 teaspoon cumin seeds
- 1 teaspoon brown mustard seeds
- 1 teaspoon turmeric powder
- 3 pounds boneless, skinless chicken thighs (cut into pieces)
- 1 tablespoon coconut oil
- 2 minced garlic cloves
- 2 sliced tomatoes
- 2 sliced yellow onions
- 1 inch minced ginger
- 1 tablespoon vinegar
- 3 teaspoons salt

Directions:
1. We'll tackle the first ingredient list right away. Turn on the pressure cooker to "Sauté."
2. Throw in the chiles and shallots, and roast until parts have blackened.
3. Carefully take them out with tongs and put them in a food processor bowl. Do not blend yet.
4. Add the shredded coconut and whole spices to the cooker and stir for 1 minute. The coconut should be a pale brown, and the spices fragrant and toasty.

5. Add the turmeric and stir for a few more seconds before moving everything to the food processor.
6. Pulse with 4-6 tablespoons of water until you get a paste.
7. Keep the paste in the bowl for now.
8. Return to the pressure cooker and add oil.
9. When shiny and hot, add the ginger, onions, and garlic.
10. Cook for 10-15 minutes until onions have softened and browned.
11. Add the coconut paste and cook for 1 minute.
12. Throw in the tomatoes and cook for 5 minutes.
13. Lastly, add the vinegar, salt, and chicken.
14. Stir everything before locking the pressure cooker lid.
15. Hit "Manual," and then adjust to 10 minutes on "high pressure."
16. When time is up, hit "Cancel" and wait for the pressure to come down.
17. Serve with plain yogurt and rice.

Nutritional Info (⅙ recipe): Total calories - 320 Protein - 47 Carbs - 5 Fiber - 4 Fat - 9

Spicy Mahi-Mahi w/ Honey + Orange

Serves: 2
Time: About 5-6 minutes

Ingredients:
- 2 mahi-mahi fillets
- 2 tablespoons sriracha
- 2 tablespoons honey
- Juice of ½ lime
- 2 minced garlic cloves
- 1-inch grated ginger piece
- 1 tablespoon Nanami Togarashi
- 1 tablespoon Simply Orange Mango juice
- Salt
- Pepper

Directions:
1. Season fish with salt and pepper.
2. In a bowl, mix honey, sriracha, OJ, lime juice, and Nanami Togarashi.
3. Pour 1 cup of water into the pressure cooker.
4. Lower in the steam rack and put the fillets inside.
5. Pour sauce on top of fish.
6. Secure the pressure cooker lid.
7. Hit "Manual" and adjust time to 5 minutes.
8. When the beeper goes off, quick-release the pressure.
9. Open the lid and serve with a side dish like rice pilaf or veggies.

Nutritional Info (½ recipe): Total calories - 229 Protein - 32 Carbs - 23 Fiber - 0 Fat - 1

Pork Fried Rice

Serves: 4
Time: 40 minutes

Ingredients:
- 3 cups + 2 tablespoons water
- 2 cups white rice
- 8-ounces thin pork loin, cut into ½-inch slices
- 1 beaten egg
- ½ cup frozen peas
- 1 chopped onion
- 1 peeled and chopped carrot
- 3 tablespoons olive oil
- 3 tablespoons soy sauce
- Salt + pepper

Directions:
1. Turn your pressure cooker to "Sauté."
2. Pour in 1 tablespoon of oil and cook the carrot and onion for 2 minutes.
3. Season the pork.
4. Cook in the pot for 5 minutes.
5. Hit "Cancel" and take out the onion, carrot, and pork.
6. Deglaze with the water.
7. Add rice and a bit of salt.
8. Lock the lid.
9. Hit "Rice" and cook for the default time.
10. When time is up, hit "Cancel" and wait 10 minutes.
11. Release any leftover steam.
12. Stir the rice, making a hollow in the middle so you can see the bottom of the pot.
13. Hit "Sauté" and add 2 tablespoons of oil.
14. Add the egg in the hollow and whisk it around to scramble it while it cooks.
15. When cooked, pour in peas, onion, carrot, and pork.
16. Stir until everything has warmed together.
17. Stir in soy sauce, hit "Cancel," and serve.

Nutritional Info (¼ recipe): Total calories - 547 Protein - 22 Carbs - 81 Fiber - 3 Fat - 2

Hawaiian Pork

Serves: 8
Time: 2 hours

Ingredients:
- 5 pounds bone-in pork roast
- 6 minced garlic cloves
- 1 cup water
- 1 quartered onion
- 1 ½ tablespoons red Hawaiian coarse salt

- Black pepper

Directions:
1. Cut the meat into 3 pieces.
2. Put in the pressure cooker.
3. Add in garlic, onion, and salt.
4. Season with black pepper.
5. Pour in the water and lock the lid.
6. Hit "Manual," and cook for 1 ½ hours on "high pressure."
7. When time is done, hit "Cancel," and wait for the pressure to decrease naturally.
8. Before serving, shred the pork with two forks.

Nutritional Info (⅛ recipe): Total calories - 536 Protein - 51 Carbs - 2 Fiber - 0 Fat – 13

Spicy Barbacoa

Serves: 4
Time: About 1 hour, 15 minutes

Ingredients:
- 2-3 pounds beef chuck roast
- 3 bay leaves
- 3 chipotle peppers + 1 tablespoon adobo sauce from can
- 1 cup beef broth
- Juice of ½ lime
- ⅓ cup apple cider vinegar
- 2 tablespoons cooking fat
- 1 ½ tablespoons ground cumin
- 1 ½ tablespoons salt
- 1 tablespoon black pepper
- 1 tablespoon tomato paste
- 2 teaspoons oregano
- 1 teaspoon onion powder
- 1 teaspoon cinnamon
- ¼ teaspoon ground cloves

Directions:
1. Turn your cooker to "Sauté."
2. Trim the beef and dry with a paper towel.
3. Season with ½ tablespoon salt and ½ tablespoon of pepper.
4. Put the fat in the pot and melt.
5. Add beef and sear all over.
6. In a blender, mix vinegar, peppers, adobo, lime juice, cumin, salt, pepper, tomato paste, onion powder, cloves, oregano, and cinnamon until smooth.
7. Pour the puree in the pot so the meat is covered.
8. Toss in the bay leaves and pour in broth.
9. Secure the lid and press "Manual," and then 50 minutes on "high pressure."

10. When time is up, press "Cancel" and wait for the pressure to come down naturally.
11. When the pressure is gone, open the pot and shred the meat.
12. Serve with the cooking liquid as a sauce.

Nutritional Info: Total calories - 165 Protein - 24 Carbs - 2 Fiber - 1 Fat - 7

Beef + Tortilla Casserole

Serves: 6
Time: About 45 minutes

Ingredients:
- 1 ¼ pounds lean ground beef
- 6 corn tortillas
- 14-ounces of crushed tomatoes
- 4 ½-ounces of mild green chiles (save the liquid!)
- 1 chopped yellow onion
- 2 cups shredded Cheddar
- ¼ cup chopped cilantro
- 2 tablespoons olive oil
- 1 ½ tablespoons chili powder
- 1 tablespoon minced garlic
- ½ teaspoon ground cumin

Directions:
1. Turn your pressure cooker to "Sauté" and add oil.
2. Add onion and cook for 3 minutes or until soft.
3. Add chiles and garlic.
4. After 1 minute, add in the beef and brown.
5. After 4 minutes, add chili powder and cumin.
6. Quickly add the cilantro and tomatoes.
7. Stir and cook for 2 minutes.
8. Carefully pour out the beef mixture into a bowl.
9. Wash out the pot and dry.
10. Pour in 2 cups of water and lower in a trivet.
11. Find a 2-quart baking dish that will fit in the cooker.
12. Layer ½ cup of the beef mixture in the dish, then one corn tortilla, followed by more sauce and ½ cup of cheese.
13. Keep going until the ingredients are gone.
14. Wrap the dish in parchment paper, and then foil.
15. Lower into the cooker.
16. Hit "Manual," and then 30 minutes on "high pressure."
17. When time is up, press "Cancel" and wait for the pressure to come down naturally.
18. Open the lid.
19. Take out the dish, unwrap it, and let it cool before serving.

Nutritional Info (⅙ recipe): Total calories - 447 Protein - 27 Carbs - 27.9 Fiber - 4 Fat - 24.3

Flank Steak w/ Sweet Potato Gravy

Serves: 4
Time: 1 hour, 10 minutes

Ingredients:

- 2 pounds flank steak, cut into four pieces
- 1 pound peeled and grated sweet potatoes
- 1 cup beef broth
- 1 chopped yellow onion
- 3 tablespoons tomato paste
- 1 tablespoon butter
- 1 tablespoon olive oil
- 1 tablespoon sweet paprika
- 2 teaspoons fresh thyme
- ½ teaspoon salt
- ¼ teaspoon cayenne
- ¼ teaspoon ground cloves

Directions:
1. Turn your pressure cooker to "Sauté" and melt the butter.
2. Add beef and brown. You probably have to brown the meat in two batches.
3. When all the meat is browned, move to a bowl.
4. Add onion and soften for 3 minutes.
5. Throw in the sweet potato, cloves, thyme, salt, and cayenne.
6. Cook for 1 minute before pouring in the broth.
7. Stir in the tomato paste and let the mixture simmer.
8. Add the meat back into the pot.
9. Secure the lid.
10. Press "Manual," and then "high pressure" for 60 minutes.
11. When time is up, hit "Cancel" and wait for the pressure to come down naturally.
12. To serve, spoon up meat, veggies, and sauce into a bowl.

Nutritional Info (¼ recipe): Total calories - 594 Protein - 67 Carbs - 28 Fiber - 4 Fat - 22

Beef Brisket w/ Veggies

Serves: 5
Time: About 1 hour

Ingredients:

- 2 pounds brisket
- 2 ½ cups beef broth
- 5-6 red potatoes
- 4 bay leaves

- 2 cups carrots cut into chunks
- 2 chopped celery stalks
- 1 big yellow onion
- 3 tablespoons Worcestershire sauce
- 3 tablespoons chopped garlic
- 2 tablespoons olive oil
- Black pepper
- Knorr Demi-Glace sauce to taste

Directions:
1. Turn on the pressure cooker to the "sauté" setting.
2. Pour in 1 tablespoon of oil and onion.
3. Caramelize.
4. When ready, move to a bowl.
5. Season brisket on both sides with black pepper.
6. Pour in another tablespoon of oil into pot and sear brisket all over.
7. Close the lid.
8. Select "Manual" and then 50 minutes on "high pressure."
9. In the meantime, prepare the veggies.
10. When the meat is done, hit "Cancel" and quick-release the pressure.
11. Carefully take off the lid and add all the veggies.
12. Select "Manual" again and 10 minutes on "high pressure."
13. When the beeper sounds, hit "Cancel" and quick-release again.
14. Take out the meat and veggies, leaving the cooking liquid in the pot. Pick out the bay leaves.
15. Turn on "sauté" and bring to a boil.
16. Add about 1 tablespoon of Demi-Glace and whisk in.
17. Serve!

Nutritional Info ($\frac{1}{5}$ recipe): Total calories - 400 Protein - 28 Carbs - 10 Fiber - 1 Fat – 18

Sweet-Spicy Meatloaf

Serves: 4
Time: About 50 minutes

Ingredients:
- 1 pound lean ground beef
- ⅔ cup bread crumbs
- ⅔ cup diced onion
- 6 sliced black olives
- 1 egg white
- 2 tablespoons ketchup
- 2 fresh, chopped basil leaves
- 1 teaspoon minced garlic
- ½ teaspoon salt
- Black pepper

- ¼ cup ketchup
- 1 tablespoon brown sugar
- 1 tablespoon spicy brown mustard

Directions:
1. Prepare a round, one-quart dish with a bit of olive oil.
2. Mix everything in the first ingredient list and form a loaf in the dish.
3. In a separate bowl, mix the brown sugar, ketchup, and spicy brown mustard together.
4. Brush on top of the meatloaf.
5. Cover the dish tightly with foil.
6. Pour one cup of water into the pressure cooker and lower in the trivet.
7. Place the meatloaf dish on top and close the pressure cooker lid.
8. Select "Meat/Stew," and then 45 minutes.
9. When the beep sounds, quick-release.
10. Carefully take out the hot dish.
11. Holding the meat in place, pour out any excess liquid.
12. Rest the meat before serving.

Nutritional Info (¼ recipe): Total calories - 261 Protein - 25 Carbs - 19.2 Fiber - 0 Fat - 7.5

Pressure Cooker Pot Roast

Serves: 8
Time: About 50 minutes

Ingredients:

- 4 pounds bottom roast cut into cubes
- 1 cup beef broth
- 5 minced garlic cloves
- 1 peeled and chopped Granny Smith apple
- 1 thumb of grated ginger
- ½ cup soy sauce
- Juice of one big orange
- 2 tablespoons olive oil
- Salt and pepper to taste

Directions:
1. Season the roast with salt and pepper.
2. Turn on your pressure cooker to "sauté."
3. When hot, pour in the olive oil and brown the roast all over.
4. Move the meat to a plate.
5. Pour in the beef broth and scrape any stuck bits of meat.
6. Pour in soy sauce and stir.
7. Put the roast back into the pot.
8. Arrange the cut apple, garlic, and ginger on top.
9. Pour in the orange juice.

10. Close the pressure cooker lid.
11. Select "Manual" and then 45 minutes on "high pressure."
12. Hit "Cancel" and quick-release the pressure when the timer beeps.
13. Serve!

Nutritional Info (⅛ recipe): Total calories - 492 Protein - 46 Carbs - 3 Fiber - 0 Fat - 37

Teriyaki Short Ribs

Serves: 4
Time: About 45 minutes

Ingredients:
- 4 big beef short ribs
- 1 cup water
- ¾ cup soy sauce
- 1 big, halved orange
- ½ cup brown sugar
- 1 full garlic bulb, peeled and crushed
- 1 large thumb of peeled and crushed fresh ginger
- ½ tablespoon sesame oil
- Dried pepper flakes
- A bunch of chopped green onions

Directions:
1. In a Ziploc bag, mix water, sugar, and soy sauce.
2. Squish around until the sugar has dissolved.
3. Add the orange juice and stir, before adding the orange slices as well.
4. Lastly, throw in the garlic, ginger, onions, and dried pepper flakes.
5. Stir before adding the ribs.
6. Stir one last time and marinate in the fridge for at least 4 hours.
7. When ready to cook the ribs, coat the bottom of the pressure cooker with olive oil and heat.
8. Remove the ribs from the bag (save the liquid!) with tongs and quickly sear for 2-3 minutes on both sides.
9. Pour in the marinade and close the lid.
10. Select the "Meat/Stew" setting and select 30 minutes.
11. When time is up, hit "Cancel" and quick-release the pressure.
12. Serve!

Nutritional Info (¼ recipe): Total calories - 603 Protein - 43 Carbs – 76 Fiber - 1 Fat - 10

Beefy Lasagna

Serves: 6
Time: About 30 minutes

Ingredients:

- 2 pounds ricotta cheese
- 1 pound of ground beef
- 24-ounces pasta sauce
- 8-ounces of no-boil lasagna noodles
- 1 package shredded mozzarella cheese
- 2 big eggs
- ¼ cup water
- ⅓ cup grated Parmesan
- 1 diced onion
- 1 tablespoon olive oil
- 2 teaspoons minced garlic
- 1 teaspoon Italian seasoning
- Salt and pepper to taste

Directions:
1. Pour olive oil in your pressure cooker and heat until it starts to smoke.
2. Quickly add the ground beef, onions, salt, and pepper.
3. When the meat is brown and onions clear, pour in the water and pasta sauce.
4. Stir before pouring out into a bowl.
5. In a separate bowl, mix the ricotta, garlic, Italian seasoning, eggs, Parmesan, salt, and pepper together.
6. Fill the pressure cooker with ¼ inch of water.
7. Layer ⅕ of the beef mixture into the bottom before adding the noodles.
8. Pour in ⅓ of the ricotta mixture, and then more beef sauce.
9. Top with noodles, and keep going until you've used everything. The last layer should be beef sauce.
10. Close the pressure cooker lid.
11. Select "Manual," and then 7 minutes on "high pressure."
12. When the beep sounds, hit "Cancel" and quick-release the pressure.
13. Open the lid and sprinkle on the mozzarella.
14. Cool for a few minutes before serving.

Nutritional Info (⅙ recipe): Total calories - 408 Protein - 25.1 Carbs - 27.4 Fiber - 2.6 Fat - 22.1

Corned Beef + Cabbage in Spiced Cider

Serves: 6
Time: 1 hour, 30 minutes

Ingredients:
- 3 ½ pounds rinsed corned beef
- 1 ½ cups unsweetened apple cider
- 8 whole cloves
- 6 big carrots, cut in half widthwise
- One, 4-inch cinnamon stick
- 1 big cored green cabbage, cut into 6 wedges
- ¼ cup honey mustard

Directions:
1. Pour cider and put the cloves and cinnamon stick into the pressure cooker.
2. Lower in the steamer basket.
3. Put the corned beef on top.
4. Rub honey mustard on top.
5. Lock the lid.
6. Select "Manual," and then "high pressure" for 80 minutes.
7. When time is up, hit "Cancel" and wait for the pressure to come down by itself.
8. Open the lid and move the meat to a cutting board.
9. Take out the rack as well as the cloves and cinnamon stick.
10. Put the carrots and cabbage into the pot.
11. Lock the lid.
12. Hit "Manual," and then "high pressure" for just 8 minutes.
13. When time is up, press "Cancel" and quick-release.
14. Carve the meat into slices.
15. Serve in bowls with the meat, cabbage, carrots, and broth.

Nutritional Info (⅙ recipe):
Total calories: 473 Protein: 59 Carbs: 18 Fiber: 4.6 Fat: 19

Top Round w/ Bacon, Bourbon, + Potatoes

Serves: 6
Time: 1 hour, 30 minutes

Ingredients:
- 3 pounds beef top round
- 1 ½ pounds Yukon Gold potatoes
- 1 ½ cups beef broth
- 1 stemmed, cored, and chopped green bell pepper
- 4 chopped bacon slices
- ¼ cup bourbon
- One, 6-inch rosemary sprig
- 2 teaspoons black pepper

Directions:
1. Roll the roast in the ground black pepper.
2. Turn your pressure cooker to "Sauté" and fry the bacon.
3. Move bacon to a plate.
4. Put the roast in the cooker and brown all over.
5. Move the roast to the plate.
6. Add the bell pepper and soften for 3 minutes.
7. Pour beef broth into the pot, then the bourbon, and deglaze.
8. Toss in the rosemary sprig and then add the bacon and beef back into the pot.
9. Lock the lid.
10. Press "Manual," and then cook for 55 minutes on "high pressure."

11. When time is up, hit "Cancel" and quick-release.
12. Open the lid and add the potatoes.
13. Lock the lid.
14. Hit "Manual" again and cook for 15 minutes on "high pressure."
15. When time is up, press "Cancel" and let the pressure decrease naturally.
16. To serve, pick out the rosemary and take out the meat to rest for 5 minutes.
17. Slice, and serve with potatoes and lots of sauce.

Nutritional Info (⅙ recipe):
Total calories: 553 Protein: 73 Carbs: 21 Fiber: 1.6 Fat: 13

Corn Pudding

Serves: 4
Time: 45 minutes

Ingredients:
- 1 ½ cups water
- 2 chopped shallots
- 1 cup fresh corn
- 2 beaten eggs
- ¾ cup whole milk
- ¼ cup sour cream
- 3 tablespoons cornmeal
- 1 tablespoon sugar
- Salt
- Pepper

Directions:
1. Turn on your pressure cooker to "Sauté."
2. Add butter and melt.
3. Add shallots and hit "Cancel." The hot butter will cook the shallots.
4. While that cooks, mix corn, sour cream, cornmeal, milk, sugar, eggs, pepper, and salt in a bowl.
5. Add the melted butter and shallots and stir together.
6. Pour water into the cooker and lower in the trivet.
7. Grease a 6-7 inch baking dish (round) and pour the corn pudding in.
8. Wrap in foil and place into the steamer rack.
9. Close the pressure cooker lid.
10. Press "Manual" and cook for 30 minutes at "low pressure."
11. When time is up, hit "Cancel" and quick-release the pressure.
12. Cool before serving.

Nutritional Info (¼ recipe): Total calories -207 Protein - 6 Carbs - 19 Fiber - 1 Fat - 7

Beets w/ Goat Cheese

Serves: 4

Time: 30 minutes

Ingredients:
- 1 cup water
- 4 medium-sized, whole beets
- ½ cup crumbled goat cheese
- ½ lemon, juiced
- Olive oil
- Salt + pepper

Directions:
1. Pour water into the pressure cooker.
2. Lower in the steamer basket.
3. Wash and trim the beets.
4. Put them in the steamer basket and lock the pressure cooker lid.
5. Hit "Manual" and 20 minutes on "high pressure."
6. When time is up, quick-release the pressure.
7. Check the beets by poking them with a knife. If soft, they're done.
8. Run the beets under cold water and peel.
9. Slice.
10. To serve, plate the beets and sprinkle on the goat cheese, lemon juice, olive oil, salt, and pepper.

Nutritional Info (¼ recipe): Total calories -112 Protein - 6 Carbs - 10 Fiber - 2 Fat - 4

Brown-Butter Fingerling Potatoes

Serves: 4
Time: 35 minutes

Ingredients:
- 1 ½ pounds small fingerling potatoes
- ½ cup chicken broth
- 2 tablespoons butter
- Minced leaves of 1 small rosemary sprig
- Salt + pepper

Directions:
1. Turn on the pressure cooker's "Sauté" function.
2. When hot, add the butter and melt.
3. When melted, add potatoes and stir.
4. Keep stirring for 10 minutes until the potato skins start to crisp up and the butter has become golden and nutty.
5. Pour in the broth and close the pot lid.
6. Hit "Manual" and 7 minutes on "high pressure."
7. When time is up, hit "Cancel" and wait for the pressure to decrease naturally for 10 minutes.
8. Quick-release any leftover pressure.
9. Open the lid.

10. Serve the potatoes with salt, pepper, and rosemary.

Nutritional Info (¼ recipe): Total calories -175 Protein - 4 Carbs - 27 Fiber - 3 Fat - 4

Ricotta-Stuffed Zucchini

Serves: 6
Time: 7 minutes

Ingredients:
- 3 big zucchinis
- 1 ¾ cups crushed tomatoes
- 1 cup ricotta
- 1 yellow onion
- ½ cup breadcrumbs
- 2 tablespoons olive oil
- 1 tablespoon minced fresh oregano
- 1 large egg yolk
- 2 teaspoons minced garlic
- 2 teaspoons fresh thyme
- ¼ teaspoon grated nutmeg
- Salt + pepper

Directions:
1. Mix breadcrumbs, ricotta, egg yolk, nutmeg, and thyme in a bowl.
2. Prepare the zucchini by cutting them into 2-inch long pieces. With a melon baller, hollow out the middles with about ¼-inch flesh on the sides and ½-inch on the bottom, so they don't fall apart.
3. Stuff 2 tablespoons of the ricotta mixture into the hollows.
4. Turn your pressure cooker to "Sauté," and cook onion until soft.
5. Add garlic and cook another 30 seconds.
6. Add oregano, tomatoes, salt, and pepper.
7. Put the zucchinis in the cooker, stuffed-side up.
8. Close and lock the lid.
9. Select "Manual," and then 5 minutes on "high pressure."
10. When time is up, hit "Cancel" and quick-release.
11. Serve with the sauce.

Nutritional Info (⅙ recipe):
Total calories: 209 Protein: 10 Carbs: 18 Fiber: 2 Fat: 11

Risotto w/ Peas + Brie Cheese

Serves: 6
Time: 10 minutes

Ingredients:
- 4 cups chicken broth

- 1 ½ cups white Arborio rice
- 1 cup peas
- 4-ounces chopped Brie cheese, rind removed
- ¼ cup unsweetened apple cider
- 3 tablespoons butter
- 1 chopped yellow onion
- 1 tablespoon apple cider vinegar
- 1 tablespoon minced sage leaves
- ¼ teaspoon grated nutmeg

Directions:
1. Turn your pressure cooker to "Sauté" and melt the butter.
2. Toss in the chopped onion and soften for 4 minutes.
3. Add rice and stir until the rice is coated in butter.
4. Pour in apple cider and vinegar.
5. Stir until the rice has absorbed the liquid, which should take about 2 minutes.
6. Pour in the broth, and add sage and nutmeg.
7. Stir.
8. Close and secure the lid.
9. Select "Manual," and cook for 10 minutes on "high pressure."
10. When time is up, hit "Cancel" and quick-release.
11. Open the lid.
12. Stir in the peas and Brie cheese.
13. Close the lid to let the residual warmth melt the cheese and warm up the peas.
14. Stir right before serving.

Nutritional Info (⅙ recipe):
Total calories: 298 Protein: 9 Carbs: 44 Fiber: 3 Fat: 11

Asparagus + Rice w/ Brown Butter

Serves: 5-6
Time: 30 minutes

Ingredients:
- 4 cups chicken stock
- 2 cups Arborio rice
- 1 pound asparagus, cut into 1-inch pieces
- 5 tablespoons butter
- 4 minced garlic cloves
- 4 chopped shallots
- ½ cup dry white wine
- ½ cup grated Parmesan cheese
- ¼ cup cream
- 1 tablespoon olive oil
- Salt + pepper

Directions:
1. Preheat your normal oven to 400-degrees.
2. Toss asparagus in olive oil, season, and layer on a baking sheet.
3. Roast for 10-15 minutes until tender and a bit crispy.
4. Turn your pressure cooker to "Sauté" and melt butter.
5. Stir occasionally until butter becomes brown and fragrant.
6. Toss in the shallots and cook for 2 minutes.
7. Add garlic and cook for another minute.
8. Pour in the wine and simmer until the wine has mostly evaporated.
9. Pour in the broth and rice.
10. Season before locking the pressure cooker lid.
11. Press "Manual" and then 6 minutes on "high pressure."
12. When time is up, hit "Cancel" and quick-release.
13. If there's still too much liquid, turn on "Sauté" and simmer.
14. Add cream and cheese.
15. Add the asparagus and serve!

Nutritional Info: Total calories -441 Protein - 14 Carbs - 50 Fiber - 2 Fat - 11

Whole-Wheat Mac 'n Cheese

Serves: 12
Time: About 10 minutes

Ingredients:
- 1 pound dry whole-wheat macaroni
- 4 cups water
- 10-ounces shredded sharp cheddar
- 8-ounces shredded Monterey Jack cheese
- 12-ounce can of evaporated milk
- 2-ounces grated Parmesan
- 1 cup breadcrumbs
- 3 tablespoons butter
- 1 tablespoon salt
- 1 teaspoon yellow mustard
- ¼ teaspoon black pepper

Directions:
1. Put the macaroni, mustard, salt, pepper, butter, and water into the pressure cooker and stir.
2. Lock the lid.
3. Press "Manual" and cook for half the time that the pasta box says. If the box recommends 10 minutes, cook in the pressure cooker for "4 minutes."
4. When the timer goes off, hit "Cancel" and quick-release.
5. If the pasta isn't done, just "Sauté" until it reaches your desired doneness.
6. With "Sauté" on, add the evaporated milk and stir.
7. Throw in the cheeses and stir until thoroughly blended.

8. Move the mac and cheese to a baking dish and sprinkle with breadcrumbs.
9. Broil in the oven for a few minutes.
10. Serve!

Nutritional Info (1/12 serving): Total calories - 377 Protein - 19.5 Carbs - 32 Fiber - 3 Fat - 12.5

Classic Potato Salad

Serves: 8
Time: 10 minutes

Ingredients:
- 6 peeled and cubed russet potatoes
- 1 ½ cups water
- 4 eggs
- 1 cup mayonnaise
- ¼ cup chopped onion
- 2 tablespoons chopped parsley
- 1 tablespoon mustard
- 1 tablespoon dill pickle juice
- Salt + pepper

Directions:
1. Pour water into the pressure cooker and lower in the steamer basket.
2. Put eggs and potatoes in the basket.
3. Lock the lid and hit "Manual," then "high pressure" for 4 minutes.
4. When time is up, hit "Cancel" and quick-release.
5. Put the eggs in ice water.
6. In a bowl, mix mayo, parsley, onion, mustard, and pickle juice.
7. Add the potatoes and mix.
8. Peel and cut eggs and mix into the potato salad.
9. Season.
10. Chill one hour before serving.

Nutritional Info (⅛ serving): Total calories - 262 Protein - 5.3 Carbs - 30.8 Fiber - 2.9 Fat – 13

Broccoli Pesto

Makes: 2 ½ cups
Time: 20 minutes

Ingredients:
- 1 pound broccoli florets
- 3 cups water
- 3 minced garlic cloves
- 1 cup fresh basil leaves
- ⅓ cup toasted walnuts
- ¼ cup olive oil

- ¼ cup grated Parmesan
- 2 tablespoons lemon juice
- Salt + pepper

Directions:
1. Add broccoli and water to the pressure cooker.
2. Press "Manual" and cook for 3 minutes on "high pressure."
3. While that cooks, pulse walnuts and garlic in a food processor.
4. When crumbly, stop.
5. When the pot timer goes off, hit "Cancel."
6. Quick-release the pressure in the cooker.
7. Take out the broccoli and rinse in cold water.
8. Drain and pulse in the food processor with oil, basil, and lemon juice.
9. Pulse and add ¼ cup of cooking liquid, cheese, salt, and pepper.
10. Keep pulsing until smooth, adding cooking liquid if needed.
11. Serve with pasta.

Nutritional Info (½ cup serving): Total calories - 248 Protein - 9 Carbs - 10 Fiber - 4 Fat - 3

Cranberry Sauce

Makes: 2 cups
Time: 35 minutes

Ingredients:
- 4 cups washed cranberries
- 1 cup sugar
- 1-inch peeled and sliced ginger
- ½ cup orange juice
- Zest from ½ orange
- Juice and zest from ½ lemon

Directions:
1. Put cranberries, sugar, orange juice, orange zest, ginger, lemon juice, and lemon zest into the pressure cooker.
2. Close the lid.
3. Hit "Manual" and then 15 minutes on "high pressure."
4. When time is up, press "Cancel" and wait 10 minutes for the pressure to come down.
5. If there's any leftover, release it.
6. Let the sauce cool.
7. Pick out the ginger if you want.
8. Store in the fridge for up to 3 weeks.

Nutritional Info (⅓ cup serving): Total calories - 177 Protein - 0 Carbs - 43 Fiber - 3 Fat - 0

Italian-Style Meat Sauce

Serves: 6-8

Time: 1 hour, 15 minutes

Ingredients:
- 3 crushed garlic cloves
- 1 peeled and diced carrot
- 1 diced celery stalk
- 1 diced onion
- 1 tablespoon olive oil
- ½ teaspoon salt
- ¼ teaspoon crushed red pepper flakes
- 1 ¼ pounds sweet Italian sausage
- 1 ¼ pounds hot Italian sausage
- 1 cup chicken broth
- ½ cup red wine
- 28-ounce can crushed tomatoes
- 2-3 sprigs fresh thyme
- 1 sprig fresh basil
- 1 sprig rosemary
- 1 teaspoon black pepper

Directions:
1. Let's focus on the first ingredient list, beginning by heating the oil in the pressure cooker on "Sauté."
2. Throw in the celery, carrot, onion, and garlic.
3. Add the salt and red pepper flakes immediately after, and stir for about 8 minutes, or until the onion has softened.
4. Pour in the wine and deglaze the pot.
5. Simmer for 1 minute.
6. Time for the second ingredient list. Add the raw sausage and brown for 5 minutes.
7. Pour in the chicken broth and crushed tomatoes.
8. To **Make** it easier to pick them out later, tie the herb sprigs together before adding to the pot.
9. Close and lock the pressure cooker lid.
10. Select "Manual," and then 20 minutes at "high pressure."
11. Sprinkle in the black pepper.
12. Serve!

Nutritional Info (1 cup serving): Total calories - 302 Protein - 20 Carbs - 6 Fiber - 1 Fat - 21

Homemade BBQ Sauce

Makes: 2 ½ cups
Time: 20 minutes

Ingredients:
- 1 chopped onion
- ¾ cup prunes
- ½ cup water
- ½ cup tomato puree

- 4 tablespoons vinegar
- 4 tablespoons honey
- 1 tablespoon sesame seed oil
- 1 teaspoon liquid smoke
- 1 teaspoon hot sauce
- 1 teaspoon salt
- ½ teaspoon ground ginger
- ⅛ teaspoon cumin

Directions:
1. Turn your pressure cooker to "Sauté."
2. Add the oil and onion.
3. Cook and stir occasionally until the edges of the onion brown.
4. In a mixing bowl, pour in water, tomato puree, vinegar, and honey.
5. Add in garlic, hot sauce, salt, liquid smoke, ginger, and cumin.
6. Mix everything well, so the honey dissolves.
7. Pour into the pressure cooker and add prunes.
8. Lock the pressure cooker lid.
9. Hit "Manual," and then 10 minutes on "high pressure."
10. When the timer goes off, hit "Cancel" and quick-release.
11. Blend the sauce well till smooth.

Nutritional Info (1 tablespoon serving): Total calories - 20 Protein - 0 Carbs - 4.5 Fiber - .3 Fat - .4

Goat Cheese Mashed Potatoes

Serves: 8-10
Time: 45 minutes

Ingredients:

- 3 pounds scrubbed Yukon Gold potatoes
- 8-ounces goat cheese w/ herbs
- ½ cup sour cream
- ½ cup milk
- 2 tablespoons butter
- 1 tablespoon salt
- Pepper to taste

Directions:
1. Put the potatoes with 1 tablespoon of salt into the pressure cooker.
2. Pour in just enough water so they are halfway covered.
3. Close the lid.
4. Choose "Manual," and then 20 minutes on "high pressure."
5. When the timer beeps, hit "Cancel" and wait for the pressure to come down on its own.
6. When ready, take out the potatoes and drain.
7. Return to the pot, along with milk, sour cream, butter, and ¾ of the goat cheese.

8. Mash everything well to your desired consistency.
9. Scoop out the mashed potatoes into an 8-inch baking dish.
10. Swirl on the rest of the goat cheese on top.
11. Broil in the oven for 5 minutes.
12. Devour!

Nutritional Info (1/10 recipe): Total calories - 254 Protein - 8.5 Carbs - 36 Fiber - 3.6 Fat - 8.5

Butternut Squash

Serves: 8
Time: 35 minutes

Ingredients:
- One butternut squash
- 1 cup of water
- Salt
- Pepper
- Nutmeg

Directions:
1. Pour 1 cup of water into your pressure cooker and lower the steamer rack inside.
2. Wash the butternut squash.
3. Cut so it can fit in the pot.
4. When the squash is in the pot, close and lock the lid.
5. Push "Manual" and cook for 17 minutes on "high pressure."
6. When the timer beeps, hit "Cancel" and quick-release the pressure.
7. Open the lid so the squash can cool for 5 minutes.
8. If the squash is cut in half, take out the seeds from the bottom part and cut in half again.
9. If the top part is big, cut that in half, too.
10. Poke the squash to determine how cooked it is. If the squash still has a way to go, return the squash to the pot and cook for another 17 minutes.
11. When time is up, hit "Cancel" and quick-release again.
12. Carefully take out the squash, scoop, mash, and season. Some salt, pepper, and nutmeg are a good start.

Nutritional Info (1 cup serving): Total calories - 63 Protein - 1.4 Carbs - 16 Fiber - 2.8 Fat – 0

Brown-Sugar Carrots

Serves: 2
Time: About 20 minutes

Ingredients:
- 2 cups carrots
- ½ cup water
- 1 tablespoon brown sugar
- ½ tablespoon butter

- Dash of salt

Directions:
1. Put the butter, brown sugar, salt, and water into the pressure cooker.
2. Hit the "sauté" button and stir until the butter melts.
3. Throw in the carrots and stir them around.
4. Close the lid.
5. Hit "Steam" and select 15 minutes.
6. When time is up, press "Cancel" and then quick-release.
7. Open up the lid and sauté until all the liquid is gone.
8. Take out the carrots and serve!

Nutritional Info (1 cup serving): Total calories - 104 Protein - 1 Carbs - 19 Fiber - 3.4 Fat - 4

Quick Baked Potatoes

Serves: 4
Time: 30 minutes

Ingredients:
- 1 cup of water
- Up to 5 pounds of potatoes (4 potatoes for 4 servings)
- Seasonings

Directions:
1. Pour water into the pressure cooker and lower in the steamer rack.
2. Add the potatoes and secure the lid.
3. Click "Manual" and then the "-" button to 10 minutes.
4. When time is up, hit "Cancel" and wait 20 minutes for the pressure to come down on its own.
5. Open the lid and serve potatoes.

Nutritional Info (1 potato): Total calories - 110 Protein - 4 Carbs - 26 Fiber - 2 Fat - 0

Buttery Orange Brussels Sprouts

Serves: 8
Time: 5 minutes

Ingredients:
- 2 pounds Brussels sprouts
- ¼ cup orange juice
- 2 tablespoons maple syrup
- 1 tablespoon butter
- 1 teaspoon grated orange zest
- ½ teaspoon salt
- ¼ teaspoon black pepper

Directions:

1. Trim ¼ off of the bottom of every sprout and rinse in cold water.
2. Put them in the pressure cooker.
3. Cover with ¾ cup water.
4. Secure the lid on the pressure cooker.
5. Hit "Manual" and then 4 minutes.
6. While the sprouts cook, mix the sauce ingredients in a skillet over low heat, just to melt the butter and get the maple syrup integrated.
7. When the timer beeps, hit "Cancel" and quick-release.
8. Serve coated in sauce.

Nutritional Info (⅛ serving): Total calories - 65 Protein - 3 Carbs - 12 Fiber - 3 Fat - 2

Red Beans

Serves: 8
Time: Overnight soak + 35 minutes

Ingredients:
- 2 quarts water
- 1 pound rinsed red kidney beans
- 1 tablespoon salt
- 5 cups water
- 1 pound smoked sausage, cut into quarters lengthwise and then cut into ¼-inch pieces
- 4 sliced garlic cloves
- 2 bay leaves
- 1 big minced onion
- 1 seeded and minced green bell pepper
- 1 minced celery stalk
- 1 teaspoon olive oil
- 1 teaspoon dried thyme
- 1 teaspoon kosher salt
- ½ teaspoon salt
- Black pepper

Directions:
1. The night before you plan on having the beans, go through them and throw out any bad ones.
2. Pour 2 quarts of water into a big bowl, add beans and salt, and soak overnight.
3. The next day, cook the aromatics. Pour 1 teaspoon oil into the pressure cooker and heat.
4. When shiny, add the celery, onion, pepper, thyme, garlic, sausage, and ½ teaspoon salt.
5. Stir while it's cooking, for 8 minutes, until the sausage and onions are starting to brown.
6. Drain and rinse off the beans.
7. Put them in the pressure cooker along with 1 teaspoon of salt and bay leaves.
8. Secure the lid and hit "Manual." Select 15 minutes.
9. When time is up, hit "Cancel" and wait 20 minutes.
10. Open the cooker and pick out the bay leaves.
11. Take out 2 cups of the beans and liquid and blend until smooth.

12. Pour them back into the cooker.
13. You can simmer for another 15 minutes if you want, but it's not necessary.
14. Serve!

Nutritional Info (⅛ serving): Total calories - 235 Protein - 11 Carbs - 11 Fiber - 14 Fat - 17

Simple Spaghetti Squash

Serves: 4
Time: 10 minutes

Ingredients:
- One 3-pound spaghetti squash
- 1 cup water

Directions:
1. Cut off the end of the squash with the stem and then cut in half.
2. Scoop out the seeds.
3. Pour water into your pressure cooker and lower in the steamer basket.
4. Put the cut squash in the basket and secure the lid.
5. Hit "Manual" and then cook for 8 minutes on "high pressure."
6. When the timer goes off, hit "Cancel" and then quick-release.
7. When you can handle the squash without burning yourself, scrap the insides out with a fork.
8. Serve!

Nutritional Info (1-cup serving): Total calories - 31 Protein - .6 Carbs - 7 Fiber - 1.5 Fat - .6

Cheesy Potatoes

Serves: 4
Time: 15 minutes

Ingredients:
- 6 peeled and ⅛-inch thick sliced potatoes
- 1 cup chicken broth
- 1 cup shredded cheese
- 1 cup panko bread crumbs
- ½ cup sour cream
- ½ cup chopped onion
- 2 tablespoons butter + 3 tablespoons melted butter
- Pepper
- Salt

Directions:
1. Hit the "sauté" button on your pressure cooker and put in 2 tablespoons butter.
2. When melted, add the onion and cook for about 5 minutes.
3. Pour in 1 cup of chicken broth, salt, and pepper.
4. Lower in the steamer basket with the sliced potatoes inside.

5. Lock the lid.
6. Hit "Manual," and then select 5 minutes on "high pressure."
7. While the potatoes cook, melt 3 tablespoons of butter and mix with the panko.
8. Grease a 9x13 baking dish.
9. When the potatoes are ready, hit "Cancel" and quick-release.
10. Remove the potatoes and layer them in the baking dish.
11. In the pressure cooker, mix cheese and sour cream into the cooking liquid.
12. Pour over potatoes and stir so they're thoroughly coated.
13. Pour over the panko/butter topping.
14. Broil in the oven for 5-7 minutes.

Nutritional Info (¼ serving): Total calories - 358 Protein - 11 Carbs - 32 Fiber - 2 Fat - 22

Steamed Crab Legs w/ Garlic Butter

Serves: 4
Time: 15 minutes

Ingredients:
- 2 pounds crab legs, fresh or frozen
- 1 cup water
- 4 tablespoons salted butter
- 1 halved lemon
- 1 big minced garlic clove
- 1 teaspoon olive oil

Directions:
1. Pour water into the pressure cooker and insert the steamer basket.
2. Put the crab legs inside and lock the lid.
3. Hit "Steam" and 3 minutes at "high pressure" for fresh, and 4 minutes for frozen.
4. Take a saucepan and heat olive oil on the stove.
5. Toss in the garlic and cook for 1 minute.
6. Add the butter and stir to melt.
7. Turn off the heat and squeeze in lots of lemon juice.
8. When the pressure cooker timer beeps, hit "Cancel" and quick-release.
9. Serve the crab and dipping sauce!

Nutritional Info (¼ serving): Total calories - 346 Protein - 44 Carbs - 2 Fiber - 0 Fat – 7

Tuna Noodles

Serves: 2
Time: About 20 minutes

Ingredients:
- 8 ounces of uncooked dry, wide egg noodles
- 1 ¼ cups water
- 1 can drained tuna

- 1 can diced tomatoes
- 1 jar drained (save the liquid!) marinated, chopped artichoke hearts
- ½ cup chopped red onion
- 1 tablespoon oil
- Feta cheese
- Dried parsley
- Dried basil
- Salt
- Pepper

Directions:
1. Turn on your pressure cooker and hit "sauté."
2. Heat a little olive oil until shiny.
3. Toss in the chopped red onion and cook, stirring, for 2 minutes.
4. Add water, noodles, tomatoes, and seasonings.
5. Hit "Soup" and then 10 minutes.
6. When time is up, hit "Cancel" and quick-release the pressure.
7. Add the tuna, artichokes, and the saved liquid.
8. Hit "Sauté" and stir for 4 minutes.
9. Serve with feta cheese and parsley.

Nutritional Info (½ serving): Total calories - 547 Protein - 8 Carbs - 18 Fiber - 2 Fat - 3

White Fish w/ Beer and Potatoes

Serves: 6
Time: 40 minutes

Ingredients:
- 1 pound white fish (like cod or pollock)
- 4 peeled and diced potatoes
- 1 cup beer
- 1 sliced red pepper
- 1 tablespoon sugar
- 1 tablespoon oil
- 1 tablespoon oyster sauce
- 1 teaspoon salt

Directions:
1. Put everything in the pressure cooker.
2. Secure the lid.
3. Push "Bean/Chili."
4. Cook for 40 minutes.
5. When time is up, quick-release.
6. Serve and enjoy!

Nutritional Info (⅙ serving): Total calories - 172 Protein - 16 Carbs - 22 Fiber - 2 Fat - 2

Spicy Lemon Salmon

Serves: 4
Time: About 5 minutes

Ingredients:
- 3-4, 1-inch thick salmon fillets
- 1 cup water
- 1 juiced lemon
- 1 sliced lemon
- 1-2 tablespoons Nanami Togarashi
- Sea salt
- Pepper

Directions:
1. Season the salmon generously with lemon juice, spices, pepper, and salt.
2. Lower the steamer rack into the pressure cooker and pour in 1 cup of water.
3. Place the fillets in the rack, without overlapping.
4. Secure the pressure cooker lid.
5. Hit "Manual" and then "-" until you get to 5 minutes.
6. Seal the lid.
7. When ready, quick-release the pressure.
8. Serve!

Nutritional Info (¼ serving): Total calories - 118 Protein - 24 Carbs - 1 Fiber - 0 Fat - 2

One-Pot Shrimp Scampi

Serves: 4
Time: 5 minutes

Ingredients:
- 1 pound frozen wild-caught shrimp
- 1 cup jasmine rice
- 1 ½ cups water
- 4 minced garlic cloves
- ¼ cup chopped parsley
- ¼ cup butter
- 1 medium, juiced lemon
- 1 pinch saffron
- Salt
- Pepper
- Red pepper flakes

Directions:
1. Mix everything in your pressure cooker, leaving the shells on the shrimp.
2. Close the lid and select "Manual," and 5 minutes on "high pressure."

3. When time is up, quick-release.
4. When you can touch the shrimp, peel off the shells.
5. Serve with parsley and grated cheese.

Nutritional Info (¼ serving): Total calories - 225 Protein - 14 Carbs - 10 Fiber - 0 Fat – 12

Seafood Gumbo

Serves: 6-8
Time: 75 minutes

Ingredients:
- 6 cups fish stock
- 1 pound crab meat
- 1 pound peeled and cleaned shrimp
- 24 shucked oysters
- 2 chopped smoked sausages
- 3 chopped celery stalks
- 2 chopped red bell peppers
- 1 chopped onion
- ½ cup flour
- ½ cup chopped green onions
- ½ cup veggie oil
- ¼ cup chopped parsley
- 2 tablespoons dried thyme
- 2 tablespoons minced garlic cloves
- Salt and pepper to taste

Directions:
1. Turn on your pressure cooker to "sauté" and pour in 2 tablespoons of vegetable oil.
2. Add red pepper, celery, garlic, and onions.
3. When the veggies are browned, pour in the fish stock and add sausages, pepper, and thyme.
4. Close the pressure cooker lid and hit "Manual" and then 10 minutes.
5. When time is up, hit "Cancel." Quick-release.
6. In another skillet, heat up the rest of the oil and mix in the flour to **Make** a roux.
7. Stir constantly until the flour becomes golden.
8. Take the skillet off the heat and mix in a bowl with some fish stock.
9. Pour into the pressure cooker and stir until the gumbo thickens.
10. Throw in the shrimp, oysters, and crab.
11. Lock the lid again and cook for just 1 minute on high pressure.
12. Quick-release.
13. Serve the gumbo with greens onions, parsley, and rice.

Nutritional Info (⅙ serving): Total calories - 135 Protein - 13 Carbs - 5 Fiber - 0 Fat - 7

Scallop Chowder

Serves: 4-6
Time: 10 minutes

Ingredients:
- 2 pounds cut Yukon Gold
- 1 ½ pounds bay scallops
- 3 thin bacon slices
- 2 chopped celery stalks
- 1 chopped yellow onion
- 2 cups chicken broth
- 1 cup heavy cream
- 1 cup clam juice
- ½ cup dry white wine
- ¼ cup chopped parsley
- 2 bay leaves
- 2 tablespoons butter
- 2 tablespoons minced chives
- 1 tablespoon fresh thyme leaves

Directions:
1. Fry the bacon in your pressure cooker on the "Sauté" setting.
2. Move to a plate.
3. Add butter to the pot and melt.
4. Toss in celery and onion. Cook until soft.
5. Pour in clam juice, broth, and wine.
6. Deglaze.
7. Add potatoes, thyme, and bay leaves.
8. Secure and lock the lid.
9. Hit "Manual," and select "high pressure" for 7 minutes.
10. When time is up, hit "Cancel" and quick-release.
11. Open the lid.
12. Stir and turn to the "Sauté" setting.
13. Crumble in the bacon and add scallops, cream, chives, and parsley.
14. Cook for 2 minutes while stirring the whole time.
15. Pick out bay leaves.
16. Serve!

Nutritional Info (¼ recipe):
Total calories: 396 Protein: 26.7 Carbs: 46.1 Fiber: 3.9 Fat: 13.1

Shrimp + Corn Stew

Serves: 4
Time: 10 minutes

Ingredients:

- 1 pound peeled and cleaned shrimp, cut in half
- 2 cups chicken broth
- 1 cup corn kernels
- 2 chopped bacon slices
- 1 chopped yellow onion
- 1 stemmed, cored, and chopped yellow bell pepper
- ½ cup heavy cream
- 2 tablespoons butter
- 1 tablespoon minced oregano leaves
- 2 teaspoons lemon zest
- ½ teaspoon celery seeds

Directions:
1. Turn your pressure cooker to "Sauté" and melt the butter.
2. Cook the bacon for about 3 minutes, until crispy.
3. Add bell pepper and onion. Cook until softened.
4. Toss in the lemon zest, oregano, and celery seeds, and cook for about 30 seconds.
5. Pour in the broth.
6. Stir before locking the lid.
7. Select "Manual," and then 5 minutes on "high pressure."
8. When time is up, hit "Cancel" and quick-release.
9. Open the cooker.
10. Turn the pot back to "Sauté."
11. Stir in the corn, cream, and shrimp.
12. Keep stirring as the shrimp cooks, which should take about 3 minutes, or until the shrimp becomes firm and pink.
13. Serve!

Nutritional Info (¼ recipe):
Total calories: 258 Protein: 19 Carbs: 12 Fiber: 1 Fat: 15

Clam Rolls

Serves: 4
Time: 5 minutes

Ingredients:
- 4 hot dog buns
- 8 romaine lettuce leaves
- 24 scrubbed littleneck clams
- 3 sliced celery stalks
- 1 stemmed, cored, and chopped red bell pepper
- 4 tablespoons melted and cooled butter
- ¼ cup plain Greek yogurt
- ¼ cup mayonnaise
- 2 tablespoons lemon juice

- ½ teaspoon black pepper
- ½ teaspoon dried dill

Directions:
1. Pour 1 ½ cups water into the pressure cooker and add the clams.
2. Close and lock the lid.
3. Select "Manual," and then "high pressure" for 4 minutes.
4. When time is up, hit "Cancel" and quick-release.
5. Pour the pressure cooker contents into a colander in a sink.
6. Cool.
7. In a bowl, mix the bell pepper, yogurt, mayo, celery, lemon juice, pepper, dill, and a few dashes of hot sauce.
8. Pull the meat from their shells, chop, and mix into the dressing.
9. Brush the inside of the hot dog buns with butter.
10. Heat a skillet and toast the buns.
11. Fill buns with lettuce and clam salad.

Nutritional Info (¼ recipe):

Total calories: 408 Protein: 17 Carbs: 29 Fiber: 1 Fat: 26

Lobster Casserole

Serves: 4
Time: 10 minutes

Ingredients:
- 6 cups water
- Three, 6-ounce lobster tails
- 8-ounces dried ziti
- 1 cup half-and-half
- ¾ cup Gruyere cheese
- ½ cup dry white wine
- 1 tablespoon chopped tarragon leaves
- 1 tablespoon Worcestershire sauce
- 1 tablespoon flour
- ½ teaspoon black pepper

Directions:
1. Pour 6 cups of water into the pressure cooker.
2. Add lobster tails and pasta.
3. Lock the lid.
4. Select "Manual," and then cook for 8 minutes on "high pressure."
5. When time is up, hit "Cancel" and quick-release.
6. Drain the pasta and lobster in a colander in the sink.
7. Cool.
8. Take out the meat from their shells, chop, and put back into the pasta.
9. Turn the pressure cooker to "Sauté."

10. Pour in wine, half-and-half, Worcestershire, tarragon, flour, and pepper.
11. Let the liquid simmer while stirring, so the flour dissolves.
12. Add pasta and lobster back into pot, stirring for 30 seconds.
13. Sprinkle on the cheese and stir until melted.
14. Hit "Cancel" and cover halfway with the lid, so the casserole thickens.
15. Serve hot!

Nutritional Info (¼ recipe):
Total calories: 441 Protein: 28 Carbs: 44 Fiber: 0 Fat: 15

Vegan Strawberries + Cream Oats

Serves: 2
Time: 13 minutes

Ingredients:
- 6 large strawberries
- 2 cups of water
- 1 cup steel-cut oats
- 1 cup full-fat coconut milk
- ½ vanilla bean

Directions:
1. Scrape the vanilla bean so you get the seeds out.
2. Add everything (except the strawberries) to your pressure cooker, including the vanilla bean pod.
3. Select "Manual" on your pot and decrease the time to 3 minutes at "high pressure."
4. When time is up, unplug the cooker and wait 10 minutes.
5. Cut up the strawberries and serve.
6. To sweeten, use a vegan-friendly option like maple syrup or agave.

Nutritional Info: Total calories - 264 Protein - 5 Carbs - 31 Fiber - 10 Fat – 13

Buckwheat Porridge w/ Rice Milk

Serves: 3-4
Time: 26 minutes

Ingredients:
- 3 cups rice milk
- 1 cup raw buckwheat groats
- ¼ cup raisins
- 1 sliced banana
- 1 teaspoon ground cinnamon
- ½ teaspoon vanilla

Directions:
1. Rinse the buckwheat and put in the pressure cooker.
2. Pour in rice milk, and add raisins, bananas, vanilla, and cinnamon.

3. Lock the lid.
4. Select "Manual," and then "high pressure" for 6 minutes.
5. When time is up, hit "Cancel" and wait for the pressure to come down naturally.
6. Open the lid and stir.
7. Serve with a little more rice milk and any desired toppings.

Nutritional Info (¼ recipe): Total calories - 297 Protein - 6 Carbs - 66 Fiber - 4 Fat - 3

Vegan Yogurt

Makes: 2 pints
Time: 12+ hours

Ingredients:
- 1 quart room-temperature organic plain soy milk
- 1 packet Cultures for Health vegan yogurt starter

Directions:
1. Pour the soy milk into a pitcher and stir in yogurt starter.
2. Pour into two clean pint jars.
3. Put jars into the pressure cooker.
4. Lock the lid.
5. Hit "Yogurt" and set for 12 hours.
6. When time is up, hit "Cancel" and let the pressure come down on its own for 20 minutes. Carefully quick-release the rest of the pressure.
7. Chill in the fridge overnight before serving.

Nutritional Info (½ cup recipe): Total calories - 50 Protein - 4 Carbs - 4 Fiber - .5 Fat - 2

No-Dairy Mashed Potatoes

Serves: 8
Time: About 20 minutes

Ingredients:
- 4 pounds of peeled and rinsed red + yellow potatoes
- 1 ½ cups water + ½ cup water
- 2 tablespoons olive oil Earth Balance
- ⅛ cup pine nuts
- 1 teaspoon salt
- Soy milk

Directions:
1. Pour 1 ½ cups of water into your pressure cooker, lower in the trivet, and add the potatoes.
2. Press "Steam" and then 15 minutes on "high pressure."
3. As the potatoes cook, puree ½ cup water and pine nuts.
4. When the pressure cooker timer goes off, quick-release the cooker.
5. Take out the potatoes and roughly chop in a bowl.

6. Add the pine nut mixture, Earth balance, ¼ cup soy milk, and salt to the bowl.
7. Mash till smooth, adding soy milk as needed.

Nutritional Info (⅛ recipe): Total calories - 213 Protein - 5 Carbs - 41 Fiber - 3 Fat – 5

Minestrone Soup

Serves: 4-6
Time: 18 minutes

Ingredients:
- 28-ounce can of tomatoes
- 3 minced garlic cloves
- 4 cups veggie broth
- 2 cups cooked white beans
- 2 diced celery stalks
- ½ cup fresh spinach, torn
- 1 bay leaf
- 1 diced onion
- 1 diced carrot
- 1 cup elbow pasta
- 2 tablespoons olive oil
- 1 teaspoon dried basil
- 1 teaspoon dried oregano
- Salt + pepper

Directions:
1. Turn your pressure cooker to "Sauté."
2. Add in the olive oil, carrot, celery, garlic, and onion.
3. When softened, add in basil, oregano, pepper, and salt.
4. Pulse the can of tomatoes (along with its liquid) in a processor to break them down.
5. Pour into the pot, along with broth, spinach, pasta, and the bay leaf.
6. Secure the pressure cooker lid and press "Manual," and then 6 minutes on "high pressure."
7. When the timer beeps, hit "Cancel" and wait 2 minutes.
8. Quick-release.
9. Add in the beans and stir.
10. Serve!

Nutritional Info: Total calories - 82 Protein - 4.3 Carbs - 11 Fiber - 1 Fat - 2.5

Three-Bean Chili

Serves: 6-8
Time: About 26-30 minutes

Ingredients:
- 3 ½ cups vegetable broth
- 2 cups chopped onion

- 1 ½ cups of cooked black beans
- 1 ½ cups cooked red beans
- 1 ½ cups cooked pinto beans
- ¾ cup chopped carrots
- ¼ cup chopped celery
- 14.5-ounces of diced tomatoes
- 14.5-ounces of tomato sauce
- 1 chopped red bell pepper
- 2 tablespoons mild chili powder
- 1 tablespoon minced garlic
- 1 ½ teaspoons dried oregano
- 1 ½ teaspoons cumin
- 1 teaspoon cumin seeds
- 1 teaspoon smoked paprika
- ½ teaspoon coriander

Directions:
1. Drain and rinse the beans.
2. In your pressure cooker, select "sauté" and cook the cumin seeds, onion, and minced garlic for 5 minutes. Pour in vegetable broth to avoid burning the spices.
3. Once fragrant, add in everything except the tomatoes and tomato sauce.
4. Stir before securing the lid.
5. Select "Manual" and choose 6 minutes on "high pressure."
6. When time is up, unplug the cooker (or press "cancel") and wait 10 minutes for the pressure to decrease naturally.
7. Open the lid and stir in the tomatoes and tomato sauce.
8. Let the chili rest and thicken, leaving the lid off.
9. When it reaches your desired texture, serve with toppings like green onions, parsley, vegan cheese, and so on.

Nutritional Info (⅙ recipe): Total calories - 456 Protein - 27.6 Carbs - 80 Fiber - 24 Fat - 4

Vegan Feijoada

Serves: 6
Time: 40 minutes (+ overnight soak time)

Ingredients:
- 2 ½ cups veggie broth
- 2 cups dried black beans (soaked overnight)
- 1 cup soy curls (softened in hot water for 15 minutes and drained)
- 2 peeled and cut carrots
- 2 sliced onions
- 4 minced garlic cloves
- 2 bay leaves
- 1 chopped red bell pepper

- 1 spicy chopped vegan sausage
- ⅓ cup dry red wine
- 1 tablespoon cumin
- ½ tablespoon smoked paprika
- ½ tablespoon dried thyme
- ½ tablespoon liquid smoke
- ½ teaspoon black pepper

Directions:
1. Turn on your pressure cooker to "sauté" and pour in a little water.
2. Add onions, bell pepper, carrots, and garlic and stir for 5 minutes.
3. Add spices and cook for a few minutes.
4. Pour in the red wine, wait 2 minutes, and then add the sausage, broth, beans, soy curls, and bay leaves.
5. Stir.
6. Lock the pressure cooker.
7. Hit "Bean/Chile" and adjust time to 30 minutes.
8. When the timer goes off, hit "Cancel" and wait for the pressure to come down.
9. Carefully open the lid and **Make** sure the beans are soft.
10. Serve with herbs like parsley or cilantro!

Nutritional Info (⅙ recipe): Total calories - 328 Protein - 20 Carbs - 54 Fiber - 13 Fat - 4

Spicy-Sweet Braised Cabbage

Serves: 4
Time: About 10 minutes

Ingredients:
- 1 ¼ cups of water + 2 teaspoons of water
- 3 pounds of cabbage, divided into 8 wedges
- ¾ cup grated carrots
- ¼ cup apple cider vinegar
- 1 tablespoon sesame oil
- 2 teaspoons cornstarch
- 1 teaspoon raw demerara sugar (Bob's Red Mill is a good brand)
- ½ teaspoon red pepper flakes
- ½ teaspoon cayenne powder

Directions:
1. Turn on the pressure cooker to the "sauté" function.
2. Pour in sesame oil and lay down the cabbage wedges to brown for 3 minutes on one side.
3. Remove the wedges.
4. Pour in 1 ¼ cups of water, sugar, cayenne, pepper flakes, and vinegar.
5. Return the cabbage wedges to the pot along with the grated carrot.
6. Secure the lid and select the "Manual" setting. Choose "high pressure" and cook for 5 minutes.
7. Quick-release the pressure.

8. Remove the cabbage wedges.
9. Turn the cooker back on to "sauté" and bring the cooking liquid to a bowl.
10. In a bowl, mix 2 teaspoons of **cold** water with the cornstarch.
11. Pour into the pressure cooker.
12. Keep boiling, allowing the liquid to thicken.
13. Pour over the cabbage wedges before serving.

Nutritional Info (¼ recipe): Total calories - 127 Protein - 4 Carbs - 22 Fiber - 6 Fat - 4

Chipotle-Pumpkin Soup

Serves: 6
Time: 18 minutes

Ingredients:
- 2 cups veggie broth
- 2 cups water
- 2 cups diced red potatoes
- 2 cups diced green apples
- 15-ounce can of pumpkin puree
- 1 diced onion
- 3 diced garlic cloves
- 1 seeded chipotle in adobe sauce
- ¼ cup uncooked red lentils run through a food processor
- ¼ cup walnuts run through a food processor
- 1 teaspoon salt
- 1 teaspoon black pepper
- 1 teaspoon cinnamon
- ¼ teaspoon nutmeg

Directions:
1. Turn on the pressure cooker's "sauté" setting and cook the garlic and onion for about 3-4 minutes.
2. When brown and fragrant, toss in all the spices, including the chipotle pepper, and stir.
3. Pour in the water and veggie broth, along with the potatoes, apples, pumpkin puree, and ground lentils and walnuts.
4. Choose the "Manual" setting and select a 4-minute cook time on "high pressure."
5. When the beep sounds, hit "Cancel" or unplug the cooker.
6. Wait 10 minutes for the pressure to come down by itself,
7. Before opening, release any leftover pressure.
8. Open up the lid and blend the soup, either with an immersion hand blender, or by carefully pouring it into a blender.
9. When smooth, serve right away!

Nutritional Info: Total calories - 147 Protein - 5 Carbs - 26.5 Fiber - 4.2 Fat - 3.7

Sweet Potato + Kidney Bean Stew

Serves: 6
Time: About 25 minutes

Ingredients:

- 1.5 pounds of diced sweet potatoes
- 4 cups veggie broth
- 2, 15-ounce cans of cooked kidney beans (drained and rinsed)
- 28-ounces of diced tomatoes (with liquid)
- 1, 15-ounce can of full-fat coconut milk
- 1 cup of dried brown lentils
- ½ cup chopped cilantro
- 2 minced garlic cloves
- 1 big diced onion
- 1 can green chilis
- 2 tablespoons red curry paste
- 2 tablespoons chili powder
- 1 tablespoon lime juice
- 1 teaspoon sea salt

Directions:
1. Select the "Sauté" setting on the pressure cooker and add garlic and onion.
2. When the aromatics are soft, add the sweet potatoes and stir for a few minutes.
3. Press "Cancel" and add the rest of the ingredients.
4. Secure the lid.
5. Choose "Manual" and a cook time of 10 minutes on "high pressure."
6. When the timer beeps, hit "Cancel" again and wait 10 minutes.
7. Quick-release any remaining pressure.
8. Stir and serve right away!

Nutritional Info: Total calories - 111 Protein - 5 Carbs - 23 Fiber - 5 Fat - 8

Vegan Taco Mix

Serves: 8
Time: Overnight + about 45 minutes

Ingredients:

- 1 pound soaked dried pinto beans
- 3 cups water
- 2 chopped garlic cloves
- 1 chopped medium-sized onion
- 2 whole dried red chilis
- 2 tablespoons tomato paste
- 1 minced green pepper
- 2 teaspoons oregano

- 2-3 teaspoons chili powder
- ½ teaspoon ground cumin
- Salt

Directions:
1. The beans should be soaked overnight. The night before you plan on making this recipe, rinse the beans and cover them with water. Drape a cloth towel over the bowl and store on the counter.
2. The next day, drain the beans
3. Pour 3 cups of water into your pressure cooker and add the beans, along with the garlic, onion, oregano, chilies, and cumin.
4. Close the lid.
5. Select "Manual" and choose 5 minutes at "high pressure."
6. When ready, unplug the cooker and wait 10 minutes for the pressure to decrease naturally.
7. Open the cooker and take out the dried chilies.
8. Add the remaining ingredients and cook without the lid for another 20-30 minutes in order for the flavors to deepen.
9. Serve in a corn tortilla or on top of fresh lettuce.

Nutritional Info: Total calories - 215 Protein - 12.9 Carbs - 39.5 Fiber - 10 Fat - 8

Spaghetti Squash Lasagna w/ Cashew Cheese Sauce

Serves: 6
Time: 1 hour, 30 minutes

Ingredients:
- 3 pounds spaghetti squash
- 8-ounces sliced mushrooms
- 1 ½ cups spaghetti sauce
- 1 minced garlic clove
- Salt and pepper to taste
- 1, 14-ounce package of extra-firm tofu (not silken)
- 2 peeled garlic cloves
- 2 tablespoons nutritional yeast
- 1 cup packed fresh basil
- 1 cup plain nut milk
- ¼ cup raw cashews
- ¼ cup nutritional yeast
- 2 tablespoons cornstarch
- 1 tablespoon lemon juice
- ½ teaspoon dry mustard

Directions:
1. Begin by pressure-cooking the squash. Cut it in half lengthwise and remove the seeds.
2. Pour 1 cup of water into your pressure cooker and lower in the steamer basket.

3. Put the squash in the basket.
4. Close the cooker.
5. Select "Manual," and then "high pressure" for 8 minutes.
6. Unplug the cooker and quick-release when time is up, and cool before removing the squash.
7. Scrape the spaghetti strands using a fork and store in a colander that's resting over a bowl.
8. Heat a stovetop saucepan and toss in the chopped garlic, mushrooms, and 1 tablespoon of water.
9. Stir and cover. Stir every minute or so for 3 minutes.
10. Take off the lid and cook until the liquid evaporates.
11. Season and set aside for now.
12. Put the 2 peeled garlic cloves in a food processor and chop.
13. Add the rest of the ingredients in the second ingredient list and process till creamy and smooth.
14. Using a blender, pour everything in the third ingredient list and smooth.
15. Time to assemble. Pour in ¼ cup of the spaghetti sauce along with ¼ cup of veggie stock in the pressure cooker. Put ½ of the spaghetti squash right on top.
16. Spoon the tofu filling over the squash and spread, so it's even.
17. Add mushrooms and then half of the cashew "cheese" sauce on top.
18. Add the rest of the squash and then the rest of the spaghetti sauce.
19. Close the pressure cooker lid.
20. Select "Manual" and cook for just 5 minutes on "low pressure." You're really just heating everything up.
21. When the timer beeps, let the pressure come down naturally for 10 minutes.
22. Open the cooker and pour the rest of the cashew "cheese" on top.
23. Let the lasagna rest for a few minutes before serving.

Nutritional Info: Total calories - 254 Protein - 18.3 Carbs - 30.5 Fiber - 3.3 Fat - 8.4

Black-Eyed Peas + Kale Bowl

Serves: 6
Time: About 50 minutes

Ingredients:
- 5 cups water + 2 tablespoons water
- 1 ½ cups of rinsed, dried black-eyed peas
- 1 tablespoon chopped garlic
- 1 tablespoon chopped ginger root + 2 teaspoons chopped ginger root
- 1 tablespoon coconut aminos
- 2 minced garlic cloves
- ½ teaspoon salt
- ¼ teaspoon red pepper flakes
- 2 cups brown rice
- 2 ½ cups water
- 1 big bunch of kale, with stems removed and leaves chopped up
- 1 minced garlic clove
- 1 chopped, small onion
- ½ chopped red bell pepper

- ¼ cup water
- 1 tablespoon coconut aminos

Directions:
1. Pour 5 cups of water into the pressure cooker.
2. Add the peas, 1 tablespoon of garlic, 1 tablespoon of ginger, and ½ teaspoon of salt.
3. Secure the lid and select "Manual," and then cook for 10 minutes at "high pressure."
4. When ready, unplug the cooker and wait 10 minutes before quick-releasing any remaining pressure.
5. Drain the peas, leaving 1 cup of the cooking liquid.
6. Take out a saucepan and pour the 2 tablespoons of water into it.
7. Heat over the stove.
8. Add 2 teaspoons of ginger root and the 2 cloves of garlic.
9. After two minutes of cooking, add ⅓ cup of the pea cooking liquid, the beans, 1 tablespoon coconut aminos, and red pepper flakes.
10. Now is a good time to **Make** the brown rice. To **Make** brown rice in the pressure cooker, pour in 2 ½ cups of water with 2 cups of brown rice.
11. Close the lid and choose "Manual," and then 22 minutes on "high pressure."
12. Let this simmer for 20-30 minutes, without a liquid. If the peas start to dry out, add more of their cooking liquid.
13. The rice should be done now. The cooker will automatically go to "keep warm." Keep this position for 10 minutes before hitting "cancel" and quick-releasing any leftover steam. You can keep the rice in the cooker for now.
14. Take out another skillet and add the onion.
15. Cook until it starts to brown, and then add garlic and the red bell pepper.
16. Add the kale and ¼ cup of water and cover.
17. After 3-6 minutes, the kale should still be very green, but tender.
18. Take the skillet off the hot burner and add 1 tablespoon coconut aminos.
19. Serve the peas with the kale and rice. Sriracha is a good condiment.

Nutritional Info (⅙ recipe): Total calories - 186 Protein - 12.5 Carbs - 34.4 Fiber - 6.2 Fat - 1

Sweet Potato Peanut Butter Soup

Serves: 4
Time: 10-15 minutes

Ingredients:
- 3 big sweet potatoes, cubed
- 3 chopped garlic cloves
- 1 chopped onion
- 15-ounce can of diced tomatoes (liquid saved)
- 14-ounce can of full-fat coconut milk
- 4-ounce can of green chilis
- 2 cups veggie broth
- ½ cup peanut butter
- 1 tablespoon lime juice

- ½ teaspoon allspice
- ¼ teaspoon ground cilantro

Directions:
1. Turn on the pressure cooker and hit "Sauté."
2. Pour in a little oil and cook the garlic and onion, stirring, until soft.
3. Hit "Cancel."
4. Add the rest of the ingredients and stir.
5. Lock the lid.
6. Press "Manual" and adjust time to 4 minutes on "high pressure."
7. When the timer beeps, hit "Cancel" again and wait for the pressure to decrease naturally.
8. Stir.
9. Puree until smooth and serve!

Nutritional Info (¼ recipe): Total calories - 286 Protein - 8 Carbs - 29 Fiber - 6 Fat - 16

Vegan Chocolate Cheesecake

Serves: 8
Time: 6 hours

Ingredients:
- 1 ½ cups almond flour
- ¼ cup vegan sweetener
- ¼ cup melted coconut oil
- 1 ¾ cups water (for the Instant Pot)
- 1 ½ cups soaked and drained cashews
- 1 cup chocolate nut milk
- ⅔ cups sugar
- ¼ cup non-dairy chocolate chips
- 2 tablespoons coconut flour
- 2 teaspoons vanilla
- ½ teaspoon salt

Directions:
1. Mix the ingredients in the first list (the crust) and press into a silicone, 7-inch cheesecake pan, covering the bottom and a little way up the sides.
2. Store in the fridge while you're making the filling.
3. Mix all the ingredients (except the chips) in a blender for about 2 minutes or until smooth.
4. Add in the chips and mix again just to distribute them.
5. Pour the batter into the pan.
6. Pour 1 ¾ cups of water into the pressure cooker and lower in the trivet.
7. Place the cheesecake pan into the cooker and close the lid.
8. Select "Manual" and choose "high pressure" for 55 minutes.
9. When the timer beeps, unplug the cooker and wait 10 minutes.
10. Quick-release any leftover pressure.
11. Open the lid and carefully remove the pan.

12. Cool for 1 hour
13. Store in the fridge, covered, for at least 4 hours to chill.
- **Nutritional Info:** Total calories - 396 Protein - 8 Carbs - 36 Fiber - 1 Fat – 26

Chocolate-Chip Zucchini Bread w/ Walnuts

Serves: 24
Time: 35 minutes

Ingredients:
- 3 eggs
- 2 ½ cups flour
- A little less than 2 cups of sugar
- 2 cups grated zucchini
- 1 cup applesauce
- ½ cup baking cocoa
- ½ cup chocolate chips
- ½ cup chopped walnuts
- 1 tablespoon pure vanilla extract
- 1 teaspoon baking soda
- 1 teaspoon salt
- 1 teaspoon cinnamon
- ¼ teaspoon baking powder

Directions:
1. In a bowl, beat the applesauce, vanilla, sugar, and eggs together.
2. Mix in the zucchini.
3. Mix all the dry ingredients together in a separate bowl.
4. Add in the zucchini wet mixture and mix thoroughly.
5. Grease an 8-inch Bundt pan and pour in the bread mix.
6. Pour 1 ½ cups of water into your pressure cooker and lower in the trivet.
7. Place the Bundt pan on top of the trivet.
8. Secure the lid.
9. Choose the "Manual" setting and cook for 25 minutes on "high pressure."
10. When done, turn off the cooker and wait 10 minutes.
11. Carefully open the lid and remove the pan.
12. Cool before serving.

Nutritional Info (1/24 of recipe): Total calories - 221 Protein - 4.4 Carbs - 28.1 Fiber - 1.6 Fat - 11

Chocolate-Chip Cheesecake w/ Brownie Crust

Serves: 6
Time: 6 hours, 50 minutes

Ingredients:
- 2 eggs
- 2 cups of water
- ½ cup butter
- ½ cup sugar
- ¾ cup white flour
- ¼ cup cocoa powder
- 2 tablespoons honey
- ¾ teaspoon baking powder
- ¼ teaspoon salt
- 24-ounces of softened cream cheese
- 14-ounces of sweetened condensed milk
- 3 eggs
- ½ cup chocolate chips
- 2 teaspoons vanilla

Directions:
1. Melt the butter and mix in cocoa powder.
2. Cool.
3. Mix the flour, baking powder, sugar, and salt together.
4. Beat the eggs, not too much, and add to the sugar/flour mixture along with the honey and butter/cocoa.
5. Mix everything well.
6. Grease an 8-inch springform pan and pour in the brownie batter.
7. Cover completely with foil.
8. Pour 2 cups of water into the pressure cooker and lower in the trivet.
9. Place the pan on top of the trivet and lock the lid.
10. Cook on "high" for 35 minutes.
11. While this cooks, **Make** your cheesecake filling.
12. Beat the cream cheese until smooth and fluffy.
13. Slowly beat in the sweetened condensed milk until just combined.
14. Add the eggs and vanilla.
15. Mix again until just combined; cheesecake fillings should not be overmixed, or they get holes.
16. Add chocolate chips.
17. Once the brownie crust is done, quick-release the pressure.
18. Remove the pan, unwrap it, and pour the filling on top.
19. Don't wrap the pan again in foil, just lower back into the cooker and secure the lid.
20. Cook for another 15 minutes on "high pressure."
21. When time is up, the pressure cooker should switch to the "keep warm" setting. Check to **Make** sure.
22. Do not touch the pot for 6 hours.
23. When ready, take out the cheesecake and let it cool.
24. Chill in the fridge before enjoying!

Nutritional Info: Total calories - 184 Protein - 3.2 Carbs - 18 Fiber - 0 Fat - 11.2

Graham-Cracker Crust Lemon Cheesecake

Serves: 6
Time: 4 hours, 15 minutes

Ingredients:
- ½ cup finely-crushed graham cracker crumbs
- 2 tablespoons sugar
- 2 tablespoons melted butter
- 32-ounces of room-temperature cream cheese
- 3 big eggs
- ½ cup sugar
- 1 tablespoon fresh-squeezed lemon juice
- 2 tablespoons of flour (optional - if you want a denser cake)
- 1 teaspoon grated lemon zest
- ½ teaspoon pure vanilla extract
- Pinch of salt

Directions:
1. Put the graham cracker crumbs in a bowl and mix in the melted butter and sugar.
2. Take your 7-inch springform pan and coat the sides with the crust mixture on the bottom and a little way up on the side. Press down firmly.
3. To **Make** the filling, begin by mixing the cream cheese (softened at room temperature) and sugar until completely smooth.
4. Add the eggs in one at a time and mix.
5. Mix in the lemon zest, lemon juice, salt, and vanilla until just combined. If you're using flour, add it in now and mix.
6. Pour into the pan over the crust.
7. Pour 2 cups of water into the pressure cooker and lower in the trivet.
8. Place the pan on top of the trivet and secure the lid.
9. Select "Manual," and cook on "high pressure" for 15 minutes.
10. After 15 minutes, turn off the cooker and wait 10 minutes.
11. Carefully remove the pan and let the cheesecake cool.
12. If there's water on top, just blot with a napkin.
13. When no longer hot, cover with plastic wrap and refrigerate for at least 4 hours to chill.

Note
Some people have found that 15 minutes is too short for their cheesecake. If when you remove the pan after letting the pressure come down naturally and it's still liquidy, put back into the pressure cooker for another 5 minutes at a time, before another natural-pressure release. It may take some experimenting to find the perfect time, but then you won't have to experiment next time.

Nutritional Info (⅙ recipe): Total calories - 719 Protein - 13 Carbs - 34 Fiber - 0 Fat - 60

Greek Yogurt Cheesecake

Serves: 8
Time: 45 minutes (+ 6 hour cooling time)

Ingredients:
- 1 ½ cups graham-cracker finely-ground crumbs
- 1 ½ cups whole-milk Greek yogurt
- 4-ounces softened, regular cream cheese
- 4 tablespoons melted butter
- 2 big eggs
- ¼ cup sugar
- 1 teaspoon vanilla

Directions:
1. Mix the cracker crumbs with melted butter.
2. Press down into the bottom of a 7-inch springform pan, so the bottom is covered and the crust is halfway up the pan.
3. Mix the cream cheese, sugar, yogurt, and vanilla until very smooth.
4. Add the eggs one at a time and mix. Be careful not to overmix.
5. Pour into the pan, covering the crust completely up the sides.
6. Lower a trivet into the pressure cooker, along with 1 cup of water.
7. Put the pan on the trivet and lock the lid.
8. Select "Manual," and then 30 minutes on "high pressure."
9. When time is up, hit "Cancel" and wait for the pressure to come down on its own.
10. Carefully open the lid.
11. With a paper towel, blot any excess moisture from the cake.
12. Take out the cake and let it cool on the counter for 1-2 hours.
13. Chill in the fridge for at least 4 hours before serving.

Nutritional Info (⅛ serving): Total calories - 280 Protein - 6 Carbs - 26 Fiber - 1 Fat - 9

Ricotta + Ginger Cheesecake

Serves: 8
Time: About 45 minutes

Ingredients:
- 1 ¼ cups gingersnap crumbs
- 8-ounces softened, regular cream cheese
- 8-ounces ricotta
- 5 tablespoons melted and cooled butter
- 2 big, room-temperature eggs
- ½ cup packed light brown sugar
- ¼ cup minced candied ginger
- 2 tablespoons plain, whole-milk (non-Greek) yogurt
- 1 tablespoon flour
- 1 teaspoon vanilla

Directions:
1. Pour 2 cups of water into the pressure cooker and lower in the trivet.
2. Mix butter and gingersnap crumbs.
3. Grease a 7-inch springform pan.
4. Press in the crumb mixture on the bottom and halfway up the pan's sides.
5. In a food processor, mix cream cheese, brown sugar, and ricotta until smooth.
6. As the machine runs, add in eggs one at a time.
7. When it's totally mixed, add in yogurt, and blend again.
8. Using a garlic press, squeeze the candied ginger into the food processor and blend till smooth.
9. Add in flour and vanilla, and mix.
10. Pour into the cheesecake pan.
11. Put the pan on top of the trivet in the pressure cooker.
12. Lock and secure the lid.
13. Press "Manual," and then 25 minutes at "high pressure."
14. When time is up, hit "Cancel" and wait for the pressure to come down naturally.
15. Take out the cheesecake and cool for 1 hour.
16. Remove from the pan and cool in the fridge for at least 6 hours.

Nutritional Info (⅛ serving): Total calories - 330 Protein - 6 Carbs -17 Fiber - 1 Fat - 27

Sea-Salt Dulce de Leche

Serves: 8
Time: 40 minutes (+ overnight cooling time)

Ingredients:
- 15-ounce can of sweetened condensed milk
- ½ teaspoon sea salt
- ½ teaspoon pure vanilla extract

Directions:
1. Take the label off the milk can, but don't open it.
2. Put the steam rack into your pressure cooker and lower in the milk can so it doesn't touch the sides.
3. Pour enough water into the pot so the can is totally submerged.
4. Close the lid.
5. Press "Manual" and then 20 minutes at "high pressure."
6. When time is up, hit "Cancel" and wait 10 minutes for the pressure to come down.
7. Open the pot lid, but don't touch anything.
8. Let it sit overnight.
9. The next day, open the milk can and pour into a bowl.
10. Whisk in the vanilla and salt.
11. Serve on ice cream, waffles, cake, and so on.

Nutritional Info (¼ cup serving): Total calories - 171 Protein - 4 Carbs - 29 Fiber - 0 Fat - 3

Orange-Chocolate Bread Pudding

Serves: 4-5
Time: 40 minutes

Ingredients:
- 2 cups water
- 3 ½ cups stale French bread, cut into ¾-inch pieces
- 3 big eggs
- 3-ounces chopped dark chocolate
- ¾ cups heavy cream
- ½ cup whole milk
- ⅓ cup sugar + 1 tablespoon
- Zest and juice of one orange
- 1 teaspoon butter
- 1 teaspoon almond extract
- Pinch of salt

Directions:
1. Pour water into the pressure cooker and insert the steamer rack.
2. Grease a 6-7 inch round baking dish.
3. In a bowl, mix the eggs and ⅓ cup of sugar.
4. Pour in the milk, cream, almond extract, orange juice, orange zest, and salt.
5. Mix.
6. Toss the bread pieces in the mixture. Let it soak for 5 minutes.
7. Add the chopped chocolate and stir.
8. Pour in the baking dish and **Make** sure all the bread is submerged.
9. Sprinkle on 1 tablespoon of sugar.
10. Put on the steamer rack (do **not** wrap in foil) and close the lid.
11. Hit "Manual" and cook for 15 minutes on "high pressure."
12. When time is up, hit "Cancel" and wait for the pressure to come down by itself.
13. When depressurized, open the lid and take out the pudding.
14. Serve!

Nutritional Info: Total calories - 467 Protein - 12 Carbs - 51 Fiber - 1 Fat - 14

Mini Pumpkin Puddings

Serves: 4
Time: 35 minutes (1 ½ hours cooling time)

Ingredients:
- 1 cup water
- 1 cup pumpkin puree
- ¼ cup sugar
- ¼ cup half-and-half
- 1 egg yolk
- 1 beaten egg
- 1 tablespoon butter

- ½ teaspoon ground cinnamon
- ½ teaspoon pure vanilla extract
- ¼ teaspoon ground ginger
- ¼ teaspoon salt
- Pinch ground cloves

Directions:
1. Pour the water into the pressure cooker and lower in the steam rack.
2. Grease four heat-safe mugs.
3. In a bowl, whisk the sugar, pumpkin, and spices together.
4. Add the egg, egg yolk, vanilla, and half-and half, and whisk until thoroughly blended.
5. Pour into the containers.
6. Place on the steam rack in the pressure cooker.
7. Lock the lid.
8. Press "Manual," and select 15 minutes on "high pressure."
9. When the timer goes off, hit "Cancel" and wait for the pressure to go down on its own.
10. Open the lid.
11. Wait till the steam dissipates before taking out the puddings.
12. Cool for 1 ½ hours on the counter.

Nutritional Info (¼ serving): Total calories - 174 Protein - 4 Carbs - 18 Fiber - 1 Fat - 6

Blueberry-Peach Cobbler

Serves: 4-6
Time: 35 minutes

Ingredients:
- 2 cups peeled, sliced frozen peaches
- 2 cups frozen blueberries
- 1 cup flour
- ⅓ cup buttermilk
- ⅓ cup sugar + 1 tablespoon
- ⅓ cup water
- 2 tablespoons cubed cold butter
- 1 tablespoon cornstarch
- 1 ½ teaspoons baking powder
- 1 teaspoon lime juice
- ½ teaspoon salt
- ¼ teaspoon baking soda
- Pinch of nutmeg

Directions:
1. In a bowl, mix flour, 1 tablespoon of sugar, baking soda, baking powder, and salt.
2. Add butter and work with your hands to form a cornmeal-like texture.
3. Pour in the buttermilk and mix until just moistened.
4. Form into a dough ball.

5. Hit "sauté" on your pressure cooker and add blueberries, peaches, ⅓ cup sugar, water, lemon juice, cornstarch, and nutmeg.
6. Cook for about 2-3 minutes until the frozen fruit has softened and started to leak juice.
7. Hit "Cancel."
8. Tear 1-inch dough balls out of the big dough ball and put on top of the fruit in the pressure cooker, making about 8 balls in total.
9. Close the lid.
10. Hit "Manual" and select 10 minutes on "high pressure."
11. When time is up, hit "Cancel" and wait for the pressure to decrease naturally.
12. When all the pressure is gone, open the lid and wait a few minutes for the liquid to thicken.
13. Serve!

Nutritional Info: Total calories - 330 Protein - 5 Carbs - 66 Fiber - 3 Fat - 4

Apple Dumplings

Serves: 6-8
Time: 30 minutes

Ingredients:
- 1 can of crescent rolls
- 1 big cored, peeled and cut green apple (8 big wedges)
- ¾ cup apple cider
- ½ cup brown sugar
- 4 tablespoons butter
- 1 teaspoon ground cinnamon
- ½ teaspoon vanilla extract
- Pinch of ground nutmeg

Directions:
1. Hit "Sauté" on your pressure cooker.
2. Prepare the dough by opening the crescent rolls and rolling out flat.
3. Take the apple wedges and wrap each piece in one crescent roll.
4. Put the butter in the pot and hit "Cancel."
5. Throw in the sugar, vanilla, nutmeg, and cinnamon.
6. Stir until everything melts together.
7. Put the dumplings in the pot.
8. Pour the apple cider along the edges of the dumplings.
9. Lock the lid.
10. Press "Manual" and then 10 minutes at "high pressure."
11. When time is done, hit "Cancel" and wait for pressure to come down on its own.
12. Serve dumplings with the cooking liquid spooned on top.

Nutritional Info: Total calories - 267 Protein - 4 Carbs - 41 Fiber - 2 Fat - 5

Creamy Rice Pudding w/ Golden Raisins

Serves: 6

Time: 15-20 minutes

Ingredients:
- 5 cups milk
- 2 eggs
- 1 ½ cups Arborio rice
- 1 cup half and half
- 1 cup golden raisins
- ¾ cup sugar
- 1 ½ teaspoons pure vanilla extract
- ½ teaspoon salt
- Cinnamon as desired

Directions:
1. In your pressure cooker, mix rice, salt, sugar, and milk.
2. Select the "sauté" button and bring to a boil while stirring constantly.
3. Once boiling, secure the lid and seal the steam release valve.
4. Press "Rice."
5. Meanwhile, mix eggs, vanilla, and half and half together in a bowl.
6. When the pressure cooker is ready, push "Cancel" and wait 15 minutes.
7. Quick-release any remaining pressure and take off the lid.
8. Pour in the egg mixture and raisins.
9. Push "sauté" again and let the pudding come to a boil, without putting on the lid.
10. Push "Cancel."
11. Serve hot or put in the fridge to chill.
12. Sprinkle on cinnamon.

Nutritional Info (⅙ recipe): Total calories - 518 Protein – 14 Carbs - 94 Fiber - 0 Fat - 11

Red-Wine Baked Apples

Serves: 6
Time: 30-40 minutes

Ingredients:
- 6 cored apples
- 1 cup red wine
- ½ cup sugar
- ¼ cup raisins
- 1 teaspoon cinnamon

Directions:
1. Set the apples inside the pressure cooker.
2. Pour in wine and add the sugar, cinnamon, and raisins.
3. Secure the lid.
4. Select "Manual" and cook for 10 minutes on "high pressure."
5. When the timer beeps, hit "cancel" and wait 20-30 minutes for the pressure to come down.

6. Serve the apples in a bowl with the cooking liquid spooned over.

Nutritional Info: Total calories - 188.7 Protein - 0 Carbs - 41.9 Fiber - 3.8 Fat - 0

Cinnamon-Crumble Stuffed Peaches

Serves: 5
Time: About 15 minutes

Ingredients:
- 5 medium-sized peaches
- ¼ cup brown sugar
- ¼ cup flour
- 2 tablespoons butter
- ½ teaspoon ground cinnamon
- 1/2 teaspoon pure almond extract + ¼ teaspoon almond extract
- Pinch of sea salt

Directions:
1. Carefully slice about ¼ inch off the top of your peaches.
2. With a sharp knife, cut into the top and take out the pits, so the peaches have a little hollow.
3. In a bowl, mix the flour, sugar, cinnamon, and salt.
4. Melt the butter and add, along with the ½ teaspoon of almond extract.
5. Mix until crumbly.
6. Fill peaches.
7. Pour 1 cup of water into the pressure cooker and add ¼ teaspoon of almond extract right into the water.
8. Lower in the steamer basket and arrange the peaches inside.
9. Secure the lid.
10. Press "Manual" and decrease the time to 3 minutes.
11. When the timer sounds, press "Cancel" and unplug.
12. Quick-release the pressure.
13. Remove the peaches with tongs and cool for 10 minutes.
14. Serve with vanilla ice cream or devour as is!

Nutritional Info (1 peach w/ crumble): Total calories - 162 Protein - 2 Carbs - 30 Fiber - 2.3 Fat - 5

Individual Brownie Cakes

Serves: 4
Time: 28 minutes

Ingredients:
- 2 eggs
- ⅔ cup sugar
- ½ cup flour
- 4 tablespoons cocoa powder
- 4 tablespoons unsalted butter

- 2 tablespoons chocolate chips
- 2 tablespoons powdered sugar
- ¼ teaspoon vanilla extract

Directions:
1. Melt the butter and chocolate chips together in a heatproof bowl.
2. Add the sugar and beat until mixed.
3. Add in the eggs and vanilla and beat again.
4. Sift in the flour and cocoa into the wet ingredients and blend.
5. Pour 1 cup of water into the pressure cooker and insert the steamer rack.
6. Pour the brownie batter into 4 ramekins and cover the top with foil.
7. Lower into the pressure cooker on top of the rack.
8. Select "Manual" and choose "high pressure" for 18 minutes.
9. When time is up, quick-release the pressure.
10. Remove the ramekins and cool for a few minutes.
11. Dust on some powdered sugar and serve!

Nutritional Info (1 cake): Total calories - 377 Protein - 6 Carbs - 56 Fiber - 0 Fat - 17

Homemade Yogurt

Makes: About 24 servings
Time: 8 hours, 10 minutes (10 minutes active time, 8 hours cook time)

Ingredients:
- 1 gallon of 2% milk
- ½ cup honey
- 3 tablespoons powdered milk
- ¼ cup yogurt with active cultures
- 1 vanilla bean

Directions:
1. Pour the 2% milk in the pressure cooker and add powdered milk.
2. Stir well.
3. Close the pot lid and hit "yogurt."
4. Hit "adjust" until you reach the "boil" setting.
5. The cycle should take about one hour.
6. When time is up, check the temperature and then hit "sauté" until the pot contents reach 185-degrees.
7. Then, unplug the pressure cooker and carefully remove the pot part to a cooling rack.
8. When it has reached 110-degrees, stir in the yogurt with active cultures and honey.
9. Return the pot to its normal position and secure the lid again.
10. Press "yogurt" and set the time for 8 hours.
11. When done, chill in the pot (in the fridge) overnight, or at least 6 hours.
12. Now it's time to strain the yogurt. Put the yogurt in nut milk bags, and hang from a cupboard knob over a bowl, to catch the whey.

13. If you want a really thick yogurt, strain for an hour.
14. When that's done, discard the whey and empty the bags into the pressure cooker again.
15. Stir well and scrape the vanilla bean into the yogurt.
16. Spoon the finished yogurt into Mason jars and refrigerate overnight before eating.

Nutritional Info (1 serving)
Total calories: 109 Protein: 6 Fat: 3 Carbs: 14 Fiber: 0

Sweet 'n Easy Peachy-Cream Oatmeal

Serves: 4
Time: 13 minutes

Ingredients:
- 4 cups water
- 2 cups rolled oats
- 1 chopped peach
- 1 teaspoon pure vanilla extract
- Cream to taste
- Maple syrup to taste

Directions:
1. Pour the water into your pressure cooker.
2. Add oats, chopped peach, and vanilla.
3. Seal the pressure cooker.
4. Hit the "porridge" setting and adjust to 3 minutes.
5. When time is up, unplug the cooker or hit "cancel" and wait 10 minutes while the pressure comes down on its own.
6. Quick-release any remaining pressure before opening the lid.
7. Stir well.
8. Serve in four bowls, with maple syrup and cream.

Nutritional Info (¼ recipe)
Total calories: 155 Protein: 6 Fat: 3 Carbs: 25 Fiber: 4

Cheesy Egg Bake

Serves: 8
Time: 15 minutes (5 minutes active time, 10 minutes cook time)

Ingredients:
- 8 eggs
- 6 slices chopped bacon
- 2 cups frozen hash browns
- 1 cup shredded cheddar cheese
- ¼ cup milk
- 1 teaspoon salt

- ½ teaspoon pepper

Directions:
1. Turn your pressure cooker to "sauté" and cook the chopped bacon until nice and crispy.
2. Add the hash browns and stir until they've begun to thaw.
3. In a separate bowl, whisk the milk, eggs, cheese, salt, and pepper together before pouring into the pot.
4. Secure the lid.
5. Select "manual" and adjust to 5 minutes on high pressure.
6. When time is up, unplug the cooker or hit "cancel."
7. Quick-release the pressure.
8. Carefully turn the pot upside down to remove the egg bake.
9. Slice up and serve!

Nutritional Info (⅛ recipe)
Total calories: 208 Protein: 11 Fat: 14 Carbs: 4 Fiber: 1

Berry Breakfast Cake

Serves: 6
Time: About 45 minutes (20 minutes active time, 25 minutes cook time)

Ingredients:

For the cake
- 5 eggs
- 1 cup whole-wheat flour
- ¾ cup vanilla yogurt
- ¾ cup ricotta cheese
- ¼ cup sugar
- 2 tablespoons melted butter
- ½ cup berry compote
- 2 teaspoons vanilla
- 2 teaspoons baking powder

For the glaze
- ¼ cup yogurt
- 1-2 tablespoons powdered sugar
- 1 teaspoon milk
- ½ teaspoon pure vanilla

Directions:
1. Spray a 6-cup Bundt pan.
2. In a bowl, mix the sugar and eggs.
3. Add ricotta cheese, melted butter, vanilla, and yogurt, and mix.
4. In another bowl, mix the salt, baking powder, and flour.
5. Pour into the wet ingredients and mix.

6. Pour into the Bundt pan.
7. With a tablespoon, swirl ½ cup of the berry compote on top of the batter.
8. Pour 1 cup of water into the pressure cooker and lay down a trivet.
9. Put the Bundt pan on top.
10. Secure the lid.
11. Select "manual" and cook at high pressure for 25 minutes.
12. While that cooks, mix yogurt, vanilla, milk, and powdered sugar for the glaze.
13. When the pressure cooker timer goes off, hit "cancel" or unplug the cooker, and wait 10 minutes.
14. Quick-release any leftover pressure.
15. Take out the Bundt pan and cool for 10 minutes or so.
16. With a knife, loosen the edges before turning upside down on a plate.
17. Drizzle on the glaze and serve!

Nutritional Info (⅙ recipe)
Total calories: 323 Protein: 13 Fat: 13 Carbs: 42 Fiber: 1

Mushroom-Thyme Steel Cut Oats

Serves: 4
Time: About 30 minutes (5 minutes active time, 25 minutes cook time)

Ingredients:
- 8 ounces of sliced crimini mushrooms
- 14-ounces of chicken broth
- 1 cup steel-cut oats
- ½ diced onion
- ½ cup water
- ½ cup finely-grated smoked gouda cheese
- 3 sprigs of thyme
- 2 minced garlic cloves
- 2 tablespoons butter
- Salt and pepper to taste

Directions:
1. Melt the butter in your pressure cooker on the "sauté" setting.
2. When melted, toss in the diced onion and mushrooms, and cook for 3 minutes.
3. Add garlic and cook for another minute.
4. Add the oats and toast for about 1 minute before pouring in the water, broth, thyme sprigs, and salt.
5. Secure the lid.
6. Select "manual" and set for 10 minutes on high pressure.
7. When time is up, unplug the cooker and wait 10 minutes.
8. Quick-release any remaining pressure.
9. Open the lid and mix in the cheese until melted.
10. Season to taste with salt and pepper.
11. Enjoy!

Nutritional Info (¼ recipe)

Total calories: 266 Protein: 9 Fat: 12 Carbs: 31 Fiber: 5

Vanilla Latte Oatmeal

Serves: 4
Time: About 25 minutes

Ingredients:
- 2 ½ cups water
- 1 cup milk
- 1 cup steel-cut oats
- 2 tablespoons sugar
- 1 tablespoon finely-grated dark chocolate
- 2 teaspoons pure vanilla extract
- 1 teaspoon espresso powder
- ¼ teaspoon salt
- A dollop of whipped cream

Directions:
1. Pour the milk and water into your pressure cooker.
2. Add oats, sugar, espresso powder, and salt.
3. Stir well until the espresso has dissolved.
4. Close the lid.
5. Select "manual" and then cook on high pressure for 10 minutes.
6. When time is up, unplug or turn off the cooker by hitting "cancel."
7. Wait 10 minutes while the pressure comes down naturally. You can use this time to grate your chocolate.
8. Quick-release any leftover pressure before opening the pot.
9. Add the vanilla extract and put the lid back on, but without sealing it.
10. After another 5 minutes, the oats should be at a good texture.
11. Serve with the chocolate and a dollop of whipped cream.

Nutritional Info (¼ recipe)
Total calories: 212 Protein: 6 Fat: 6 Carbs: 34 Fiber: 5

Tomato-Spinach Quiche

Serves: 6
Time: About 35 minutes (5 minutes active time, 30 minutes cook time)

Ingredients:
- 12 eggs
- 3 cups chopped baby spinach
- 4 tomato slices
- 3 sliced green onions
- 1 cup diced tomato

- ½ cup milk
- ¼ cup shredded Parmesan cheese
- Salt and pepper to taste

Directions:
1. Put a trivet in the pressure cooker and pour in 1 ½ cups of water.
2. In a bowl, mix the milk, eggs, salt, and pepper.
3. Put the chopped spinach, diced tomato, and green onion in a 1 ½-quart baking dish (that you know fits in the pressure cooker) and mix.
4. Pour the eggs in the dish over the veggies and stir.
5. Place the tomato slices evenly on top and top with cheese.
6. Without covering the dish, lower into the pressure cooker and secure the lid.
7. Hit "manual" and then choose high pressure for 20 minutes.
8. When the timer goes off, unplug the cooker or hit "cancel."
9. After ten minutes, quick-release any remaining pressure.
10. Serve!

Tip: If you want, you can stick the baking dish under a broiler after everything is cooked for a few minutes to brown the top.

Nutritional Info (⅙ recipe)
Total calories: 177 Protein: 15 Fat: 11 Carbs: 3 Fiber: 0

Homemade Bacon Hash Browns

Serves: 4
Time: 35 minutes (20 minutes active time, 15 minutes cook time)

Ingredients:
- About 2 pounds of washed and peeled russet potatoes
- Just under 1 cup of crumbled bacon
- 2 tablespoons chopped parsley
- 2 tablespoons olive oil
- Salt and pepper to taste

Directions:
1. Take your potatoes and either grate them, or pulse them through a food processor.
2. Put the hash in a strainer and rinse in cold, running water for 30 seconds.
3. Squeeze-dry really well using paper towels.
4. Pour the olive oil into your pressure cooker and heat on "sauté."
5. When shiny, add the potatoes and sprinkle on salt and pepper.
6. Cook for 5-6 minutes until the potatoes are brown.
7. Add in your parsley and bacon and mix.
8. With a spatula, flatten the potatoes into the normal hash brown shape.
9. Secure the pressure cooker lid and select low pressure for about 6 ½ minutes.
10. When time is up, hit "cancel" and quick-release the pressure.
11. Serve right away!

Nutritional Info (¼ recipe)

Total calories: 303 **Protein:** 16 **Fat:** 15 **Carbs:** 34 **Fiber:** 0

Breakfast Burritos

Serves: 6
Time: About 45 minutes (10 minutes active time, 35 minutes cook time)

Ingredients:
- 1 ½ cups + 1 tablespoon water
- 8 eggs
- 8-ounces of seasoned, ground pork sausage
- 6 burrito-style tortillas
- ¼ cup milk
- Salt and pepper to taste

Directions:
1. Mix the ground pork sausage with 1 tablespoon of water in a bowl.
2. Cover with plastic wrap and set aside for now.
3. Take out a sheet of foil and brush with a little olive oil, so your tortillas don't stick.
4. Put your tortillas in the center of the foil, and top with another sheet of foil, also brushed with oil.
5. Fold and seal the corners well.
6. In a bowl, mix the eggs.
7. Add milk and some salt and pepper.
8. Add the pork sausage and break up, so the meat is dispersed in the eggs.
9. Cover tightly with foil.
10. Pour 1 ½ cups of water into your pressure cooker and lower in a trivet.
11. Put the bowl of eggs/meat into the cooker on top of the trivet.
12. Place the wrapped tortillas on top.
13. Secure the lid and select "manual." Cook for 15 minutes on low pressure.
14. When time is up, turn off the cooker and wait 10 minutes.
15. Quick-release any leftover pressure.
16. Carefully remove the food.
17. Assemble your burritos! Add cheese and salsa before wrapping up and serving.
18. If you're freezing, assemble with just the pork/egg mixture, and then wrap back up in foil and stick in the freezer.

Nutritional Info (⅙ recipe)
Total calories: 406 **Protein:** 21 **Fat:** 20 **Carbs:** 35 **Fiber:** 0

Coconut Steel-Cut Oatmeal

Serves: 4
Time: About 30 minutes (10 minutes active time, 20 minutes cook time)

Ingredients:
- 2 cups water
- 1 cup steel-cut oats

- 1 cup full-fat coconut milk
- ½ cup unsweetened coconut flakes
- 2 tablespoons brown sugar
- ½ teaspoon ground cinnamon
- Dash of salt

Directions:
1. Toss the coconut into the pressure cooker to toast.
2. Stir, so the coconut doesn't burn.
3. When the coconut is becoming golden, take out half and set aside in a bowl.
4. Add the oats into the coconut still in the pot and stir for 2 minutes.
5. Put in 1 cup of coconut milk and the other ingredients, except the cinnamon.
6. Stir well and secure the lid.
7. Select "manual," then cook for 2 minutes on high pressure.
8. When the timer goes off, unplug or hit "cancel," and wait 10 minutes.
9. Open the lid.
10. Serve with the coconut you set aside earlier and any leftover coconut milk.

Nutritional Info (¼ recipe)
Total calories: 239 Protein: 5 Fat: 9 Carbs: 37 Fiber: 4

Huevos Rancheros

Serves: 1-2
Time: 25 minutes (5 minutes active time, 20 minutes cook time)

Ingredients:
- 3 eggs
- ½ cup of salsa
- Salt and pepper to taste
- Tortillas (or tortilla chips)

Directions:
1. Pour your salsa into a ramekin.
2. Crack the eggs on top of the salsa.
3. With foil, wrap the ramekin tightly.
4. Pour 1 cup of cold water into the pressure cooker and lower in a steamer basket.
5. Place the ramekin in the basket.
6. Secure the lid and select "manual" and then 20 minutes on low pressure.
7. When time is up, hit "cancel" and quick-release the pressure.
8. Carefully remove the ramekin from the basket.
9. Serve the breakfast in the ramekin and dip in chips, or pour over warm tortillas.

Nutritional Info (½ recipe)
Total calories: 195 Protein: 12 Fat: 10 Carbs: 14 Fiber: 0

Stone-Ground Cheesy Grits

Serves: 4
Time: About 30-35 minutes (5 minutes active time, 25 minutes cook time)

Ingredients:
- 3 cups water
- 1 ¾ cups of cream
- 1 cup stone-ground grits
- 2 tablespoons coconut oil
- 4 ounces of cheddar cheese
- 3 tablespoons butter
- 2 teaspoons salt
- Black pepper to taste

Directions:
1. Turn your pressure cooker to "sauté" and preheat.
2. Add the oil.
3. When shiny and hot, pour in the grits and stir so they toast, but do not burn.
4. Turn off the cooker.
5. Pour in the rest of the ingredients.
6. Close the lid, select "manual," and then cook on high pressure for 10 minutes.
7. When the timer goes off, unplug the cooker and wait 15 minutes.
8. Quick-release any leftover pressure.
9. Stir before serving, and season to taste with salt and pepper.

Nutritional Info (¼ recipe)
Total calories: 532 Protein: 13 Fat: 38 Carbs: 34 Fiber: 0

Cranberry-Apple Chicken w/ Cabbage

Serves: 4
Time: 35 minutes (5 minutes active time, 30 minutes cook time)

Ingredients:
- 2 pounds boneless, skinless chicken thighs
- 2 cored and sliced apples
- 1 small head of cored and shredded cabbage
- 1 cup frozen (or fresh) cranberries
- ½ cup chicken broth
- 1 tablespoon pure maple syrup
- 1 tablespoon apple cider vinegar
- 1 teaspoon ground ginger
- 1 teaspoon cinnamon
- Salt to taste

Directions:
1. Put the ingredients in your pressure cooker, with the shredded cabbage on the bottom.
2. Close and secure the lid.

3. Select the "poultry" button and adjust time to 20 minutes.
4. When time is up, hit "cancel" or unplug the cooker.
5. Let the pressure come down naturally for 10 minutes before opening the pressure cooker.
6. Serve and enjoy!

Nutritional Info (¼ recipe)
Total calories: 409 Protein: 35 Fat: 22 Carbs: 16 Fiber: 1

Chicken Pot "Pie"

Serves: 6
Time: 14 minutes (10 minutes active time, 4 minutes cook time)

Ingredients:
- 2 pounds of cubed boneless, skinless chicken breasts
- 16-ounces of frozen mixed veggies
- 3 cups chicken stock
- 3 medium-sized peeled and chopped potatoes
- 1 can of biscuit dough, torn into four pieces
- ¼ cup diced onion
- 1 teaspoon salt
- 1 teaspoon Herbes de Provence

For the cream of chicken soup
- 1 ½ cups cold milk
- 2 tablespoons room temp butter
- 2 tablespoons potato starch
- 2 teaspoons salt
- 1 ½ teaspoons chicken bouillon
- 1 ½ teaspoons Herbes de Provence
- Black pepper

Directions:
1. Whisk all the ingredients in the second list together. This is your homemade cream of chicken soup.
2. Put the chicken in the pressure cooker and pour in the stock.
3. Add veggies and potatoes.
4. Pour in the cream of chicken soup.
5. Arrange the four biscuit dough pieces on top.
6. Season with salt and Herbes de Provence.
7. Secure the lid.
8. Hit "manual" and cook for 4 minutes on high pressure.
9. When time is up, wait 10 minutes for the pressure to come down.
10. Turn off the cooker and quick-release leftover pressure.
11. To Make a thicker sauce, scoop out ¼ cup of liquid and mix with 1 tablespoon of potato starch.
12. Whisk until smooth and pour back into the pot.
13. Let the pot sit and simmer in its own heat until the sauce has thickened to your liking.

14. Serve!

Nutritional Info (⅙ recipe)

Total calories: 458 Protein: 55 Fat: 12 Carbs: 32 Fiber: 1

Chipotle Chicken w/ Rice and Black Beans

Serves: 6
Time: Less than 10 minutes

Ingredients:
- 1 pound boneless, skinless, diced chicken breasts
- 4 cups diced tomatoes (in juice)
- 1 chopped onion
- 1 can drained and rinsed black beans
- 1 cup uncooked Jasmine rice
- ½ cup water
- 1 tablespoon butter
- 1 tablespoon pureed chipotle peppers in adobo sauce
- ½ juiced lime
- 2 teaspoons sea salt
- ½ teaspoon black pepper

Directions:
1. Put the chicken, onion, tomatoes (and their juice), chipotle peppers, rice, butter, water, and seasonings in your pressure cooker.
2. Secure the lid.
3. Hit "manual" and select "high pressure."
4. Adjust time to 6 minutes.
5. When time is up, quick-release the pressure.
6. Pour in the can of black beans and stir to heat them through.
7. Season to taste with more salt and pepper if necessary.
8. Serve!

Nutritional Info (⅙ recipe)

Total calories: 678 Protein: 93 Fat: 13 Carbs: 44 Fiber: 4

Pressure Cooker Chicken Lo Mein

Serves: 6
Time: About 22-25 minutes (10 minutes active time, 12 minutes cook time)

Ingredients:
- ½ pound boneless, skinless, diced chicken breasts
- 13-16 ounce box of linguini pasta
- 4 cups chicken broth
- 4 minced garlic cloves

- 4 peeled medium-sized carrots, cut into strips
- 1 medium-sized red bell pepper, cut into strips
- 1 bunch of green onions, cut into strips
- ¼ cup soy sauce
- 1 tablespoon sugar
- 2 teaspoons extra-virgin olive oil
- 1 teaspoon garlic powder
- ½ teaspoon red pepper flakes

Directions:
1. Break the pasta in half so it all fits in the pressure cooker, but don't put it in just yet.
2. Hit "sauté" on the cooker and add olive oil.
3. Brown the chicken all over and set aside.
4. In a bowl, mix the broth, soy sauce, sugar, garlic powder, and red pepper flakes.
5. Put the garlic cloves in the pressure cooker and pour in the liquid.
6. Lay down the broken noodles in the pot, followed by the veggie strips (minus the green onion) and diced chicken.
7. Secure the lid.
8. Reset the cooker (by pushing "cancel") and then press "manual."
9. Adjust time to 12 minutes on high pressure.
10. When time is up, quick-release the cooker.
11. Add the green onion and stir well.
12. Taste and season as desired with salt and pepper.
13. Serve!

Nutritional Info (⅙ recipe)
Total calories: 332 Protein: 17.6 Fat: .3 Carbs: 53.9 Fiber: 7.2

Easy Teriyaki Chicken

Serves: 8
Time: 40 minutes (20 minutes active time, 20 minutes cook time)

Ingredients:
- 3 pounds boneless, skinless
- chicken thighs
- 1 cup chicken broth
- 1 can crushed pineapple
- ¾ cup brown sugar
- ¾ cup soy sauce
- ¼ cup apple cider vinegar
- 2 tablespoons cold water
- 2 tablespoons cornstarch
- 2 tablespoons ground ginger
- 2 tablespoons garlic powder
- 1 teaspoon black pepper

Directions:
1. Put the chicken in the pressure cooker.
2. In a bowl, mix the soy sauce, vinegar, brown sugar, pineapple with its juice, chicken broth, ginger, pepper, and garlic.
3. When the brown sugar is dissolved, pour over the chicken and mix so the meat is thoroughly coated.
4. Select "manual" and cook for 20 minutes on high pressure.
5. While that cooks, stir the cold water and cornstarch together.
6. When time is up on the pressure cooker, unplug or hit "cancel" before quick-releasing.
7. Move the chicken to a plate.
8. Turn on the cooker again, this time to "sauté."
9. Pour the cornstarch/water mixture into the sauce and whisk.
10. Keep stirring until the sauce is boiling, then turn the cooker off again.
11. Return the chicken and stir.
12. Serve!

Nutritional Info (⅛ recipe)
Total calories: 352 Protein: 30.7 Fat: 11.4 Carbs: 31 Fiber: 1.2

Honey-Sesame Chicken

Serves: 6
Time: 15 minutes (7 minutes active time, 8 minutes cook time)

Ingredients:
- 4 big, boneless, skinless and
- diced chicken breasts
- 1 cup honey
- 2 chopped green onions
- 2 minced garlic cloves
- ½ cup diced onion
- ½ cup soy sauce
- ¼ cup ketchup
- 3 tablespoons water
- 2 tablespoons cornstarch
- 1 tablespoon veggie oil
- 2 teaspoons sesame oil
- ¼ teaspoon red pepper flakes
- Salt and pepper to taste
- A sprinkle of toasted sesame seeds

Directions:
1. Season your chicken with salt and pepper.
2. Turn your pressure cooker to "sauté" and add oil.
3. When hot and shiny, add the garlic, onion, and chicken.
4. Keep stirring for about 3 minutes, or until the onion is soft.
5. Pour in the soy sauce, ketchup, and red pepper flakes.

6. Stir well.
7. Close the pressure cooker lid, select "manual," and cook on high pressure for 3 minutes.
8. When the timer goes off, hit "cancel" and quick-release.
9. Add sesame oil and honey, and stir until the honey dissolves.
10. In a small bowl, mix the cornstarch and cold water.
11. Pour into the cooker and turn back to "sauté."
12. When the sauce thickens, add the green onions.
13. Serve the chicken with sauce and sesame seeds on top.

Nutritional Info (⅙ recipe)
Total calories: 261 Protein: 18 Fat: 5.3 Carbs: 37.4 Fiber: 0

Chicken Alfredo w/ Broccoli

Serves: 4
Time: About 15 minutes (5 minutes active time, 8 minutes cook time)

Ingredients:
- 1 pound of cubed boneless, skinless chicken breasts
- 16-ounces of pasta
- 16-ounces of Asiago cheese
- 16-ounces of frozen broccoli
- 2 cups water
- 1 cup white wine
- 8-ounces of heavy cream
- 2 garlic cloves
- 1 tablespoon olive oil
- Salt and pepper to taste

Directions:
1. Turn your pressure cooker to the "sauté" setting.
2. Add olive oil and garlic, and when hot and fragrant, add the chicken.
3. Brown on all sides for 1-2 minutes.
4. Pour in the white wine and scrape up any browned chicken bits.
5. Next, pour in 2 cups of water and the pasta. If the water doesn't quite cover the pasta, add a little more.
6. Toss in the broccoli before closing up the lid.
7. Select "manual," and then high pressure for 8 minutes.
8. When time is up, hit "cancel" and quick-release.
9. Check the pasta. If it isn't done yet, close up the cooker again and cook for another 2 minutes.
10. When the noodles are done, keep the pot lid off and hit "sauté" again.
11. Pour in the heavy cream and stir.
12. When the sauce begins to thicken, add the cheese and turn off the cooker.
13. The cheese will melt quickly, and it's time to eat!

Nutritional Info (¼ recipe)
Total calories: 309 Protein: 8.5 Fat: 20.9 Carbs: 21 Fiber: 2.6

Chicken, Black Bean, and Rice Bowl

Serves: 4-6
Time: About 30 minutes (5 minutes active time, 6 minutes cook time)

Ingredients :
- 1 pound of skinless, boneless chicken breasts
- 1 medium-sized, chopped red onion
- 1 medium-sized, chopped yellow bell pepper
- 2 cups shredded lettuce
- 1 ½ cups parboiled rice
- 1 ½ cups water
- 1 cup black beans (soaked overnight)
- 1 bay leaf
- 1 tablespoon lime juice
- 1 tablespoon lime zest
- 1 tablespoon olive oil
- 1 ½ teaspoons salt
- 1 teaspoon cayenne pepper
- 1 teaspoon garlic powder
- 1 teaspoon cumin

Directions:
1. Find a 4-cup bowl that will work in a pressure cooker.
2. Fill with the rice, water, and lime zest.
3. Set aside for now.
4. Turn your pressure cooker to "sauté" and pour in the olive.
5. When hot and shiny, brown the chicken on one side for 5 minutes.
6. Take out the chicken.
7. Add and mix the bell pepper, beans, onion, seasonings, bay leaf, and 1 ½ cups water.
8. Put the chicken (brown side up) on top.
9. Lower your steamer basket into the pot on top of the chicken and put in the bowl of rice.
10. Secure the pot lid.
11. Cook for 6 minutes on high pressure.
12. When the timer goes off, hit "cancel" or unplug the cooker, and wait for the pressure to come down all the way.
13. When safe, open the lid.
14. Take out the rice bowl and mix with some lime juice.
15. Take out the chicken and shred.
16. Return the meat to the pot and mix with the beans.
17. Pick out the bay leaf before serving.

Nutritional Info (⅙ recipe)
Total calories: 415 Protein: 28.8 Fat: 5.1 Carbs: 64 Fiber: 10

Chicken and Cornbread Stuffing

Serves: 5-6
Time: About 25 minutes

Ingredients:
- 4 big frozen, skinless, boneless chicken breasts
- 23-ounces of cream of chicken soup
- 1 bag of frozen green beans
- 14-ounce bag of cornbread stuffing
- 1 cup chicken broth

Directions:
1. Pour 1 cup of broth into the pressure cooker and add the chicken.
2. Cook on high pressure for 15 minutes.
3. When finished, unplug the cooker and quick-release the pressure.
4. Open the lid and put the green beans right on top of the chicken.
5. Close the lid again and cook for 2 minutes on high pressure.
6. Quick-release.
7. Add the cornbread stuffing and pour over the cream of chicken soup.
8. Secure the lid and cook for 4 minutes.
9. Quick-release.
10. Stir everything together before seasoning with salt and pepper, and serving.

Nutritional Info ($\frac{1}{5}$ recipe)
Total calories: 374 Protein: 34 Fat: 12 Carbs: 36 Fiber: 2

Homemade Chicken + Gravy

Serves: 2-4
Time: 45 minutes (5 minutes active time, 40 minutes cook time)

Ingredients:

For the chicken
- 6 chicken thighs
- 1 sliced onion
- 4 chopped garlic cloves
- 2 beaten eggs
- 1 cup + 2 ½ tablespoons cold water
- 1 ½ cups toasted panko crumbs*
- 1 cup flour
- 2 tablespoons cornstarch
- 1 tablespoon soy sauce
- 1 pinch of rosemary
- Salt and pepper to taste

For the breading
- 1 ½ cups panko crumbs
- 2 tablespoons butter
- 2 tablespoons olive oil
- Salt to taste

Directions:
1. Put the garlic, onion, and rosemary in your pressure cooker.
2. Pour in 1 cup of cold water and lower in the steamer basket.
3. Add the chicken thighs in the basket.
4. Secure the lid.
5. Hit "Manual" and cook on high pressure for 6 minutes for small thighs, and 9 minutes for bigger ones.
6. Let the pressure come down naturally when the timer goes off.
7. While the chicken cooks, **Make** the breading.
8. Heat a skillet and add olive oil and butter.
9. Toss in the panko crumbs to toast until a golden color.
10. Season with salt.
11. Preheat the oven to 400-degrees.
12. When the cooker is pressure-free, take out the chicken thighs and pat dry with a paper towel.
13. Season.
14. Coat in flour, dip in beaten eggs, and then coat with the toasted panko breading.
15. Bake for 5-10 minutes.
16. In the meantime, turn your pressure cooker to "sauté" to heat up the chicken cooking liquid.
17. Add 1 tablespoon of soy sauce, salt, and pepper.
18. In a small bowl, mix cornstarch and water, and pour into the gravy to thicken.
19. Serve the chicken with lots of gravy!

Nutritional Info (¼ recipe)

Total calories: 1047 Protein: 64 Fat: 44 Carbs: 145 Fiber: 0

Easy Orange Chicken

Serves: 6
Time: Under 10 minutes (3 minutes cook time)

Ingredients:
- 4 big, boneless, skinless, and diced chicken breasts
- ¼ cup + 3 tablespoons water
- ¼ cup soy sauce
- 2 chopped green onions
- ½ cup orange marmalade
- 3 tablespoons cornstarch
- 2 tablespoons brown sugar
- 1 tablespoon rice wine vinegar

- 1 teaspoon sesame oil
- ¼ teaspoon chili garlic sauce
- Red pepper flakes

Directions:
1. Mix soy sauce, ¼ cup water, brown sugar, sesame oil, chili garlic sauce, rice wine vinegar, and chicken in your pressure cooker.
2. Secure the lid.
3. Select "manual" and cook for 3 minutes on high pressure.
4. When ready, turn off the cooker and quick-release.
5. Stir in the marmalade.
6. In a separate bowl, mix 3 tablespoons of cold water and cornstarch until smooth.
7. Pour into the cooker.
8. Turn the cooker to "sauté" and heat until the sauce becomes thick.
9. Serve with a dash of red pepper flakes and sprinkle of green onions.

Nutritional Info (⅙ recipe)
Total calories: 322 Protein: 29 Fat: 7 Carbs: 32 Fiber: .7

Pulled Turkey w/ BBQ Mustard Sauce

Serves: 4
Time: 1 hour, 15 minutes (15 minutes active time, 1 hour cook time)

Ingredients:
- 2-3 pounds of turkey breast
- ½ cup yellow mustard
- ½ cup beer
- ½ cup apple cider vinegar
- 2 tablespoons olive oil
- 2 tablespoons honey
- 1 tablespoon molasses
- 1 tablespoon Worcestershire sauce
- 2 teaspoons hot sauce
- 1 teaspoon garlic powder
- 1 teaspoon onion powder
- 1 teaspoon mustard powder
- 1 teaspoon Liquid Smoke
- Salt and pepper

Directions:
1. In a bowl, mix the vinegar, mustard, molasses, honey, Worcestershire, onion powder, garlic powder, mustard powder, salt, pepper, hot sauce, and liquid smoke.
2. Take your turkey breast and season with salt.
3. Turn your pressure cooker to "sauté" and heat olive oil.
4. When shiny, brown the turkey on both sides.

5. When golden, take out of the pot.
6. Pour in beer and deglaze, which means to scrape off any bits of burned meat off the pot sides.
7. Pour in the BBQ mustard sauce.
8. Return meat and stir to coat well.
9. Secure the lid and select "manual," and cook for 50 minutes on high pressure.
10. When the timer goes off, hit "cancel" and wait for the pressure to come down on its own.
11. When the pressure is all released, take out the turkey.
12. Turn the cooker back to sauté and let the sauce reduce.
13. Pull the turkey apart with two forks.
14. When your sauce has thickened, put the shredded meat back in and stir to coat.
15. Serve!

Nutritional Info (¼ recipe)
Total calories: 504 Protein: 51 Fat: 25 Carbs: 17 Fiber: 0

Smoked Turkey + Black Bean Soup

Serves: 8
Time: About 1 hour, 20 minutes (10 minutes active time, 70 minutes cook time)

Ingredients:
- 6 cups water
- 11 ounces of smoked turkey
- 1 big, chopped onion
- 1 chopped carrot
- 1 chopped celery stalk
- 3 smashed garlic cloves
- 2 bay leaves
- 2 cups dried black beans
- ½ cup chopped parsley
- ½ tablespoon olive oil
- Salt and pepper to taste

Directions:
1. First, sauté the aromatics. Heat the oil until shiny and then add the carrots, parsley, celery, and onion.
2. After 8-10 minutes or until the ingredients are fragrant, add the garlic and cook for another minute.
3. Pour in the water, bay leaves, beans, and turkey.
4. Sprinkle in black pepper.
5. When boiling, lock the pressure lid.
6. Hit "manual," and then cook for 45 minutes on high pressure.
7. Turn off the cooker when the timer goes off, and wait for the pressure to come down naturally.
8. When the pressure is gone, open the lid and pick out the bay leaf.
9. Take out the turkey. If it's on the bone, cut it off.
10. With an immersion blender, puree the soup until it reaches the texture you want.
11. Salt to taste, add the turkey back in, and serve!

Nutritional Info (⅛ recipe)
Total calories: 133 Protein: 19 Fat: 2 Carbs: 26 Fiber: 16

Cranberry-Spiced Beef Roast

Serves: 4-6
Time: 2 hours, 10 minutes (10 minutes active time, 2 hours cook time)

Ingredients:
- 3-4 pounds beef arm roast
- 6 whole cloves
- 2 cups bone broth
- 1 cup whole cranberries
- ½ cup white wine
- ½ cup water
- ¼ cup honey
- 1, 3-inch cinnamon stick
- 2 peeled, whole garlic cloves
- 2 tablespoons olive oil
- 1 teaspoon horseradish powder
- Salt and pepper to taste

Directions:
1. Begin by patting the roast dry with paper towels and seasoning with salt and pepper.
2. Hit "sauté" on your pressure cooker and pour in the olive oil.
3. When hot and shiny, brown the roast all over. It should take 8-10 minutes.
4. Take out the meat.
5. Pour in the wine and deglaze.
6. Stir for 4-5 minutes.
7. Pour in the water, honey, cranberries, garlic, cloves, horseradish powder, and cinnamon stick.
8. Stir until 4-5 minutes. The cranberries should begin to burst.
9. Add the meat back in.
10. Pour in the bone broth, so it almost covers the meat.
11. Secure the pressure cooker lid.
12. Hit "manual" and select high pressure for 75 minutes.
13. When time is up, unplug or hit "cancel."
14. Wait for the pressure to come down naturally for 15 minutes.
15. If there's any pressure left, quick-release it.
16. Take out the meat, plate, and pour some of the sauce on top.
17. Pour the rest of the juice in a gravy pitcher for the table.
18. Enjoy!

Nutritional Info (¼ recipe)
Total calories: 362 Protein: 25 Fat: 15 Carbs: 31 Fiber: 1

Maple-Balsamic Beef

Serves: 8
Time: About 1 hour (20 minutes active time, 35 minutes cook time)

Ingredients:
- 3 pounds of trimmed, sliced boneless chuck steak
- 1 cup bone broth
- 1 cup maple syrup
- ½ cup balsamic vinegar
- 2 tablespoons olive oil
- 1 ½ teaspoons salt
- 1 teaspoon ground ginger
- 1 teaspoon finely-chopped garlic

Directions:
1. After trimming and slicing the meat, season with salt and ground ginger.
2. Turn your pressure cooker to "brown," and add the olive oil.
3. When hot and shiny, add the beef and brown all over.
4. Set aside for now.
5. Turn the pot to "sauté" and cook garlic for 1 minute.
6. Pour in the broth, maple syrup, and balsamic vinegar, and stir until mixed.
7. Add the beef strips back into the pot and secure the lid.
8. Select "manual" and choose high pressure for 35 minutes.
9. When ready, unplug or hit "cancel."
10. Carefully quick-release the pressure.
11. Serve!

Tip: If you want a thicker sauce, plate the meat after you've quick-released the pressure, and pour in a mixture of cold water and cornstarch (about 2 tablespoons of each) into the pot. Turn the cooker back on to "sauté" and bring to a boil to thicken. Pour over the meat and serve.

Nutritional Info (⅛ recipe)
Total calories: 1112 Protein: 43 Fat: 29 Carbs: 33 Fiber: 0

Teriyaki-Garlic Flank Steak

Serves: 6
Time: About 1 hour (10 minutes active time, 45 minutes cook time)

Ingredients:
- 2 pounds of flank steak
- 2 finely-chopped garlic cloves
- ¼ cup soy sauce
- ¼ cup maple syrup
- 2 tablespoons Red Boat fish sauce
- 1 tablespoon honey
- 1 ½ teaspoons ground ginger

Directions:

1. Slice the steak into ½-inch strips
2. Mix soy sauce, syrup, fish sauce, honey, and ginger together in the pressure cooker.
3. Add the meat and garlic, and stir to coat.
4. Secure the lid.
5. Hit "manual" and cook on high pressure for 40 minutes.
6. When time is up, unplug the cooker and let it depressurize naturally for just 5 minutes.
7. Quick-release the remaining pressure.
8. Serve the meat with lots of sauce and rice!

Nutritional Info (⅙ recipe)
Total calories: 395 Protein: 43 Fat: 18 Carbs: 15 Fiber: 0

Beef Stroganoff

Serves: 6
Time: 1 hour, 35 minutes (5 minutes active time, 90 minutes cook time)

Ingredients:
- 2 pounds of beef stew meat
- 16-ounces of cooked egg noodles
- 3 cups of halved mushrooms
- 3 minced garlic cloves
- 1 cup of beef broth
- ¼ cup flour
- 1 chopped onion
- 8-ounces of sour cream
- 2 tablespoons olive oil
- 1 tablespoon of Dijon mustard
- Salt and pepper to taste

Directions:
1. Mix flour, salt, and pepper in a plastic bag and shake.
2. Add your beef to coat evenly.
3. Turn your pressure cooker to "sauté" and pour in oil.
4. When hot and shiny, add the beef and brown all over for 3-5 minutes.
5. Throw in the chopped onion and garlic and cook for another 2 minutes.
6. Pour in the beef broth.
7. Close the lid.
8. Press "Meat/Stew" and adjust to 35 minutes.
9. When the timer goes off, turn off the cooker and quick-release the pressure.
10. Add the sour cream, mushrooms, and Dijon.
11. Turn the pot back to sauté and simmer for 10 minutes.
12. Add salt and pepper to taste.
13. Serve with the cooked noodles.

Tip: If you want a thicker sauce, mix 1-2 tablespoons of cornstarch into 2 tablespoons of cold water. Pour into the cooker before serving, and simmer for a little while until the sauce looks the way you like

it.
Nutritional Info (⅙ recipe)
Total calories: 300 Protein: 25 Fat: 6 Carbs: 41 Fiber: 5

Freezer Pulled Pepper Steak

Serves: 6
Time: 1 hour, 20 minutes

Ingredients:
- 3-4 pounds beef
- 16-ounces of banana peppers
- ½ cup beef broth
- 1 tablespoon garlic powder
- Salt and black pepper to taste

Directions:
1. Season the beef with salt, pepper, and garlic and lay in the pressure cooker.
2. Pour the jar of peppers into the cooker, and then the broth.
3. Close the lid.
4. Hit "Meat" and adjust time to 70 minutes.
5. When the timer goes off, turn off the cooker and wait for the pressure to decrease naturally.
6. When the pressure is safely reduced, open the cooker.
7. Shred the meat with two forks.
8. Serve as desired.

Nutritional Info (⅙ recipe)
Total calories: 442 Protein: 65 Fat: 18 Carbs: 3 Fiber: 0

Ground Beef, Potato, and Kale Soup

Serves: 6
Time: 44 minutes (40 minutes active time, 4 minutes cook time)

Ingredients:
- 3 quarts of water
- 1 pound ground beef
- 5 diced russet potatoes
- 8 chopped kale leaves
- 12-ounces of cooked bacon
- 3 minced garlic cloves
- 1 chopped onion
- 1 cup heavy cream
- 1-2 tablespoons butter
- 2 teaspoons sea salt
- 1 teaspoon red pepper flakes

- ½ teaspoon oregano
- ½ teaspoon basil

Directions:
1. Cook the bacon before beginning with the soup.
2. When ready, turn on the cooker to "sauté" and heat.
3. When the cooker is hot, add the onion and butter.
4. Stir until they become clear.
5. Add meat, garlic, and seasonings.
6. When the beef is cooked, add the potatoes and bacon.
7. Pour in water (to reach the 3-quarts line) and stir.
8. Close the lid and select "manual" and then cook for 4 minutes on high pressure.
9. When done, unplug and let the pressure come down by itself.
10. Add the kale and cream.
11. Stir and season with salt to taste.
12. Serve!

Nutritional Info (⅙ recipe)
Total calories: 506 Protein: 23 Fat: 31 Carbs: 34 Fiber: 4

Smoky-Maple Brisket

Serves: 3-4
Time: 1 hour, 40 minutes (35 minutes active time, 65 minutes cook time)

Ingredients:
- 1 ½ pounds beef brisket
- 2 cups bone broth
- 3 thyme sprigs
- 2 tablespoons maple sugar
- 1 tablespoon liquid smoke
- 2 teaspoons smoked sea salt
- 1 teaspoon mustard powder
- 1 teaspoon onion powder
- 1 teaspoon black pepper
- ½ teaspoon smoked paprika

Directions:
1. About 30 minutes before cooking, take out the brisket and pat dry with towels.
2. In a bowl, mix the smoked sea salt, pepper, maple sugar, mustard powder, onion powder, and smoked paprika.
3. Coat the beef well with this spice rub.
4. Turn your pressure cooker to "sauté" and heat for 2-3 minutes.
5. Pour in a little olive oil and add the brisket.
6. Brown all over until a deep gold color.
7. Turn the brisket so the fatty side is facing up, and pour in the broth, liquid smoke, and thyme sprigs.
8. Deglaze before closing the cooker.

9. Select "manual" and then adjust time to 50 minutes on high pressure.
10. When time is up, unplug the cooker and wait for the pressure to come down naturally.
11. Open the lid and take out the brisket.
12. Plate and cover with foil to rest for 10 minutes.
13. Turn the pot back to sauté to reduce the sauce.
14. To serve, cut the brisket diagonally (on a bias) and serve with sauce.

Nutritional Info (⅓ recipe)
Total calories: 577 Protein: 39 Fat: 40 Carbs: 6 Fiber: 0

Classic Spaghetti and Meatballs

Serves: 4
Time: About 28 minutes (10 minutes active time, 18 minutes cook time)

Ingredients:
- 1 pound of ground beef
- 8-10 ounces of noodles
- 1 jar of spaghetti sauce
- 2 eggs
- ¼ cup milk
- ¼ cup breadcrumbs
- ½ garlic clove
- Salt and pepper to taste

Directions:
1. In a bowl, mix the beef, egg, breadcrumbs, garlic, and seasonings.
2. Put the noodles and spaghetti sauce in your pressure cooker. Fill the empty jar with water and pour into the pot.
3. Turn the cooker to "sauté."
4. Roll the mixed meat into golf balls and put on top of the noodles.
5. Close the lid.
6. Select "manual" and then cook at high pressure for 11 minutes.
7. When done, quick-release the pressure and let the food sit (with the lid off) for about 8 minutes to blend the flavors.

Nutritional Info (¼ recipe)
Total calories: 703 Protein: 32 Fat: 29 Carbs: 71 Fiber: 0

Pressure Cooker Jambalaya

Serves: 6-8
Time: About 30 minutes (20 minutes active time, 6 minutes cook time)

Ingredients:
- 1 pound ground beef
- 1 pound smoked sausage

- 3 cups chicken broth
- 2 cups basmati rice
- 2 cups frozen okra
- 6 chopped garlic cloves
- 4 tablespoons olive oil
- 1 chopped yellow onion
- 1 chopped green bell pepper
- 1 chopped celery stalk
- 2 tablespoons red pepper flakes
- 2 tablespoons tomato paste
- 2 tablespoons black pepper
- 1 tablespoon Worcestershire sauce
- Salt to taste

Directions:
1. Begin by cooking the veggies. Pour 2 tablespoons olive oil into the pressure cooker and hit "sauté."
2. Add garlic, pepper, celery, and onion, and stir for 3 minutes.
3. Add in the tomato paste, Worcestershire, red pepper flakes, salt, and black pepper.
4. Keep stirring for 7 minutes.
5. Remove the veggies and plate for now.
6. Add more oil if necessary to the pot.
7. Add the sausage and ground beef.
8. Break it up and stir, browning, for 7-10 minutes.
9. When the meat is brown, add the okra and rice. Pour in the chicken broth.
10. Once the cooker is boiling, add the cooked veggies back in and lock the lid.
11. Select "manual," and then cook on high pressure for 6 minutes.
12. When time is up, unplug the cooker and carefully quick-release the pressure.
13. Stir well before serving.

Nutritional Info (1 cup serving)
Total calories: 500 Protein: 23 Fat: 10 Carbs: 34 Fiber: 4

Coney Island-Style Chili

Serves: 6-8
Time: 30 minutes (10 minutes active time, 20 minutes cook time)

Ingredients:
- 2 pounds ground beef
- 2 cups chicken broth
- 2 cans tomato paste
- 2 tablespoons apple cider vinegar
- 2 tablespoons Worcestershire sauce
- 1 tablespoon olive oil
- 1 tablespoon Dijon mustard
- 1 tablespoon onion powder

- 1 tablespoon garlic powder
- 1 tablespoon cumin
- 2 teaspoons allspice
- 2 teaspoons chili powder
- 1 teaspoon celery seed
- Salt and pepper to taste

Directions:
1. Turn your pressure cooker to "sauté" and pour in 1 tablespoon oil.
2. When hot, cook the brown meat just enough to break it up, do not brown.
3. Pour in the broth.
4. Stir before adding tomato paste, Dijon, Worcestershire, garlic powder, onion powder, allspice, chili powder, cumin, celery seed, vinegar, salt, and pepper.
5. Close the lid.
6. Select "manual" and cook for 10 minutes on high pressure.
7. When time is up, unplug the cooker (or hit cancel) and wait 5 minutes.
8. Quick-release the rest of the pressure.
9. Stir or use an immersion blender to get the desired consistency.
10. Serve on hot dogs with diced raw onions and yellow mustard.

Nutritional Info (⅙ recipe)
Total calories: 678 Protein: 41 Fat: 48 Carbs: 20 Fiber: 4.9

Cuban-Style Braised Beef

Serves: 4
Time: 55 minutes (15 minutes active time, 40 minutes cook time)

Ingredients:
- 1 ½ pounds of crosswise-cut flank steak, three pieces
- 28-ounces crushed tomatoes
- 2 chopped red bell peppers
- 2 minced garlic cloves
- 1 sliced onion
- 1 jalapeno
- 2 tablespoons chopped cilantro
- 2 teaspoons oregano
- 1 teaspoon cayenne pepper
- 1 teaspoon cumin
- 1 sliced avocado
- One small bunch of chopped cilantro
- Crumbled cotija

Directions:
1. Season your steak with the salt and pepper.
2. Turn your pressure cooker to "sauté" and brown the steak on all sides.
3. In a bowl, mix the crushed tomatoes, jalapeno, garlic and spices.

4. Pour over the steak.
5. Select "manual" and cook on high pressure for 35 minutes.
6. Hit "cancel" or unplug when the timer goes off.
7. Wait 10 minutes before quick-releasing the remaining pressure.
8. Serve with chopped cilantro, cotija cheese, and avocado.

Nutritional Info (¼ recipe)
Total calories: 649 Protein: 54 Fat: 22.7 Carbs: 56 Fiber: 8.5

Stuffed Flank Steak

Serves: 2
Time: About 40 minutes (5 minutes active time, 35 minutes cook time)

Ingredients:
- 1 pound flank steak
- 6 tablespoons beef broth
- 1 cup diced tomatoes
- 1 cup breadcrumbs
- 1 minced garlic clove
- ½ cup chopped celery
- ½ cup chopped onion
- 1 tablespoon butter
- ½ teaspoon salt
- ¼ teaspoon thyme
- ¼ teaspoon marjoram
- ⅛ teaspoon pepper

Directions:
1. Melt the butter in your pressure cooker on the "sauté" setting.
2. When melted, add the onion, garlic, and celery.
3. When the onion has softened and the mixture is fragrant, add the breadcrumbs and seasonings with 2 tablespoons of broth.
4. Cut your flank steak into two equal pieces.
5. Spoon the stuffing mixture evenly on one piece of steak, before laying down the other piece on top.
6. Use toothpicks to keep them together.
7. Pour the diced tomatoes and 4 tablespoons of broth into the cooker, and put in the steak.
8. Close the pressure cooker lid and select "manual," and cook for 23 minutes on high pressure.
9. When time is up, unplug the cooker (or hit "cancel") and let the pressure decrease naturally.
10. Plate the steak and let it rest for 5 minutes before cutting and serving!

Nutritional Info (½ recipe)
Total calories: 776 Protein: 69 Fat: 35 Carbs: 42 Fiber: 1

Pineapple-Pork Stew

Serves: 6

Time: About 45-50 minutes (10 minutes active time, 35 minutes cook time)

Ingredients:
- 2 pounds stewing pork, cut into cubes
- 1 sliced (wedged) onion
- 2 chopped garlic cloves
- 1 cup bone broth
- 1 cup pineapple chunks
- 1 bay leaf
- 1 bunch of Swiss chard (stems chopped, leaves halved and sliced)
- 1-2 tablespoons olive oil
- 2 tablespoons sugar-free marmalade
- 1 tablespoon soy sauce
- 1 teaspoon ground cinnamon
- ½ teaspoon turmeric powder
- ½ teaspoon ginger powder
- ½ teaspoon sea salt
- ½ teaspoon ground cloves

Directions:
1. Marinate the pork in soy sauce, salt, cloves, ginger, and turmeric for at least an hour.
2. When ready to Make the stew, hit "sauté" and add olive oil.
3. When hot and shiny, cook the onions for a minute.
4. Add garlic.
5. When onions are clear, remove them along with the garlic.
6. If necessary, pour in some more olive oil and add the pork.
7. Brown all over.
8. Remove the meat and deglaze pressure cooker with bone broth.
9. Put the pork, onions, and garlic back to the pot.
10. Mix cinnamon, pineapple, bay leaf, chard stems, and marmalade in the pot.
11. Secure the lid and select "meat/stew" setting for 35 minutes.
12. When time is up, hit "cancel" and quick-release the pressure.
13. Turn the cooker back to "sauté" and throw in the chard leaf strips.
14. Simmer for a few minutes.
15. Pick out the bay leaf.
16. Taste and season as needed.
17. Serve!

Tip: Pork shoulder is a good cut of meat for stews.

Nutritional Info (⅙ recipe)

Total calories: 339 Protein: 40 Fat: 10 Carbs: 21 Fiber: 2

Apple-Cherry Pork Loin

Serves: 4
Time: 40 minutes

Ingredients:
- 1 ⅓ pounds boneless pork loin
- 2 cups diced apple
- ⅔ cup pitted cherries
- ½ cup apple juice
- ½ cup water
- ⅓ cup diced celery
- ⅓ diced onion
- Salt and pepper to taste

Directions:
1. Put everything in your pressure cooker.
2. Close the lid.
3. Select "meat/poultry" and adjust the time to 40 minutes.
4. When time is up, hit "cancel" or unplug the cooker.
5. Quick-release the pressure.
6. Serve.

Nutritional Info (5-ounce serving)
Total calories: 237 Protein: 31 Fat: 12 Carbs: 6 Fiber: 0

Honey Pork Chops w/ Ginger

Serves: 6
Time: 25 minutes (10 minutes active time, 15 minutes cook time)

Ingredients:
- 6 boneless pork chops
- ¼ cup honey
- 2 tablespoons maple syrup
- ½ teaspoon peeled and minced fresh ginger
- ½ teaspoon sea salt
- ½ teaspoon ground garlic
- ½ teaspoon cinnamon
- ¼ teaspoon ground cloves
- ¼ teaspoon black pepper
- Splash of apple cider vinegar

Directions:
1. Season the pork chops with salt, pepper, and ground garlic.
2. Heat your pressure cooker on the "sauté" setting.
3. Brown meat on both sides.
4. In a bowl, mix the honey, mustard, syrup, ginger, cinnamon, and cloves.
5. Pour over the meat in the pressure cooker.
6. Close the lid.
7. Hit "manual" and cook on high pressure for 15 minutes.
8. When time is up, hit "cancel" and quick-release the pressure.

9. Serve with a side like a fresh green salad.

Nutritional Info (⅙ recipe)

Total calories: 239 Protein: 25.8 Fat: 10 Carbs: 10.6 Fiber: 0

Jerk-Style Pork Roast

Serves: 12
Time: 45 minutes

Ingredients:
- 4 pounds pork shoulder
- ½ cup beef stock
- ¼ cup Jamaican Jerk spice blend
- 1 tablespoon olive oil

Directions:
1. Coat the pork roast with olive oil and spice blend.
2. Turn your pressure cooker to "sauté."
3. When heated, lay down the meat to brown on all sides.
4. Pour in the beef broth.
5. Close the lid.
6. Select "manual" and cook for 45 minutes on high pressure.
7. When time is up, unplug the cooker (or hit "cancel") and let the pressure come down for 10 minutes.
8. Quick-release the remaining pressure.
9. With two forks, shred the pork.
10. Serve!

Nutritional Info (4-ounce serving)

Total calories: 282 Protein: 23 Fat: 20 Carbs: 0 Fiber: 0

Pork Chops w/ Hong-Kong Tomato Sauce

Serves: 4
Time: 30 minutes (10 minutes active time, 20 minutes cook time)

Ingredients:

For the marinade
- 4 boneless pork loin chops
- 1 tablespoon light soy sauce
- ½ tablespoon dark soy sauce
- ¼ teaspoon sesame oil
- ¼ teaspoon salt

Other
- 4 minced garlic cloves
- 1 medium-sized sliced onion

- 1 cup water
- 1 diced small shallot
- 8 sliced mushrooms
- 2 tablespoons ketchup
- 2 tablespoons water
- 1 ½ tablespoons cornstarch
- 1 tablespoon peanut oil
- 1 tablespoon white sugar
- 1 teaspoon Worcestershire
- ½ teaspoon white sugar
- 50 ml tomato paste
- Salt and black pepper

Directions:
1. With a meat tenderizer, tenderize the pork.
2. Marinate the chops for 20 minutes.
3. When ready, hit "sauté" and preheat.
4. Add the peanut oil and lay in the pork chops to brown for 1-1 ½ minutes on each side.
5. Take out the meat.
6. Add shallots and onion until softened.
7. Toss in garlic and cook for 30 seconds.
8. Season with pepper and salt.
9. Add mushrooms.
10. Pour in ¼ cup of water and deglaze.
11. In a bowl, mix water, ketchup, sugar, Worcestershire, and tomato sauce and pour into cooker.
12. Put the pork chops back in the pressure cooker and close the lid.
13. Cook on high pressure for 1 minute.
14. When done, turn off the cooker and wait 10 minutes.
15. Remove the meat and turn the cooker to sauté to thicken the sauce.
16. Season if necessary.
17. In a small bowl, mix cornstarch with cold water until smooth, and pour into the pressure cooker.
18. Serve with the thickened tomato sauce on top of the pork chops.

Nutritional Info (¼ recipe)

Total calories: 252 Protein: 24.9 Fat: 12.6 Carbs: 9.7 Fiber: 1.9

Citrus-Garlic Shredded Pork

Serves: 8
Time: About 50 minutes + 2 hours marinade time (10 minutes active time, 30 minutes cook time)

Ingredients:

For the marinade/rub
- 4 pounds cubed, boneless pork shoulder roast
- 3 tablespoons olive oil
- 2 teaspoons salt

- 1 ½ teaspoons ground cumin
- 1 teaspoon black pepper
- 1 teaspoon ground chipotle chili pepper

Other
- 2 quartered onions
- 2 cups fresh orange juice
- ¾ cup fresh lime juice
- 5 minced garlic cloves
- 2 cinnamon sticks
- 2 teaspoons dried oregano

Directions:
1. Mix the marinade/rub ingredients together and rub on the pork.
2. Stick in the fridge for 2 hours.
3. Turn the pressure cooker to sauté.
4. Brown the pork evenly.
5. When golden, add in all the "other" ingredients and cook until the onions have softened and garlic is fragrant.
6. Lock the pressure cooker lid.
7. Select "manual" and cook on high pressure for 30 minutes.
8. When time is up, unplug the cooker or hit cancel.
9. Let the pressure come down by itself.
10. Open the cooker and put the pork on a cookie sheet lined with parchment paper.
11. Stick in the broiler for 5 minutes.
12. Shred with two forks.
13. Put back in the cooker and stir in the juices.
14. Serve!

Nutritional Info (⅛ recipe)
Total calories: 506 Protein: 40 Fat: 33 Carbs: 10 Fiber: 0

Bacon-Wrapped Ribeye Steak

Serves: 4
Time: 30 minutes (5 minutes active time, 25 minutes cook time)

Ingredients:
- 4 ribeye pork steaks
- 6-8 strips of bacon
- 1 ½ cups water
- 3-4 peeled and quartered potatoes
- 4 ounces sliced mushrooms
- 1 tablespoon olive oil
- ½ chopped green pepper
- Seasoned salt to taste

Directions:
1. Season the pork with salt.
2. Roll the steaks (flatten if they're too thick) and wrap bacon around them. Secure with a toothpick.
3. Turn on the "sauté" setting on your pressure cooker and pour in the olive oil.
4. When hot and shiny, brown the bacon-wrapped pork all over.
5. When brown, add in the veggies.
6. Pour in the water and close the lid.
7. Select "manual" and adjust to high pressure for 15 minutes.
8. When time is up, unplug the cooker and wait 10 minutes.
9. Quick-release any remaining pressure.
10. Take out the meat and veggies.
11. Strain the broth.
12. Serve the broth with the meat and veggies.

Nutritional Info (¼ recipe)

Total calories: 399 Protein: 26 Fat: 25 Carbs: 21 Fiber: 0

Asian Pork Chops

Serves: 4

Time: 30 minutes (10 minutes active time, 20 minutes cook time)

Ingredients:
- 4 cups frozen broccoli
- Four, ½-inch thick pork chops
- 6 medium scallions
- 2 tablespoons brown sugar
- 1 ½ tablespoons toasted sesame oil
- 1 tablespoon rice vinegar
- ½ cup chicken broth
- ¼ cup soy sauce
- 1 teaspoon minced garlic

Directions:
1. Turn your pressure cooker to "sauté" and heat the sesame oil.
2. Brown the pork chops until they just start to become golden.
3. Add the garlic and onion.
4. Cook for 1 minute.
5. Pour in the broth, soy sauce, vinegar, and brown sugar.
6. Mix.
7. Close the pressure cooker lid and choose "manual," and then 10 minutes on high pressure.
8. When time is up, hit "cancel" and quick-release.
9. Toss in the frozen broccoli and close the lid again.
10. Let the broccoli cook in the leftover heat for 8-10 minutes.
11. Serve and enjoy!

Nutritional Info (¼ recipe)

Total calories: 199 **Protein:** 17 **Fat:** 11 **Carbs:** 9 **Fiber:** 2.4

Apricot-BBQ Pork Roast

Serves: 8
Time: 1 hour, 10 minutes (10 minutes active time, 1 hour cook time)

Ingredients:
- 3 pounds of boneless, rolled pork roast
- 2 cups water
- 1 sliced onion
- ½ cup teriyaki sauce
- ½ cup ketchup
- ⅓ cup apricot preserves
- ¼ cup packed dark brown sugar
- ¼ cup apple cider vinegar
- 1 teaspoon dry mustard
- 1 teaspoon crushed red pepper
- ¼ teaspoon black pepper

Directions:
1. The night before you plan on making the roast, put the pork in a large plastic bag with the teriyaki, apricot preserves, vinegar, ketchup, brown sugar, mustard, red pepper, and pepper.
2. The next day, take the pork out of the bag and save the marinade.
3. Turn your pressure cooker to "sauté."
4. Brown the pork all over.
5. Take out the pork.
6. Pour water into your cooker along with the onion.
7. Lower in the cooking rack and add the pork.
8. Put the rest of the onion on top of the meat.
9. Close the lid.
10. Select "manual" and adjust time to 65 minutes on high pressure.
11. When time is up, hit "cancel" and let the pressure decrease naturally.
12. In the meanwhile, pour the marinade in a saucepan and simmer over the top until it has thickened.
13. Serve the pork with the sauce and onions.

Nutritional Info (⅛ recipe)
Total calories: 617 **Protein:** 51 **Fat:** 19.7 **Carbs:** 60 **Fiber:** .7

Pork-Rib Stew

Serves: 4
Time: About 55 minutes (10 minute active time, 45 minute cook time)

Ingredients:
- 2 pounds of pork ribs

- 1 cup water + 1 tablespoon
- 4 slices of fresh ginger
- ¾ pound peeled and chopped radish
- 1 minced garlic clove
- 3 tablespoons soy sauce
- 2 tablespoons sherry
- 1 tablespoon rice wine
- ½ tablespoon raw sugar
- 3 teaspoons white vinegar
- 2 teaspoons cornstarch
- Salt to taste

Directions:
1. Boil a large pot of water on your stovetop.
2. When a rolling boiling has been reached, submerge the pork ribs for just a few seconds.
3. Drain into a colander and set the ribs aside on a plate.
4. Turn your pressure cooker to "sauté" and heat a little bit of olive oil (just enough to coat the bottom).
5. When hot, brown the pork ribs on both sides.
6. With the pork in the pot, add the garlic, ginger, soy sauce, sugar, 1 cup of water, wine, and sherry.
7. Close the lid, and select the "Meat/Stew" setting, and adjust time to 35 minutes.
8. When time is up, hit "cancel" and wait 5 minutes before quick-releasing the pressure.
9. Add the chopped radish and close the lid again.
10. Select "Meat/Stew" again and cook for just 10 minutes this time.
11. Quick-release the pressure.
12. With the lid off, hit "sauté" and let the sauce reduce.
13. In a small bowl, mix 1 tablespoon of cold water with cornstarch until smooth, and add into the sauce.
14. When thick, season with salt to taste, and serve!

Nutritional Info (¼ recipe)
Total calories: 336 Protein: 22 Fat: 18 Carbs: 17 Fiber: 1.9

Pork Shoulder w/ Dr. Pepper BBQ Sauce

Serves: 10-12
Time: 1 hour, 45 minutes (20 minutes active time, 1 hour 25 minutes cook time)

Ingredients:

For the rub
- 3-4 pounds of pork shoulder
- 3 tablespoons brown sugar
- 2 tablespoons chili powder
- 2 tablespoons paprika
- ½ teaspoon salt
- ¼ teaspoon cayenne pepper

For the BBQ sauce

- ½ cup Dr. Pepper
- ½ cup ketchup
- 1 teaspoon liquid smoke
- Salt and pepper to taste

Directions:
1. Cut the pork shoulder into 4 equal parts.
2. Mix the rub ingredients together, then coat the pork.
3. Open your pressure cooker and mix the Dr. Pepper and ketchup together.
4. Lay the pork inside and close the lid.
5. Select "manual," and cook on high pressure for 45 minutes.
6. When time is up, hit "cancel" and wait 10 minutes before quick-releasing any leftover pressure.
7. Take out the meat and cover loosely with foil on a plate.
8. Turn your pot to sauté to reduce the sauce.
9. Add in the salt, pepper, and liquid smoke.
10. When the sauce has thickened to your liking, shred the pork with two forks and mix back into the pot.
11. Serve on hamburger buns for a delicious BBQ sandwich.

Nutritional Info (1/10 recipe)
Total calories: 245 Protein: 16 Fat: 16 Carbs: 7.3 Fiber: 0

Pork Medallions with Cremini Mushrooms

Serves: 2
Time: About 30 minutes (10 minutes active time, 15 minutes cook time)

Ingredients:
- 2 pork tenderloins
- 3 cups sliced cremini mushrooms
- 2 cups chicken stock
- ½ cup flour
- 3 sprigs fresh thyme
- 2 sprigs fresh rosemary
- Olive oil
- Salt and pepper

Directions:
1. Cut the pork into 2-centimeter medallions.
2. In a bowl, mix ½ cup flour with a little salt and pepper.
3. Pour your olive oil into the pressure cooker and heat on sauté,
4. Coat the pork coins in the flour and lay in the pressure cooker when hot.
5. Brown on both sides before removing the pork.
6. Add the herbs to the pot and deglaze with chicken stock.
7. When you've gotten all the bits of meat, put the pork back into the cooker along with mushrooms.
8. Close the lid and hit "manual," and cook for 15 minutes on high pressure.
9. When time is up, hit "cancel" and carefully quick-release.

10. Pick out the herbs.
11. Serve!

Tip: If the sauce is too thin and watery for your taste, turn the "sauté" setting back on and simmer until it thickens.

Nutritional Info (½ recipe)

Total calories: 317 Protein: 30 Fat: 3 Carbs: 35 Fiber: 0

Easy Baby-Back Ribs

Serves: 4-8
Time: About 30 minutes

Ingredients:
- 1-2 slabs of baby back ribs
- Water
- Apple cider vinegar
- Salt

Directions:
1. Lay your ribs in the pressure cooker.
2. Pour about 1 inch of water into the cooker with a splash of apple cider vinegar.
3. Sprinkle in a little salt.
4. Close the pot, select "manual," and cook on high pressure for 15 minutes.
5. When the timer goes off, hit "cancel" and let the pressure come down by itself for 15 minutes.
6. Quick-release any remaining pressure before opening the pot.
7. Take out the meat and lay on a parchment-lined baking sheet.
8. Cover with sauce and stick under a hot broiler for 4-5 minutes, or until the sauce is sticky.
9. Serve!

Tip: If for some reason you don't need to eat the ribs right away, you can bake them in a 250-degree oven for 30 minutes instead of putting them under the broiler.

Nutritional Info (¼ recipe)

Total calories: 540 Protein: 38 Fat: 44 Carbs: 0 Fiber: 0

Pasta w/ Sausage + Bacon

Serves: 6
Time: 15-20 minutes (10 minutes active time, 5 minutes cook time)

Ingredients:
- 18-ounces of penne pasta
- 17 ounces of pork sausage
- 3.4-ounces bacon
- 2 cups tomato puree
- 2 minced garlic cloves
- ¼ cup Parmesan cheese

- 1 tablespoon olive oil
- Water
- Salt to taste
- A handful of chopped basil

Directions:
1. Turn your pressure cooker to sauté and wait for it to heat up.
2. Add your olive oil and bacon.
3. When bacon has become about ½ its original size, move to a plate.
4. Add the sausage meat to the pot and cook all the way through, stirring occasionally.
5. Add the garlic and onion, and cook for a few minutes.
6. Turn off the cooker.
7. Pour in the tomato puree and add a little salt.
8. Add your pasta and stir, pushing down to flatten it into the cooker.
9. Pour in enough water to cover the pasta, and no more.
10. Close the pressure cooker lid, select "manual" and cook on LOW pressure for half the time the pasta box recommends.
11. When the timer goes off, hit "cancel" and quick-release the pressure.
12. Stir in the cheese, basil, and bacon before serving.

Nutritional Info (⅙ recipe)
Total calories: 716 Protein: 32 Fat: 32 Carbs: 72 Fiber: 0

Sausage + Peppers

Serves: 4-8
Time: 30 minutes (5 minutes active time, 25 minutes cook time)

Ingredients:
- 1-2 pounds of sweet sausage
- 2 sliced sweet bell peppers
- 1 Vidalia onion
- 28-ounces crushed tomatoes
- 8-ounces of tomato sauce
- 1 tablespoon Italian seasoning
- Salt and pepper to taste

Directions:
1. Cut the sausage into thirds, and prepare the veggies. Cut the onion into rings.
2. Pour the tomatoes, tomato sauce, and Italian seasoning into your pressure cooker.
3. Put the cut sausage on top (without stirring), before adding the onions and peppers.
4. Season.
5. Close the pressure cooker lid, select "manual," and cook on high pressure for 25 minutes.
6. When time is up, press "cancel" and quick-release the pressure.
7. Serve with some Parmesan cheese!

Nutritional Info (¼ recipe)

Total calories: 420 Protein: 15 Fat: 24 Carbs: 33.7 Fiber: 5.3

Simple Lemon-Dill Cod w/ Broccoli

Serves: 4
Time: Less than 5 minutes

Ingredients:
- One, 1 pound, 1-inch thick frozen cod fillet
- 2 cups of broccoli
- 1 cup water
- Dill weed
- Lemon pepper
- Dash of salt

Directions:
1. Cut the fish into four pieces.
2. Season with lemon pepper, salt, and dill weed.
3. Pour 1 cup of water into the pressure cooker and lower in the steamer basket.
4. Put the fish and broccoli florets in the basket.
5. Close the cooker.
6. Select "manual" and cook for 2 minutes on low pressure.
7. Quick-release the pressure after time is up, and you've turned off the cooker.
8. Serve right away.

Nutritional Info (½ recipe)
Total calories: 83 Protein: 14 Fat: 8 Carbs: 6 Fiber: 2.4

Southern Shrimp Boil

Serves: 4-6
Time: 15 minutes (10 minutes active time, 5 minutes cook time)

Ingredients:
- 1 ½ pounds fresh shrimp
- 1 pound tiny potatoes
- 8 peeled and crushed garlic cloves
- 4 ears of corn
- 2 chopped sweet onions
- 12-ounces of cooked Andouille sausage
- 16-ounces of beer
- 1 big tablespoon Old Bay seasoning
- 1 teaspoon crushed red pepper
- Salt and pepper to taste

Directions:
1. Remove the heads from the shrimp, but keep the shells on.

2. Cut the corn ears into thirds.
3. Put everything in the pressure cooker, the beer and seasonings first.
4. Close the lid.
5. Select "manual," and cook for 5 minutes on high pressure.
6. When the timer beeps, hit "cancel" and quick-release the pressure.
7. Serve!

Nutritional Info (1 cup)
Total calories: 379 Protein: 30 Fat: 10 Carbs: 41 Fiber: 9

5-Minute Alaskan Cod

Serves: 2-3
Time: 7 minutes (2 minutes active time, 5 minutes cook time)

Ingredients:
- 1 big Wild Alaskan cod fillet
- 1 cup of cherry tomatoes
- 2 tablespoons butter
- Olive oil
- Salt and pepper to taste

Directions:
1. Put the tomatoes in an oven-safe glass dish.
2. Cut the fish into 2-3 pieces, depending on how many you're serving, and put on top of the tomatoes.
3. Season generously.
4. Put butter pats on top, each one about 1 tablespoon.
5. Finish with a little olive oil.
6. Pour 1 cup of water into your pressure cooker and lower in the trivet.
7. Put the dish on top and close the lid.
8. Select "manual," and then cook for 5 minutes on high pressure.
9. When ready, quick-release the pressure.
10. Serve with a side like rice pilaf and veggies.

Tip: If you're using frozen fish, cook for 9 minutes in the pressure cooker.
Nutritional Info (½ recipe)
Total calories: 174 Protein: 14 Fat: 12 Carbs: 3 Fiber: 0

Cajun-Style Shrimp w/ Broth

Serves: 4
Time: 45 minutes (10 minutes active time, 20 minutes cook time)

Ingredients:

- 6 cups chicken broth
- 1 ½ pounds shrimp, tails-on

- 1 stick butter
- 5 minced garlic cloves
- 1 cup beer
- 16-ounces clam juice
- 3-ounces tomato paste
- 1 tablespoon fresh rosemary
- 2 teaspoons dried thyme
- 1 teaspoon celery seed
- 1 teaspoon fennel seed
- 1 teaspoon black pepper
- 1 teaspoon red pepper flakes

Directions:
1. Smash the spices, thyme, and rosemary together.
2. Pour in the broth, clam juice, and tomato paste in your pressure cooker along with the crushed spices.
3. Lock the lid and select "manual," and cook for 10 minutes on high pressure.
4. When time is up, hit "cancel" and wait 15 minutes.
5. Open the lid when all the pressure is gone and pour in the beer.
6. This time, you'll cook on LOW pressure for 10 minutes.
7. Do another natural release for 15 minutes.
8. Next, hit "sauté" and let the broth reach a healthy simmer.
9. Add the shrimp and stir constantly until they become solid and pink.
10. Pour into bowls and serve!

Nutritional Info (¼ recipe)
Total calories: 349 Protein: 26 Fat: 8 Carbs: 35.7 Fiber: 2.2

Shrimp + Spinach Risotto

Serves: 4
Time: 17 minutes (10 minutes active time, 7 minutes cook time)

Ingredients:
- 2 ¼ cups chicken broth
- 15 peeled shrimp
- 2 cups spinach
- 2 bay leaves
- 1 cup Arborio rice
- 1 chopped onion
- 1 chopped celery stalk
- 1 chopped garlic clove
- ½ cup Parmesan cheese
- ¼ cup white wine
- 1 tablespoon olive oil
- 1 tablespoon butter

- 2 teaspoons ground oregano
- ¼ teaspoon ground white pepper

Directions:
1. Turn your pressure cooker to "sauté" and melt the butter and oil.
2. When hot, add in the celery, garlic, and onions.
3. After 2 minutes, or until the onions are soft and clear, add the rice.
4. Stir.
5. Cook for another minute.
6. Add the oregano, bay leaves, pepper, wine, and chicken broth.
7. When the mixture is simmering and bubbling, mix everything again before closing up the cooker.
8. Hit "manual" and cook on high pressure for 7 minutes.
9. While that cooks, chop up your spinach and peel the shrimp.
10. When time is up, quick-release the pressure.
11. Pick out the bay leaves.
12. Put the spinach and shrimp in the pot right away.
13. Keep stirring until the shrimp has become pink and solid.
14. Add the cheese and stir so it melts.
15. Serve!

Tip: You can use frozen shrimp. Just set them in a bowl of cold water before you start cooking the rice, and peel when the pressure cooker has about 4-5 minutes left.

Nutritional Info (¼ recipe)

Total calories: 224 Protein: 13 Fat: 9.3 Carbs: 20 Fiber: 1.9

Roasted Rosemary-Shrimp Risotto

Serves: 4
Time: About 15 minutes (7 minutes active time, 6 minutes cook time)

Ingredients:
- 1 pound peeled and cleaned shrimp
- 4 cups chicken broth
- 3 minced garlic cloves
- 2 cups Arborio rice
- ¼ cup Parmesan cheese
- ½ diced yellow onion
- 2 tablespoons +1 tablespoon olive oil
- 2 tablespoons butter
- 1 tablespoon chopped fresh rosemary sprigs
- ½ teaspoon salt

Directions:
1. Preheat your oven to 400-degrees.
2. Turn to your pressure cooker to "sauté" and add oil, onions, and garlic.
3. When the onions have softened, add the rice.
4. Stir, so the grains become oily.

5. Pour in the chicken broth.
6. Close the lid and select "manual," and then cook on high pressure for 6 minutes.
7. In the meantime, mix 1 tablespoon of oil, rosemary, salt, and garlic in a bowl.
8. Toss the shrimp in the bowl.
9. Spread on a baking sheet and put in the oven for 5 minutes.
10. When time is up on the cooker, hit "cancel" and quick-release.
11. Stir in the butter and parmesan cheese.
12. Serve with the baked shrimp on top.

Nutritional Info (¼ recipe)

Total calories: 544 Protein: 26 Fat: 18 Carbs: 75 Fiber: 3

Lobster Tails

Serves: 4
Time: 20 minutes (10 minutes active time, 10 minutes cook time)

Ingredients:
- 4 lobster tails (1-pound each)
- 1 cup water
- ½ cup white wine
- ¼ cup melted butter

Directions:
1. Defrost your lobster tails in a bowl of cold water.
2. Cut the tails in half tip-to tip, so the meat is exposed.
3. Pour the wine and water in your pressure cooker, so the liquid reaches the halfway point.
4. Lower in the steamer attachment.
5. Put the lobster tails shell-side down in the steamer basket.
6. Select "manual" and then steam on LOW pressure for 4 minutes.
7. When time is up, quick-release the pressure after turning off the cooker.
8. You know the meat is done when it is firm and white, not translucent.
9. Serve with melted butter.

Nutritional Info (¼ recipe)

Total calories: 190 Protein: 19 Fat: 12 Carbs: 0 Fiber: 0

Orange-Ginger White Fish

Serves: 4
Time: 17 minutes (10 minutes active time, 7 minutes cook time)

Ingredients:
- 4 white fish fillets
- 1 cup white wine
- 3-4 spring onions
- Thumb-sized piece of chopped, grated ginger

- Juice + zest of one orange
- Olive oil
- Salt and pepper to taste

Directions:
1. Pat your fish dry with a paper towel.
2. Rub on the olive oil, and season with a bit of salt and pepper.
3. Pour the white wine and orange juice into the pressure cooker, and add the ginger, zest, and spring onions.
4. Lower in the steamer basket, and lay in the fish.
5. Close the pressure cooker lid.
6. Select "manual" and cook on LOW pressure for 7 minutes.
7. When time is up, hit "cancel" and quick-release the pressure.
8. Serve with fresh greens.

Nutritional Info (¼ recipe)
Total calories: 167 Protein: 16 Fat: 5 Carbs: 8 Fiber: 0

Creole-Style Cod

Serves: 4
Time: About 10 minutes (5 minutes active time, 5 minutes cook time)

Ingredients:
- 2 pounds of cod fillet
- 2 cups chopped onion
- 2 bay leaves
- 2 minced garlic cloves
- 1 chopped green bell pepper
- 1 cup chopped celery
- 28-ounces of chopped tomatoes
- ¼ cup olive oil
- ¼ cup white wine
- 1 tablespoon paprika
- 1 teaspoon salt
- ½ teaspoon cayenne pepper

Directions:
1. Turn your pressure cooker to the sauté setting and add oil.
2. When hot and shiny, toss in the celery, onion, garlic, and green pepper.
3. Cook until the onion is clear and pepper has softened. Remove and set aside for now.
4. Drain the tomato juice from the can into the cooker, along with the wine.
5. Lower in the steamer basket.
6. Cut the fish into 4 equal parts and put in the steamer basket. **Make** sure the cooker is no more than ⅔ of the way full.
7. Close the cooker and select "manual" and cook for 4 minutes on high pressure.
8. When time is up, hit "cancel" and quick-release.

9. Add in the tomatoes, the cooked veggies from before, bay leaves, and seasonings.
10. Close the pot lid again and select "manual," and cook for just 1 minute on high pressure.
11. You will know the fish is done when it is solid, not translucent.
12. Serve with cooked rice.

Nutritional Info (¼ recipe)

Total calories: 247 Protein: 14 Fat: 20 Carbs: 14 Fiber: 1

Pressure Cooker Cod w/ Mango Salsa

Serves: 2
Time: About 40 minutes (30 minutes prep/marinade time, 10 minutes cook time)

Ingredients:

For the marinade
- 2 frozen cod fillets
- 1 cup coconut milk
- 1 tablespoon Thai green curry paste
- 1 tablespoon fresh minced ginger
- 1 tablespoon fish sauce
- 2 teaspoons brown sugar
- 1 teaspoon minced garlic
- Zest of one lime
- Juice of ½ lime

For the salsa
- ¾ cup of diced mango
- 1 minced jalapeno chile
- 1 chopped scallion
- Juice of 1 lime

Directions:
1. Mix the marinade ingredients together and pour into a bag with the fillets.
2. Store in the fridge for 30 minutes.
3. In the meantime, **Make** the mango salsa.
4. Pour 2 cups of water into the pressure cooker and lower in the steamer basket.
5. Wrap the fish tightly in foil (with a few lime slices) and put into the steamer.
6. Close the lid.
7. Select "manual" and cook on high pressure for 10 minutes.
8. In the meantime, bring the marinade from the fish to a simmer in a saucepan on the stove.
9. When the timer goes off, hit "cancel" and quick-release.
10. Serve with mango salsa, a bit of simmered marinade, and chopped scallions.

Nutritional Info (½ recipe)

Total calories: 195 Protein: 18 Fat: 4.9 Carbs: 18.7 Fiber: 3

Creamy-Tomato Haddock w/ Potatoes, Kale, and Carrots

Serves: 2
Time: About 20 minutes (4 minutes active time, 16 minutes cook time)

Ingredients:
- 1 pound frozen wild Haddock fillets
- 2 cups chicken broth
- 2 cups kale
- 2 cups whole-peeled tomatoes w/ juice
- ½ cup heavy cream
- 1 peeled and cubed red-skinned potato
- 1 chopped onion
- 1 chopped and peeled carrot
- 1 minced garlic clove
- 2 tablespoons butter
- 2 tablespoons chopped parsley
- 1 tablespoon chopped basil
- 2 teaspoons salt
- 1 pinch of crushed red pepper flakes
- Black pepper

Directions:
1. Turn your pressure cooker to "sauté" and melt the butter.
2. Cook the garlic and onion for 3 minutes.
3. Pour in the chicken broth, along with the herbs, tomatoes, carrots, and potatoes.
4. When simmering, put the fish in the steamer rack and lower into the cooker.
5. Season with salt, crushed red pepper flakes, and black pepper before closing the lid.
6. Cook on high pressure for 6 minutes.
7. Hit "cancel" and quick-release the pressure.
8. Take out the steamer basket.
9. Puree the broth till smooth.
10. Add the kale, cream, and fish back into the broth and keep on "warm" for 5-10 minutes.
11. Serve!

Nutritional Info (½ recipe)
Total calories: 550 Protein: 44 Fat: 24 Carbs: 15 Fiber: 1

Cod Fillets w/ Almonds and Peas

Serves: 4
Time: Under 10 minutes (5 minutes active time, 3 minutes cook time)

Ingredients:

- 1 pound frozen cod fish fillet
- 2 halved garlic cloves
- 10-ounces frozen peas
- 1 cup chicken broth
- ½ cup packed parsley
- 2 tablespoons fresh oregano
- 2 tablespoons sliced almonds
- ½ teaspoon paprika

Directions:
1. Take the fish out of the freezer.
2. In a food processor, pulse together garlic, oregano, parsley, paprika, and 1 tablespoon almonds.
3. Turn your pressure cooker to "sauté" and heat a bit of olive oil.
4. When hot, toast the rest of the almonds until they are fragrant.
5. Take out the almonds and put on a paper towel.
6. Pour the broth in the cooker and toss in your herb mixture.
7. Cut the fish into 4 pieces and put in the steamer basket.
8. Lower into the cooker and close the lid.
9. Select "manual," and cook on high pressure for 3 minutes.
10. Hit "cancel" and quick-release the pressure.
11. The fish is done when it is solid, not translucent.
12. Add the frozen peas and close the lid again.
13. Cook on high pressure for 1 minute.
14. Quick-release again.
15. Serve with the toasted almonds on top.

Tip: If you want a thicker sauce, remove the fish before mixing 1 tablespoon of cornstarch with 1 tablespoon of cold water, and pouring into the cooker. Turn the cooker to sauté and bring to a simmer until thickened.

Nutritional Info (¼ recipe)
Total calories: 210 Protein: 26 Fat: 6.3 Carbs: 11.7 Fiber: 3.9

Halibut w/ Dijon-Mustard Sauce

Serves: 4
Time: 10 minutes (5 minutes active time, 5 minutes cook time)

Ingredients:

For the fish
- 4, 1-inch thick halibut fillets
- 1 chopped onion
- 1 cup dry white wine
- 1 minced garlic clove
- 4 tablespoons Dijon mustard
- 1 bay leaf
- ½ teaspoon dried thyme

For the sauce
- 2 tablespoons Dijon mustard
- 1 tablespoon cornstarch

Directions:
1. Season the fish with 1 tablespoon of mustard, and sprinkle evenly with the thyme.
2. Pour a coating of olive oil into the pressure cooker, and turn on the "sauté" setting.
3. Cook the garlic and onion until the onion has softened.
4. Pour in the wine and toss in the bay leaf.
5. Put the fish in your steamer basket, and lower into the cooker.
6. Close the lid, select "manual," and cook on LOW pressure for 5 minutes.
7. When time is up, hit "cancel" and quick-release.
8. Pick out the bay leaf and plate the fish.
9. To Make the sauce, mix mustard with cornstarch.
10. Stir into the pressure cooker with the leftover liquid.
11. Simmer on sauté until the sauce begins to boil and has thickened.
12. Serve fish with sauce on top!

Nutritional Info (¼ recipe)

Total calories: 178 Protein: 21 Fat: 2 Carbs: 4 Fiber: 0

Tapioca Parfait w/ Berries

Serves: 4
Time: 25 minutes

Ingredients:
- 2 cups almond milk
- 2 cups fresh berries
- ½ cup small pearl tapioca
- ¼ cup organic sugar
- 1 teaspoon pure vanilla
- ½ teaspoon lemon zest
- Pinch of salt

Directions:
1. Put the tapioca in a fine-mesh strainer and run under water for about 30 seconds.
2. Put the milk in your pressure cooker, followed by the tapioca and a pinch of salt.
3. Stir.
4. Close the lid and select "manual," and then high pressure for 4 minutes.
5. When time is up, turn off the cooker and wait for 20 minutes while the pressure comes down naturally.
6. Quick-release any leftover pressure before opening the lid.
7. Mix in the sugar, lemon zest, and vanilla.
8. To serve, layer 2 tablespoons of berries in a glass, followed by tapioca, berries, tapioca again, and end with berries.

Nutritional Info (¼ recipe)
Total calories: 180 Protein: 2 Fat: 2 Carbs: 39 Fiber: 1

Butternut-Squash Apple Butter

Makes: 3 cups
Time: About 35 minutes (15 minutes active time, 18 minutes cook time)

Ingredients:
- 1 small butternut squash
- 4 peeled and diced apples
- ½ cup apple juice
- ½ cup golden raisins
- ½ cup applesauce
- ¼ cup maple syrup
- ¼ cup brown sugar
- 1 ½ teaspoons cinnamon
- ¾ teaspoon nutmeg
- ½ teaspoon ground ginger
- ⅛ teaspoon ground cloves
- Pinch of salt

Directions:
1. Cut the butternut squash in half and clean out the seeds.
2. Peel and cut into cubes.
3. Pour 1 cup of water into the pressure cooker before adding the squash.
4. Close the lid and cook for 10 minutes on high pressure.
5. When time is up, quick-release the pressure.
6. Move the cooked cubes to a plate, and measure out 2 cups.
7. Puree, making sure you still have 2 cups. If you want, you can add honey to **Make** the puree sweeter, which will result in a sweeter final product.
8. Add the puree and all the other ingredients (except maple syrup) to the pressure cooker.
9. Lock the lid.
10. Select "manual," and cook on high pressure for just 3 minutes.
11. When time is up, turn off the cooker and wait 15 minutes.
12. Quick-release any leftover pressure before mixing in the maple syrup.
13. Taste and season as necessary.

Nutritional Info (1 cup)
Total calories: 397 Protein: 3 Fat: 0 Carbs: 102 Fiber: 6

Black Bean Chili

Serves: 6-8
Time: Overnight bean-soak + 1 hour, 30 minutes (9 minutes active time, 48 minutes cook time)

Ingredients:
- 1 pound dried black beans
- 2 ½ cups water
- 2 cups thawed corn kernels
- 1 can crushed tomatoes
- 4 chopped garlic cloves
- 2 diced red onions
- 2 diced red bell peppers
- 3 tablespoons olive oil
- 2 tablespoons minced chipotles in adobo sauce
- 2 tablespoons chili powder
- 1 tablespoon salt
- 1 tablespoon tomato paste
- 1 tablespoon ground cumin

Directions:
1. The night before you **Make** the chili, soak the beans in about 3 inches of cold water. Leave the bowl uncovered and leave on the counter.
2. The next day, drain the beans.
3. Heat oil in your pressure cooker on "sauté" until shiny.
4. Cook the bell pepper, onion, garlic, and 1 teaspoon of salt until the veggies are soft.
5. Toss in the cumin and chili powder, stirring, for 2 minutes.
6. Spoon in the tomato paste and chipotles and mix for 1-2 minutes.
7. Add the water, tomatoes, beans, and 2 teaspoons of salt, and stir.
8. Close the lid, select "manual," and cook on high pressure for 30 minutes.
9. When time is up, hit "cancel" and wait 15 minutes.
10. Quick-release any leftover pressure.
11. Add the corn and stir to warm the kernels through.
12. Season as necessary before serving.

Nutritional Info (⅙ recipe)
Total calories: 200 Protein: 11 Fat: 2 Carbs: 31 Fiber: 15

Easy Chickpea Curry

Serves: 6
Time: 20 minutes (5 minutes active time, 15 minutes cook time)

Ingredients:
- 2 cans of rinsed and drained chickpeas
- 2 cans of diced tomatoes
- 3 big peeled and cubed potatoes
- 1 sliced onion
- ½ cup water
- 8 teaspoons olive oil
- 4 teaspoons crushed garlic

- 4 teaspoons whole cumin seeds
- 2 teaspoons garam masala
- 2 teaspoons ground turmeric
- 2 teaspoons ground coriander
- ½ teaspoon salt
- ¼ teaspoon black pepper

Directions:
1. Turn your pressure cooker to "sauté" and heat the oil.
2. When hot, stir in the cumin seeds until they begin to **Make** a crackling sound.
3. Add the onion and stir for 5 minutes until soft.
4. Stir in the garlic and spices.
5. Add the rest of the ingredients and close the lid.
6. Select "manual," and cook for 15 minutes on high pressure.
7. When done, hit "cancel" and quick-release the pressure.
8. Serve with a side like rice or naan bread.

Nutritional Info (⅙ recipe)
Total calories: 384 Protein: 11.6 Fat: 8.3 Carbs: 68.9 Fiber: 12

Lasagna Soup

Serves: 6
Time: 20 minutes (5 minutes active time, 10 minutes cook time)

Ingredients:
- 4 cooked vegan sausage links
- 28-ounces fire-roasted tomatoes
- 4 cups torn kale
- 2 cups veggie broth
- 1 cup broken-up lasagna noodles
- 4 minced garlic cloves
- 2 chopped celery stalks
- 1 chopped onion
- 1 chopped carrot
- 1 chopped zucchini
- 1 teaspoon oregano
- 1 teaspoon basil
- ½ teaspoon rosemary
- ½ teaspoon black pepper
- Dash of salt
- Dash of red pepper flakes

Directions:
1. Turn your pressure cooker to "sauté" and pour in a little veggie broth.
2. Cook the carrot, celery, and onion until soft. If it looks like the pot is getting dry, keep adding broth.
3. Add the rest of the ingredients (except the sausage) and select "manual," and then high pressure for

10 minutes.
4. When the timer beeps, hit "cancel" and wait for the pressure to come down on its own.
5. Open up the cooker and stir in the cut-up sausage to heat it through.
6. Taste and season as necessary.
7. Soup's on!

Nutritional Info (⅙ recipe)
Total calories: 180 Protein: 9 Fat: 1 Carbs: 34 Fiber: 9

Coconut-Milk Corn Chowder

Serves: 6
Time: 26 minutes (20 minutes active time, 6 minutes cook time)

Ingredients:
- 5 ears of corn, kernels removed
- 3 chopped Yukon Gold potatoes
- 4 cups veggie broth
- 1 cup coconut milk
- 3 chopped carrots
- 3 minced garlic cloves
- 1 tablespoon coconut oil
- 1 tablespoon arrowroot powder (or potato starch)
- Juice of 1 lime
- 1 teaspoon smoked paprika
- Cumin to taste
- Salt and pepper to taste
- Dash of red pepper flakes

Directions:
1. After removing the kernels from the cob, throw into the pressure cooker along with carrots, onions, and a dash of red pepper.
2. Cook for about 4 minutes until the onions begin to become clear.
3. Add the garlic and cook for another minute.
4. Pour in the broth, and add the cobs, potatoes, salt, and pepper.
5. Lock the pressure cooker lid and select "high pressure" for 6 minutes.
6. When time is up, hit "cancel" and wait 15 minutes.
7. Quick-release any remaining pressure.
8. Pick out the cobs.
9. Mix the coconut milk with arrowroot powder in a separate bowl until smooth.
10. Add in the lime juice.
11. Pour the whole thing into the pressure cooker.
12. Turn on "sauté" and blend the chowder with a hand blender until completely smooth.
13. Serve!

Nutritional Info (⅙ recipe)
Total calories: 217 Protein: 5 Fat: 6 Carbs: 41 Fiber: 3

White Vegetable Stew

Serves: 4-6
Time: 15 minutes (2 minutes active time, 13 minutes cook time)

Ingredients:
- 1 ½ cups broth
- 3 cups diced celery root
- 2 bay leaves
- 1 cup diced carrot
- 1 cup sliced leek
- 1 cup diced parsnip
- 1 sprig rosemary
- 1 sprig thyme
- ½ cup green lentils
- ½ cup peas
- Squirt of lemon juice
- Salt and pepper to taste

Directions:
1. Put the leek in your pressure cooker, no oil, and cook for 1 minute on the "sauté" setting.
2. Add garlic and cook for another minute.
3. Turn off the cooker and add carrot, parsnips, lentils, celery root, broth, and herbs.
4. Close the lid and select "manual," and then high pressure for 6 minutes.
5. When time is up, hit "cancel" and wait for the pressure to come down on its own.
6. When the pressure is gone, add the peas.
7. Stir and close the lid for 2 minutes to heat everything.
8. Season with salt, pepper, and lemon juice before serving.

Nutritional Info (¼ recipe)
Total calories: 103 Protein: 4 Fat: 0 Carbs: 23 Fiber: 5

Curried Pear and Squash Soup

Serves: 4-6
Time: 15 minutes (5 minutes active time, 10 minutes cook time)

Ingredients:
- 4 cups vegetable stock
- 3 small delicata squash
- 1 peeled and cut Comice pear
- 1 small diced onion
- 2 tablespoons parsley
- 1 tablespoon lemon juice
- 3 teaspoons curry powder
- 1 teaspoon grated ginger

- 1 teaspoon grated turmeric
- Pinch of cayenne pepper
- ½ teaspoon salt
- Black pepper

Directions:
1. Turn your pressure cooker to "sauté" and add a little oil to coat the bottom.
2. When hot, add onion and cook until soft.
3. Throw in the cut pear, ginger, turmeric, and curry powder.
4. After 2 minutes of cooking and stirring, pour in the broth and squash.
5. Close the pot lid and select "manual," and then cook on high pressure for 7 minutes.
6. When time is up, hit "cancel" and wait for the pressure to reduce.
7. Remove the lid and puree the soup.
8. Season with lemon juice, salt, pepper, cayenne, and parsley.

Nutritional Info (⅙ recipe)
Total calories: 167 Protein: 3 Fat: 6.6 Carbs: 27.5 Fiber: 6.6

Rainbow Soup

Serves: 8
Time: 21 minutes

Ingredients:
- 5 cups veggie broth
- 3 minced garlic cloves
- 3 cups cooked black beans
- 2 diced carrots
- 15-ounce can diced tomatoes
- 1 chopped small red cabbage
- 1 chopped onion
- 1 diced jalapeno chile
- 1 chopped yellow bell pepper
- 6-ounces quartered mushrooms
- 2 tablespoons tomato paste
- 1 tablespoon oregano
- 1 tablespoon chili powder
- 1 teaspoon cumin
- Salt to taste

Directions:
1. Mix everything in your pressure cooker, minus the salt.
2. Close the lid, select "manual," and cook on high pressure for 6 minutes.
3. When time is up, turn off the cooker and wait 15 minutes.
4. Release any remaining pressure.
5. Salt and serve!

Nutritional Info (⅛ recipe)

Total calories: 169 Protein: 11 Fat: 1 Carbs: 32 Fiber: 11

Lemon Polenta w/ Chickpeas and Asparagus

Serves: 4
Time: 55 minutes (15 minutes active time, 40 minutes cook time)

Ingredients:

For polenta
- 2 ¼ cups water
- 2 cups veggie broth
- 1 cup coarse-grind polenta
- 2 teaspoons minced garlic
- 1 teaspoon basil

For asparagus
- 12-ounces trimmed asparagus, cut into 1 ½-inch bits
- 4 teaspoons toasted pine nuts
- 1 teaspoon lemon zest
- Salt to taste
- Lemon juice to taste

For chickpeas
- 1 ½ cups drained and rinsed canned chickpeas
- ½ cup veggie broth
- ¼ cup water
- 2 minced garlic cloves
- ½ finely-chopped onion
- 1 teaspoon cornstarch
- 1 teaspoon lemon juice
- 1 teaspoon lemon zest
- ½ teaspoon dried basil
- ¼ teaspoon black pepper

Directions:
1. Pour 2 ¼ cups of water and 2 cups of broth to a boil in your pressure cooker on the "sauté" setting.
2. Stir in the polenta, garlic, and basil.
3. Secure the lid and select "manual," and then cook on high pressure for just 5 minutes.
4. In the meantime, take a saucepan and cook the onion on the stove for 3 minutes.
5. Add garlic and drained chickpeas and stir for one minute.
6. Pour in ½ cup veggie broth and stir for 1 minute with basil and black pepper.
7. Reduce the heat and simmer for 5 minutes.
8. Add lemon zest and lemon juice.
9. In a small bowl, mix cornstarch with ¼ cup of cold water until smooth, and pour into the pan.
10. On low, simmer until the sauce thickens.
11. To **Make** the asparagus, boil a large pot of water.

12. Submerge the asparagus for two minutes to blanch them.
13. Drain and toss in a bowl with some lemon juice, salt, and lemon zest.
14. When time is up on the pressure cooker, hit "cancel" and wait for the pressure to reduce naturally.
15. When all the pressure is gone, open the lid and salt to taste, and stir.

Nutritional Info (¼ recipe)
Total calories: 276 Protein: 10.4 Fat: 1.7 Carbs: 55.6 Fiber: 8.5

Vegan Brazilian Potato Salad

Serves: 6-8
Time: 1 hour, 15 minutes (15 minutes cook time, 1 hour chill time)

Ingredients:
- 4 cups chopped potatoes
- 2 cups water
- 1 ½ cups diced carrots
- 1 cup corn kernels
- 1 cup peas
- ¼ cup + 1 tablespoon vegan mayo
- 10 minced black olives
- ½ teaspoon salt
- ½ teaspoon black pepper

Directions:
1. Put the water, carrots, and potatoes in your pressure cooker.
2. Select "manual," and cook on high pressure for 10 minutes.
3. When time is up, quick-release the pressure after pressing "cancel."
4. Add peas and corn, and cook again, on LOW pressure this time, adjusting to "0" minutes.
5. When the timer beeps, quick-release.
6. Pour the pot contents into a colander and rinse under cold water.
7. In a separate bowl, mix olives, mayo, salt, and pepper.
8. Stir into the potato salad.
9. Chill in a covered Tupperware for one hour before serving.

Nutritional Info (⅙ recipe)
Total calories: 272 Protein: 5 Fat: 14 Carbs: 33 Fiber: 10

Easy Seitan (Vegan Meat Substitute)

Makes: 1 pound
Time: Around 20 minutes (3 minutes active time, 16 minutes cook time)

Ingredients:
- 1 cup vital wheat gluten
- ¾ cup vegan veggie broth
- 3 tablespoons nutritional yeast

- 1 tablespoon smoked paprika
- 2 teaspoons seasoning of choice (Italian seasoning, Herbes de Provence, Jamaican jerk seasoning, etc.)
- 1 teaspoon garlic powder

Directions:
1. Combine the ingredients in a big bowl and mix until you get a sticky ball.
2. Knead for a few minutes.
3. Form a sausage shape with the dough, and then cut into slices.
4. Prepare the pressure cooker by greasing the inside with coconut oil.
5. Put the seitan inside and pour in just enough water to cover them.
6. Close the lid.
7. Select "manual," and cook on high pressure for 16 minutes.
8. When time is up, turn off the cooker and quick-release the pressure.
9. Serve in whatever dish you are preparing.

Tip: To store seitan, you can put it in a Tupperware, cover with a little veggie broth so it doesn't dry out, and keep it in the fridge for about 1 week. To freeze, wrap up the slices tightly in plastic wrap and keep in the fridge for up to 2 months. To use, thaw it out like you would meat.

Nutritional Info (⅓ recipe)
Total calories: 195 Protein: 26 Fat: 2 Carbs: 15 Fiber: 1.6

Pressure Cooker Garlic Broth

Makes: About 6 cups
Time: 30 minutes (10 minutes active time, 20 minutes cook time)

Ingredients:
- 6 cups filtered water
- 1 head of garlic
- 4-6 celery stalks (w/ leaves), sliced into 3-inch pieces
- 1 big, quartered onion
- ½ cup fresh parsley
- 3 teaspoons nutritional yeast (optional)
- 1 teaspoon dried thyme
- ¼ teaspoon rubbed sage
- Salt to taste

Directions:
1. Separate the garlic cloves, but do not peel them.
2. Put the cut onion, garlic cloves, celery, sage, and thyme in the pressure cooker.
3. Pour in water and close the lid.
4. Select "manual," and cook for 10 minutes on high pressure.
5. When time is up, hit "cancel" and wait for the pressure to descend on its own.
6. Pick out the garlic cloves.
7. Pour the broth into a strainer over a big bowl.
8. If you are using yeast, add it now when the broth is still hot. Salt if desired, though you can always

salt the broth when you're using it in a specific recipe.
9. Squeeze down with the back of a spoon to get the liquid out and strained through into the bowl.
10. When you get close to 6 cups, store. It keeps in the fridge for 3 days, and can be frozen for up to 6 months.

Nutritional Info (1/6 recipe)
Total calories: 19 Protein: 1 Fat: 0 Carbs: 4 Fiber: 0

Sweet 'n Sour Mango Chicken

Serves: 4
Time: 50 minutes (10 minutes active time, 40 minutes cook time)

Ingredients:
- 8 boneless chicken thighs
- 4 chopped garlic cloves
- 1 chopped mango
- ½ chopped red onion
- ½ cup chicken broth
- ¼ cup chopped cilantro
- ¼ cup + 1 tablespoon coconut aminos
- 1-inch piece of chopped ginger
- 2 tablespoons lime juice
- 2 tablespoons apple cider vinegar
- 2 tablespoons honey
- 1 tablespoon olive oil
- 1 teaspoon fish sauce
- Salt to taste

Directions:
1. Heat the olive in your pressure cooker turned to the sauté setting.
2. Put the chicken thighs in with the skin down, and brown for three minutes.
3. Flip and brown on that side for two minutes.
4. Plate the thighs.
5. Put the mango, garlic, and onion in your cooker.
6. When the onion is translucent and mango is beginning to brown, turn off the cooker.
7. Add the chicken back in, along with the lime juice, ¼ cup coconut aminos, cilantro, honey, broth, ginger, fish sauce, and 1 tablespoon of apple cider vinegar.
8. Seal the lid.
9. Cook on high pressure for 15 minutes.
10. When time is up, turn off the cooker and quick-release.
11. Plate the thighs.
12. Pour in 1 tablespoon of coconut aminos, 1 tablespoon apple cider vinegar, and salt into your cooker.
13. Hit sauté again and reduce for 10-15 minutes, or until you get a nice thick sauce.
14. Serve chicken with sauce on top.

Nutritional Info (¼ recipe)

Total calories: 379 Protein: 38 Fat: 13 Carbs: 26 Fiber: 4

Red Chicken Soup

Serves: 6-8
Time: About 1 hour (20 minutes active time, 40 minutes cook time)

Ingredients:
- 1, 3-lb trussed chicken
- 2 smashed garlic cloves
- 2 chopped carrots
- 1 wedged red onion
- 1 lime
- ½ big cored and diced red cabbage
- ½ diced pineapple
- 1-2 tablespoons tamarind paste
- 1 teaspoon ginger powder
- 1 teaspoon turmeric powder
- 1 teaspoon cinnamon powder
- Fish sauce to taste
- Salt to taste

Directions:
1. Put the carrots in the pressure cooker, followed by the trussed (see TIPS for instruction) chicken, garlic, onion, and cabbage.
2. Cover with enough water, so that everything is covered.
3. Seal the lid and select "soup." Adjust time to 30 minutes.
4. When time is up, turn off the cooker and wait 10 minutes.
5. Release any remaining pressure.
6. Put the tamarind paste in a bowl, and spoon over ½ cup of the pressure cooker broth.
7. Take out the chicken and shred the meat.
8. Return to the pot.
9. When the paste is cool to the touch, knead until the paste has become thickened.
10. Squeeze a little, and pick out any pods.
11. Add to the pot, along with turmeric, ginger, and cinnamon.
12. Add the pineapple, and stir the soup.
13. Squeeze the lime juice into the pot.
14. Hit "sauté" and let the broth simmer.
15. Simmer for 5-10 minutes.
16. Before serving, season to taste with fish sauce and salt.

Tip: To truss a whole chicken, you first rinse in running water inside and out. Pat dry with paper towels and lay in a clean baking dish. Grab the wings and tuck them behind its back. Pull the ankles back, and loop a cooking string (should be cut a few feet long) around twice. Holding both ends of the string, one in each hand, wrap over where the thigh meets the breast, and pull string over where the wings meet the neck. Flip the chicken over and **Make** an "X" shape with the twine and flip over again, with the string on the bottom of the bird. Tie off the twine around the ankles and cut off excess string

Nutritional Info (⅙ recipe)
Total calories: 271 Protein: 52 Fat: 3 Carbs: 7 Fiber: 0

Chicken Drumstick Soup

Serves: 4
Time: About 40-45 minutes

Ingredients:
- 1 ½ pounds chicken drumsticks
- 1 quart chicken broth
- 2 big peeled and diced carrots
- 2 long sliced celery stalks
- 2 bay leaves
- 1 medium-sized peeled and diced rutabaga
- 1 big peeled and diced parsnip
- 1 small diced yellow onion
- Salt and pepper to taste

Directions:
1. Put everything in the pressure cooker, and pour the broth over on top.
2. Close the lid and select "Soup." Use the default time setting (30 minutes).
3. When time is up, turn off the cooker and wait for a natural pressure release.
4. When all the pressure is gone, take out the drumsticks and let them cool on a plate.
5. When they are cool, tear off the meat and put back in the pot.
6. Season to taste before serving.

Tip: Save the drumstick bones for stock!
Nutritional Info (¼ recipe)
Total calories: 103 Protein: 9.6 Fat: 4 Carbs: 7.8 Fiber: 2

Mexi-Meatloaf

Serves: 4
Time: 40 minutes (5 minutes active time, 35 minutes cook time)

Ingredients:
- 2 pounds ground beef
- 1 cup salsa
- 1 egg
- 1 diced yellow onion
- ¼ cup arrowroot
- 1 tablespoon olive oil
- 1 teaspoon garlic powder

- 1 teaspoon cumin
- 1 teaspoon chili powder
- 1 teaspoon paprika
- 1 teaspoon onion powder
- 1 teaspoon black pepper
- 1 teaspoon salt

Directions:
1. Mix all the ingredients (except ¼ cup of the salsa and olive oil) in a bowl.
2. With your hands, **Make** a tightly-formed loaf.
3. On "sauté," heat 1 tablespoon of oil in the pressure cooker.
4. Put the meatloaf in the cooker and ladle over ¼ cup salsa on top.
5. Seal the lid and hit "Meat/Stew." Adjust to 35 minutes on "normal" pressure.
6. When time is up, hit "cancel" and quick-release the pressure.
7. Serve!

Nutritional Info (¼ recipe)
Total calories: 494 Protein: 52 Fat: 26 Carbs: 20 Fiber:: 0

Beef + Broccoli Soup

Serves: 6-8
Time: About 30 minutes (5 minutes active time, 24 minutes cook time)

Ingredients:
- 4 ¾ cups beef stock
- 2 pounds tri-tip beef
- 2 pounds frozen broccoli florets
- 4 garlic cloves
- 1 small chopped onion
- 1 cup cheddar cheese
- 2 tablespoons salt
- Black pepper to taste

Directions:
1. Turn on your pressure cooker and when it reads "HOT," add a little bit of olive oil, just to coat the bottom.
2. Season the beef with salt and pepper.
3. Lay in the pot and brown on both sides for 5 minutes.
4. Remove meat and plate for now.
5. Add onion and garlic, and cook until softened.
6. Return beef and pour in broth.
7. Seal the lid and cook for 20 minutes on high pressure.
8. When time is up, hit "cancel" and quick-release the pressure.
9. Add broccoli florets, and stir.
10. Close lid and select "manual," and cook on high pressure again for just 4 minutes.
11. Quick-release again when time is up.

12. If you're adding cheese, stir into the pot before serving.
13. Season to taste.

Nutritional Info (⅙ recipe)
Total calories: 270 Protein: 37 Fat: 7.5 Carbs: 13 Fiber: 3

Beef + Plantain Curry

Serves: 5-6
Time: 1 hour, 50 minutes (10 minutes active time, 40 minutes cook time, 1 hour marinating time)

Ingredients:

For marinade
- 2 chopped-up pounds pot roast
- 2 peeled and sliced onions
- 1 cup coconut milk
- 2 teaspoons coconut milk
- 1 teaspoon ginger powder
- 1 teaspoon garlic powder
- 1 teaspoon turmeric powder
- 1 teaspoon salt

Other ingredients
- 1 stick cinnamon
- 1 sliced very-ripe plantain
- Salt to taste

Directions:
1. In a bowl, mix spices and coconut oil together.
2. Pour into a Ziploc bag with the beef and marinate for 1 hour.
3. Turn your pressure cooker to "sauté" and pour in 3 teaspoons coconut oil.
4. When hot, cook onions until clear.
5. Take out and plate for now.
6. Brown the cut meat all over.
7. Plate with the onions.
8. Pour in coconut milk and deglaze.
9. Add the onion and meat back in, with the cinnamon stick.
10. Secure the lid and hit "manual," then cook for 35 minutes on high pressure.
11. When time is up, hit "cancel" and wait for the pressure to come down naturally.
12. Turn the sauté setting on again and add the plantain.
13. Salt to taste and simmer for 5 minutes.
14. Pick out the cinnamon stick before serving.

Nutritional Info (⅕ recipe)
Total calories: 454 Protein: 41 Fat: 26 Carbs: 11 Fiber: 1

Easy Beef Stew

Serves: 4-5
Time: 35 minutes

Ingredients:
- 2 pounds chopped beef
- 1 acorn squash
- 6 sliced garlic cloves
- 3 tablespoons broth
- 3 big sliced carrots
- 1 peeled and sliced yellow onion
- 1 rosemary sprig
- 1 bay leaf
- Salt to taste

Directions:
1. Microwave the squash for 1 minute.
2. When it's cool to handle, peel, seed, and cube it.
3. Put everything in the pressure cooker.
4. Select "Soup/Stew" and adjust time to 35 minutes.
5. When time is up, hit "cancel" and quick-release the pressure.
6. Taste and season as needed.
7. Serve!

Nutritional Info (⅕ recipe)
Total calories: 289 Protein: 38 Fat: 8 Carbs: 14 Fiber: 0

Bone Broth

Makes: 8 cups
Time: About 50 minutes (10 minutes active time, 40 minutes cook time)

Ingredients:
- 8 cups of water
- 2.5 pounds of bones
- 2 cleaned and crosswise cut leeks
- 1 peeled carrot, cut into three pieces
- 2 tablespoons fish sauce
- 1 teaspoon apple cider vinegar

Directions:
1. Put all the veggies in the pressure cooker.
2. Put in the bones and cover with water. **Make** sure the pot is not more than ⅔ of the way full.
3. Add vinegar and fish sauce.
4. Close the lid and select "manual," and then high pressure for 30 minutes.

5. When the timer beeps, hit "cancel" and wait for the pressure to decrease naturally.
6. Pour the broth through a strainer and discard the solids.
7. It will keep frozen for up to a year, and last 2-3 days in the fridge.

Nutritional Info (1 cup):

Total calories: 160 Protein: 8 Fat: 9 Carbs: 0 Fiber: 0

Creamy Cabbage w/ Bacon

Serves: 4-6

Time: 19 minutes (10 minutes active time, 9 minutes cook time)

Ingredients:
- 2 cups bone broth
- 1 medium-sized head of finely-chopped Savoy cabbage
- 1 cup diced bacon
- 1 chopped onion
- 1 bay leaf
- 2 tablespoons parsley flakes
- ½ can of coconut milk
- ¼ teaspoon mace

Directions:
1. Cut a piece of parchment that fits in the bottom of the pressure cooker, but keep for later.
2. Press the sauté button and wait till the control panel reads, "HOT."
3. Put the onions and bacon in the pot and cook until the onions have browned and become clear.
4. Pour in the bone broth and deglaze.
5. Add the bay leaf and cabbage.
6. Cover the top with the round of parchment you cut out, and secure the lid.
7. Select "manual," and adjust time to 4 minutes on high pressure.
8. When time is up, hit "cancel" and quick-release the pressure.
9. Take off the parchment and turn your cooker to "sauté."
10. When boiling, add coconut milk and nutmeg.
11. Let the pot simmer for 5 minutes, before turning off the cooker.
12. Add parsley flakes before serving.

Nutritional Info (¼ recipe):

Total calories: 94 Protein: 7 Fat: 3.7 Carbs: 8.6 Fiber: 2

Crunchy Corn Niblets

Serves: 6

Time: 55 minutes + overnight soak time (10 minutes active time, 45 minutes cook time)

Ingredients:
- 2 cups dried corn
- 2 tablespoons olive oil

- 1 tablespoon chili powder
- 1 teaspoon salt

Directions:
1. Soak the corn overnight.
2. When ready, pour them into your pressure cooker with the minimum amount of water.
3. Hit "manual," and cook on high pressure for 30 minutes.
4. When done, hit "cancel" and quick-release.
5. When done, take out the corn and dry.
6. Heat a saucepan and pour in olive oil.
7. When hot, add the corn, salt, and chili powder.
8. Roast until crunchy and delicious.

Nutritional Info (⅙ recipe):
Total calories: 74 Protein: 0 Fat: 5 Carbs: 0 Fiber: 0

Pressure Cooker Cornbread

Serves: 8
Time: 40 minutes

Ingredients:
- Two, 8.5-ounce boxes of Jiffy Corn Muffin mix
- 2 large eggs
- 1 cup milk

Directions:
1. In a bowl, stir the muffin mix, eggs, and milk.
2. Grease a half-sized Bundt pan before pouring in the batter. You do not have to wrap it in foil.
3. Pour 1 cup of water into your pressure cooker and insert the trivet.
4. Put the Bundt pan on the trivet.
5. Secure the lid, select "manual," and then 20 minutes on high pressure.
6. When the timer goes off, hit "cancel" and wait for the pressure to go down naturally.
7. After 10 minutes, quick-release the rest of the pressure.
8. When safe, take out the Bundt pan and rest for 5 minutes.
9. When cool, cut and serve.

Nutritional Info (⅛ recipe):
Total calories: 215 Protein: 5 Fat: 7 Carbs: 30 Fiber: 0

Apple Crisp

Serves: 3-4
Time: 13 minutes (5 minutes active time, 8 minutes cook time)

Ingredients:
- 5 peeled and chopped medium-sized apples
- 4 tablespoons butter

- ¾ cup old-fashioned rolled oats
- ½ cup water
- ¼ cup flour
- ¼ cup brown sugar
- 1 tablespoon maple syrup
- 2 teaspoons cinnamon
- ½ teaspoon nutmeg
- Pinch of salt

Directions:
1. Put the chopped apples in your pressure cooker and sprinkle with nutmeg and cinnamon.
2. Pour in the water and maple syrup.
3. Melt the butter in your microwave.
4. Mix with oats, brown sugar, salt, and flour.
5. Spoon on top of the apples.
6. Close the pressure cooker.
7. Select "manual," and adjust time to 8 minutes on high pressure.
8. When time is up, hit "cancel" and wait for the pressure to decrease naturally.
9. When you open the lid, wait a few minutes, so the sauce thickens.
10. Serve with ice cream!

Nutritional Info (¼ recipe):
Total calories: 309 Protein: 4 Fat: 13 Carbs: 47 Fiber: 5

Two-Ingredient Chocolate Fondue

Serves: 2-4
Time: 2 minutes

Ingredients:
- 3.5-ounces of dark chocolate (minimum 70% cocoa)
- 3.5-ounces of cream

Directions:
1. Pour two cups of water into the pressure cooker and lower in the trivet.
2. Put chocolate chunks in a ceramic, heat-proof container that fits into the pressure cooker, and pour over the cream.
3. Put into the pressure cooker, uncovered.
4. Close the lid and select "manual," then adjust time to 2 minutes on high pressure.
5. When time is up, hit "cancel" and carefully quick-release.
6. Open the lid and remove the container.
7. Whisk quickly until the chocolate becomes smooth.
8. Serve right away!

Tip: If you want to **Make** your fondue unique, add 1 teaspoon of Amaretto liquor before closing up the pressure. Other flavor options include chili powder, peppermint extract, orange extract, or Bailey's.

Nutritional Info (¼ recipe):

Total calories: 216 Protein: 1.8 Fat: 20.3 Carbs: 11.7 Fiber: 2.6

Cranberry Bread Pudding w/ Bourbon Sauce

Serves: 6
Time: 1 hour, 10 minutes (15 minutes prep time, 55 minutes cook time)

It's time to kick bread pudding up a notch. By adding cranberries to the batter and topping off the finished product with a rich, buttery bourbon sauce, you'll have a Christmas-ready dessert that will impress everyone in your family. The best part is how easy the whole process is.

Ingredients:

For pudding
- 4 beaten eggs
- 3 cups dry bread crumbs
- 2 cups milk
- 1 ½ cups water
- ½ cup sugar
- ⅓ cup dried cranberries
- 1 teaspoon vanilla

For sauce
- ¼ cup butter
- ½ cup sugar
- 1 egg yolk
- 2 tablespoons bourbon
- 2 tablespoons water

Directions:
1. Begin by greasing a 1 ½-quart soufflé dish.
2. In a bowl, whisk the milk, eggs, sugar, and vanilla.
3. Put bread and cranberries in the greased dish, and pour over the egg mixture.
4. Wrap tightly with foil.
5. Pour 1 ½ cups of water into your pressure cooker and lower in the trivet.
6. Put the covered dish on the trivet and close the pot lid.
7. Select "manual," and cook for 25 minutes on high pressure.
8. In the meantime, **Make** your bourbon sauce. Begin by melting butter in a saucepan.
9. Remove from the stovetop and mix in sugar.
10. In a small bowl, mix the egg yolk and water, and then pour into the saucepan.
11. Return to the stove and stir constantly for 4-5 minutes, or until the sugar has completely dissolved.
12. The sauce will probably be beginning to bubble, so remove from heat and add the bourbon.
13. When time is up, hit "cancel" and wait for the pressure to come down on its own.
14. Carefully take out the dish and cool for 15 minutes before serving with the bourbon sauce.

Tip: You can serve the pudding warm or chilled for up to 24 hours.

Nutritional Info (⅙ recipe):

Total calories: 227 Protein: 9 Fat: 6 Carbs: 36 Fiber: .9

Crème brûlée

Serves: 6
Time: 2 hours, 16 minutes (16 minutes cook time, 2 hours chill time)

Ingredients:
- 8 egg yolks
- 2 cups heavy cream
- 6 tablespoons superfine sugar
- ⅓ cup white sugar
- 1 ½ teaspoons vanilla
- Pinch of salt

Directions:
1. Pour 1 ½ cups of water into your pressure cooker and lower in the trivet.
2. In a bowl, mix the egg yolks, white sugar, and a pinch of salt.
3. Add in the cream and vanilla, whisking until smooth and blended.
4. Strain this into a pitcher, and then pour into six custard cups.
5. Wrap tightly in foil and put on the trivet. You'll need a second trivet to go on top of that first layer so you can put the rest of the cups in the cooker.
6. Close the lid.
7. Hit "manual," then cook on high pressure for 6 minutes.
8. When time is up, hit "cancel" and wait for the pressure to reduce for 10 minutes.
9. Quick-release the leftover pressure.
10. Take out the cups and unwrap so they can cool.
11. Once cool, cover with plastic wrap and chill for at least 2 hours.
12. When you're ready to serve, sprinkle the superfine sugar on top.
13. Use a torch, holding it about 2 inches from the sugar, and caramelize.

Nutritional Info (⅙ recipe):
Total calories: 210 Protein: 13 Fat: 10 Carbs: 18 Fiber: 3

Orange Marble Cheesecake

Serves: 8
Time: 4 hours, 47 minutes (12 minutes active time, 35 minutes cook time, 4 hours chill time)

Ingredients:

For crust
- 12 crushed Oreos
- 2 tablespoons melted butter

For filling
- 16-ounces room-temperature cream cheese
- ½ cup melted and cooled orange candy melts
- ½ cup sugar

- 2 tablespoons sour cream
- 2 room-temperature eggs
- 1 tablespoon orange zest
- 1 teaspoon vanilla extract

Directions:
1. Grease a 7-inch springform pan.
2. In a bowl, mix the melted butter and cookie crumbs together.
3. Pour into the springform pan to **Make** the crust, pressing down on the crumbs, with it going up 1-inch on the pan's sides.
4. Refrigerate for 10 minutes to set.
5. Put 8-ounces of cream cheese in a bowl along with ¼ cup sugar.
6. Beat until smooth.
7. Add sour cream and vanilla.
8. Mix in one egg until the ingredients are just incorporated.
9. In another bowl, put the rest of the cream cheese with the rest of the sugar and mix.
10. Add the melted candy and blend.
11. Add eggs until blended, and then the orange zest.
12. Take out the springform pan, and spoon in the plain vanilla batter and orange batter.
13. With a skewer or chopstick, swirl the batters together to get the marbled look.
14. Pour 1 cup of water into your pressure cooker and lower in the trivet.
15. Put the springform pan on the trivet. You don't need to wrap it.
16. Close the lid, select "manual," and then high pressure for 25 minutes.
17. When time is up, hit "cancel" and wait 10 minutes before quick-releasing leftover pressure.
18. The cheesecake should be set, but a little wiggly, like Jell-O.
19. Soak up excess water with the corner of a paper towel.
20. Take out the pan to cool before covering with plastic wrap, and chilling in the fridge for at least 4 hours.
21. Serve!

Nutritional Info (⅛ recipe):
Total calories: 383 Protein: 8 Fat: 23 Carbs: 39.5 Fiber: 1

Cinnamon-Poached Pears w/ Warm Chocolate Sauce

Serves: 6
Time: About 11 minutes (5 minutes active time, 6 minutes cook time)

Ingredients:

For the pears
- 6 ripe, firm pears
- 3 cups water
- 2 cups white wine
- 2 cups cane sugar

- 6 cinnamon sticks
- 1 lemon, cut in half

For the chocolate sauce
- 9-ounces bittersweet chocolate (at least 70%)
- ½ cup coconut milk
- ¼ cup coconut oil
- 2 tablespoons maple syrup

Directions:
1. Pour the water, wine, and sugar into the pressure cooker along with the cinnamon sticks.
2. Hit "sauté" and bring the liquid to a simmer, stirring so the sugar can dissolve.
3. Hit the "keep warm" button while you peel the pears.
4. You want the pears peeled, with the stems still on. Rub with lemon juice from the cut lemon as soon as they're peeled.
5. Squeeze the lemon halves into the pressure cooker before dropping them in.
6. Put the pears in the pressure cooker and lock the lid.
7. Select "manual," and cook on high pressure for just 3 minutes.
8. When time is up, hit "cancel" and quick-release.
9. Take out the pears with a slotted spoon and let them cool on a plate.
10. When the cooking liquid cools, pour over the fruit.
11. To **Make** the sauce, put the chocolate (broken into pieces) in a bowl.
12. Heat the coconut milk, oil, and maple syrup in a saucepan until it starts to boil.
13. Quickly pour over the chocolate, wait a minute or so, and then whisk until smooth and creamy.
14. Pour the sauce on top of the pears and serve!

Tip: To **Make** the pears look really fancy, cut a small slice off the bottom before pouring on the chocolate, so the pears stand up on their own.

Nutritional Info (⅙ recipe):
Total calories: 738 Protein: 4 Fat: 28 Carbs: 116 Fiber: 6

Samoa Cheesecake

Serves: 6
Time: 4 hours, 55 minutes (10 minutes active time, 45 minutes cook time, 4 hours chill time)

Ingredients:

For the crust
- ½ cup crushed chocolate graham crackers
- 2 tablespoons melted butter

For the filling
- 12-ounces room-temperature cream cheese
- 2 room-temperature eggs
- 1 room-temperature egg yolk
- ½ cup sugar

- ¼ cup sour cream
- ¼ cup heavy cream
- 1 tablespoon all-purpose

For the topping
- 12 unwrapped chewy caramels
- 1 ½ cups shredded coconut
- ¼ cup chopped semisweet chocolate
- 3 tablespoons heavy cream

Directions:
1. Grease a 7-inch springform pan.
2. In a bowl, mix the cracker crumbs and melted butter.
3. Pour into the pan and press down evenly, covering the bottom and up the sides by about 1-inch.
4. Stick in the fridge for 10 minutes to set.
5. In another bowl, mix sugar and cream cheese.
6. Add and mix heavy cream, vanilla, flour, and sour cream.
7. Add eggs until just incorporated.
8. Pour into the pan and cover with foil.
9. Pour 1 cup of water into the pressure cooker and lower in the trivet.
10. Put the pan on top and close the lid.
11. Select "manual," then cook on high pressure for 35 minutes.
12. When time is up, hit "cancel" and let the pressure decrease naturally for 10 minutes.
13. Carefully take out the cheesecake and look beneath the foil. If the cheesecake looks set and jiggles a little, it's ready. If not, cover, and put back in the pressure cooker to cook on high for 5 more minutes. Quick-release this time.
14. Take out the pan to cool without the foil.
15. When cool, cover with plastic wrap and chill for at least 4 hours.
16. To **Make** the topping when you're ready to serve the cheesecake, preheat the oven to 300-degrees.
17. Spread the coconut evenly on a baking sheet lined with parchment, and toast for 20 minutes, stirring every 5 minutes to prevent burning.
18. Cool.
19. Microwave the cream and caramels for 1-2 minutes, stopping to stir every 20 seconds.
20. When totally smooth, add the coconut.
21. Spread on top of cheesecake.
22. Melt the chocolate in a microwave.
23. Pour into a Ziploc bag and use like a pastry bag, with a corner snipped off, and drizzle on top of the caramel.

Nutritional Info (⅙ recipe):
Total calories: 761 Protein: 0 Fat: 49 Carbs: 71 Fiber: 0

Sugar-Pumpkin Pie Filling

Serves: 8
Time: 20 minutes (5 minutes active time, 15 minutes cook time)

Ingredients:
- 2-3 pounds seeded and cut sugar pumpkin
- 1 cup whole milk
- ¾ cup maple syrup
- 2 eggs
- 1 tablespoon cornstarch
- 1 teaspoon cinnamon
- ½ teaspoon ginger
- ¼ teaspoon cloves
- 2 pinches salt

Directions:
1. Pour 1 cup of water into the pressure cooker.
2. Put the pumpkin chunks in the steamer basket and lower into the cooker.
3. Secure the pot lid.
4. Select "manual," and cook for 4 minutes on high pressure.
5. While that cooks, mix the milk and maple syrup in a bowl.
6. Add the egg, cinnamon, ginger, salt, and cornstarch.
7. Mix well until blended.
8. By now, the pressure cooker should be done cooking.
9. Hit "cancel" and quick-release the pressure.
10. Pour the pumpkin chunks into a strainer and carefully peel.
11. After 10 minutes and the pumpkin has cooled, press down to remove excess liquid.
12. Squeeze into a 2-cup measure and mix with the egg mixture.
13. Preheat your oven to 350-degrees.
14. Pour filling into a 9-inch baked pie crust.
15. Cover the edges with a ring of foil and bake for 45-50 minutes, or until a toothpick comes clean out of the center.
16. Serve with fresh whipped cream!

Nutritional Info (⅛ pie-filling recipe):

Total calories: 143.9 Protein: 3.3 Fat: 2.3 Carbs: 29.1 Fiber: 2.1

Mango Cake

Serves: 8
Time: 45 minutes (5 minutes active time, 40 minutes cook time)

Ingredients:
- 1 ¼ cups flour
- ¾ cup milk
- ½ cup sugar
- ¼ cup coconut oil
- 1 tablespoon lemon juice
- 1 teaspoon mango syrup
- 1 teaspoon baking powder

- ¼ teaspoon baking soda
- ⅛ teaspoon salt

Directions:
1. Grease a baking pan that will fit in your pressure cooker.
2. Mix the sugar, oil, and milk in a bowl until the sugar has melted.
3. Pour in mango syrup and mix again.
4. Pour all the dry ingredients through a sieve into the wet.
5. Add lemon juice and mix well.
6. Pour into the baking pan.
7. Pour 1 cup of water into the pressure cooker and lower in a trivet.
8. Lower the baking pan into the cooker and close the lid.
9. Select "manual," and cook on high pressure for 35 minutes.
10. When time is up, hit "cancel" and wait for the pressure to come down naturally.
11. Check the cake for doneness before cooling for 10 minutes.
12. Serve!

Nutritional Info (⅛ recipe):
Total calories: 230 Protein: 2 Fat: 7 Carbs: 39 Fiber: 0

Chocolate-Chocolate Cheesecake

Serves: 6-8
Time: 4 hours, 40 minutes (10 minutes active time, 30 minutes cook time, 4 hours chill time)

Ingredients:

For the crust
- 1 ½ cups chocolate cookie crumbs
- 4 tablespoons butter

For the batter
- 1 pound room-temperature cream cheese
- 5 ounces sifted, packed brown sugar
- 2 room temperature eggs
- 6-ounces melted and cooled bittersweet chocolate
- 2-ounces sour cream
- 2 tablespoons cocoa powder
- 1 ½ teaspoons instant coffee (dissolved in 1 ½ teaspoons water)
- 1 teaspoon vanilla extract
- ¼ teaspoon fine sea salt

Directions:
1. Grease a 6x3 springform pan and cut a piece of parchment paper, so you get a round that will go on top of the pan when you close up the cooker.
2. In a bowl, mix the cookie crumbs and melted butter.
3. Press the crust down evenly into the bottom of the pan and 1-inch up the sides. Store in the fridge

until it's time to pour in the batter.
4. To **Make** the batter, begin by creaming the cream cheese in a low mixer until smooth.
5. Add the salt, vanilla, and sugar and continue to beat on low until combined.
6. Add 1 egg and mix completely.
7. Add the second egg and mix.
8. Add the instant coffee/water mixture.
9. In a separate bowl, whisk the cocoa and sour cream together until you get a whipped-cream like consistency.
10. Add the mixer and slowly incorporate.
11. Pour in the melted (and cooled) chocolate and mix until just combined.
12. Pour into the pan. Wrap completely in foil, including the bottom and sides.
13. Pour 2 cups of water into the pressure cooker and lower in the trivet.
14. Close the lid.
15. Select "manual," and cook on high pressure for 25 minutes.
16. When time is up, hit "cancel" and wait 10 minutes for the pressure to come down on its own.
17. Chill the cheesecake for at least four hours before serving.

Tip: Remember to keep scraping the bowl when you're mixing the ingredients. You don't want there to be unmixed stuff on the bottom of the bowl.
Nutritional Info (⅙ recipe):
Total calories: 498 Protein: 8.5 Fat: 31 Carbs: 49 Fiber: 2

Key Lime Pie

Serves: 6-8
Time: 4 hours, 40 minutes (15 minutes active time, 25 minutes cook time, 4 hours chill time)

Ingredients:

For the crust
- ¾ cup graham cracker crumbs
- 3 tablespoons melted butter
- 1 tablespoon sugar

For the batter
- 14-ounces sweetened condensed milk
- 4 big egg yolks
- ⅓ cup sour cream
- 2 tablespoons grated lime zest
- ¼ cup lemon juice
- ¼ cup lime juice

Directions:
1. Grease a 7-inch springform pan.
2. In a bowl, mix the graham crumbs, butter, and sugar.
3. Press down into the bottom of the pan and up 1-inch on the sides. Stick in the freezer to set.

4. In the meantime, mix the egg yolks until they become light yellow. Slowly mix in the condensed milk.
5. Slowly add the citrus juice, mixing, until smooth.
6. Lastly, mix in the lime zest and sour cream until just incorporated.
7. Pour into the springform pan and cover with foil.
8. Pour 1 cup of water into the pressure cooker and lower in the trivet.
9. Put the pan in the cooker on top of the trivet and lock the lid.
10. Select "manual," and cook on high pressure for 15 minutes.
11. When time is up, hit "cancel" and wait 10 minutes.
12. Release any leftover pressure with a quick-release.
13. Take out the pan and check to see if the middle is set.
14. If not, put back in the cooker and set for 5 more minutes. Quick-release.
15. Cool the pie, uncovered, before covering with plastic wrap and storing in the fridge for 4 hours.

Nutritional Info (⅙ recipe):

Total calories: 553 Protein: 11 Fat: 21 Carbs: 85 Fiber: 1

Cheesy Egg Bake

Serves: 4

Time: 15 minutes (5 minutes prep time, 10 minutes cook time)

Ingredients:

- 1 ½ cups water
- 2 cups frozen hash browns
- 6 eggs
- ½ cup shredded cheddar cheese
- ¼ cup milk

Directions:

1. Hit "sauté" and add hash browns to thaw for 3 minutes.
2. 2. Mix eggs, milk, and cheese together in a cooker-safe bowl.
3. Add hash browns to the bowl.
4. Pour water into your pressure cooker and lower in trivet.
5. Put the bowl on top and seal the lid.
6. Hit "manual" and adjust time to 10 minutes.
7. When time is up, hit "cancel" and quick-release.
8. Serve hot!

Nutritional Info (¼ recipe per serving):

Total calories: 217 Protein: 15 Carbs: 12 Fat: 12 Fiber: 2

Creamy Eggs with Prosciutto

Serves : 4

Time : About 6 minutes (2 minutes prep time, 4 minutes cook time)

Ingredients :
- 4 eggs
- 4 slices of prosciutto
- 1 cup of water
- A splash of cream per ramekin
- Olive oil

Directions :
1. Put 1 cup of water into your pressure cooker and lower in the trivet.
2. Grease the insides of four ramekins with a bit of olive oil.
3. Put a slice of prosciutto on the bottom of the ramekin, and then crack in an egg.
4. Pour in a bit of cream and then wrap ramekin tightly in foil.
5. Lower ramekins into the steamer basket, and then put inside the cooker.
6. Seal the lid.
7. Hit "manual" and adjust time to 4 minutes on LOW pressure.
8. When time is up, hit "cancel" and quick-release.
9. Serve right away!

Nutritional Info (1 ramekin per serving):

Total calories: 116 Protein: 11 Carbs: 1 Fat: 8 Fiber: 0

Coconut Milk Steel-Cut Oats

Serves : 8

Time : 20 minutes (10 minutes cook time, 10 minutes natural pressure release)

Ingredients :
- 4 cups water
- 2 cups coconut milk
- 2 cups steel-cut oats

Directions :
1. Pour water and coconut milk into your pressure cooker.
2. Stir in oats and seal the lid.
3. Select "manual," and adjust time to 10 minutes.
4. When the timer beeps, hit "cancel" and wait 10 minutes before quick-releasing.
5. Stir the oats thoroughly before serving; they may appear soupy until you stir.
6. Serve sweet or savory!

Nutritional Info (⅛ recipe, not including sugar):

Total calories: 189 Protein: 4 Carbs: 28 Fat: 6 Fiber: 5

Freeze-Dried Strawberry Oats

Serves : 1
Time : 20 minutes (10 minutes cook time, 10 minutes natural pressure release)

Ingredients :

- 2 cups water
- ⅔ cup whole milk
- ⅓ cup rolled oats
- 2 tablespoons freeze-dried strawberries
- ½ teaspoon sugar

Directions :

1. Pour water into your pressure cooker and lower in the steamer basket.
2. In a cooker-safe bowl, mix oats, milk, and strawberries.
3. Put the bowl in the steamer basket and seal the lid.
4. Hit "manual" and adjust time to 10 minutes.
5. When the timer beeps, hit "cancel" and wait 10 minutes for a natural pressure release.
6. Mix in sugar and serve!

Nutritional Info (1 bowl per serving):
Calories: 207.8 Protein: 8.6 Fat: 7.3 Carbs: 28.3 Fiber: 2.8

Homemade Vanilla Yogurt

Makes : About 24 servings
Time : 25 hours, 20 minutes (1 hour boil time, 20 minutes cool time, 8 hours yogurt time, 6 hours fridge time, 1 hour strain time, overnight wait time)

Ingredients:

- 1 gallon of 2% milk
- ½ cup honey
- ¼ cup yogurt with active cultures
- 3 tablespoons powdered milk
- 1 vanilla bean

Directions:

1. Pour milk and powdered milk into the pressure cooker and stir well.
2. Seal the lid.
3. Hit "yogurt" and then the "adjust" button, until you reach "boil."
4. After an hour, the cycle will be done, so check the temperature. It should be 185-degrees, so "sauté" until that's reached.
5. Hit "cancel" and remove the pot from the base.
6. When mixture has descended to 110-degrees, stir in honey and active culture yogurt.

7. Return the pot to the base and seal the lid.
8. Hit "yogurt" again and adjust time to 8 hours.
9. When time is up, hit "cancel" and store the whole pot (without the base) in the fridge for at least 6 hours.
10. To strain the yogurt, pour into nut milk bags and hang on a cupboard knob with kitchen string over a bowl, to catch the straining whey.
11. For a thick yogurt, strain for one hour.
12. When ready, throw out the captured whey and pour bags into the pressure cooker.
13. Stir and scrape in vanilla bean.
14. Store in Mason jars in the fridge overnight before serving.

Nutritional Info (1 serving)
Total calories: 109 Protein: 6 Carbs: 14 Fat: 3 Fiber: 0

Peach + Cream Oatmeal

Serves : 4

Time : 13 minutes (3 minutes cook time, 10 minutes natural pressure release)

Ingredients :
- 4 cups water
- 2 cups rolled oats
- 1 chopped peach
- 4 tablespoons heavy cream
- 1 teaspoon pure vanilla extract

Directions :
1. Pour water into the pressure cooker.
2. Add peach, oats, and vanilla extract.
3. Seal the lid.
4. Hit "manual" and cook for 3 minutes.
5. When the timer beeps, hit "cancel" and wait 10 minutes.
6. If there's any leftover pressure, quick-release.
7. Stir and serve with cream, 1 tablespoon per bowl.

Nutritional Info (¼ recipe)
Total calories: 240 Protein: 7 Carbs: 33 Fat: 9 Fiber: 4

Blackberry-Coconut Breakfast Quinoa

Serves : 4

Time : 9 minutes (7 minutes cook time, 2 minutes additional time)

Ingredients :

- 2 cups of water
- 2 cups blackberries
- 1 ½ cups quinoa
- ½ cup shredded coconut
- Honey to taste

Directions :

1. Pour water into the cooker, and add quinoa right into the pot.
2. Seal the lid.
3. Hit "manual" and adjust cook time to 7 minutes.
4. When time is up, hit "cancel" and quick-release.
5. Drain quinoa.
6. Divide between four bowls and add honey.
7. Mix in ½ blueberries per bowl.
8. Sprinkle on coconut and serve!

Nutritional Info (1 bowl per serving):
Calories: 526 Protein: 11 Fat: 28 Carbs: 64 Fiber: 16

Freezer Egg-and-Sausage Burritos

Serves : 6
Time : 30 minutes (5 minutes active time, 15 minutes cook time, 10 minutes natural pressure release)

Ingredients :

- 1 ½ cups + 1 tablespoon water
- 6 burrito-style tortillas
- 8 eggs
- 8-ounces of seasoned, ground pork sausage
- Brush of olive oil

Directions :

1. Mix sausage with 1 tablespoon of water.
2. Cover the bowl with plastic wrap.
3. Take two pieces of foil and brush both with a little olive oil.
4. Put tortillas in the foil and top with another sheet, sealing the corners.
5. Whisk eggs in a bowl.
6. Add sausage and break up with a fork, so the meat disperses evenly in the eggs.
7. Wrap bowl in foil.
8. Pour 1 ½ cups water into your pressure cooker, lowering in a trivet.
9. Put the bowl on the trivet, with the wrapped tortillas on top of the bowl.
10. Seal the lid.
11. Hit "manual" and adjust time to 15 minutes on LOW pressure.
12. When the timer beeps, hit "cancel" and wait 10 minutes before quick-releasing.

13. Remove food.
14. Wrap egg/sausage mixture in tortillas and eat right away, or wrap in foil and freeze for later.

Nutritional Info (⅙ recipe)
Total calories: 455 Protein: 21 Carbs: 39 Fat: 23 Fiber: 0

Huevos Rancheros

Serves : 1-2
Time : 25 minutes (5 minutes prep time, 20 minutes cook time)

Ingredients :
- 1 cup water
- 3 eggs
- ½ cup of your favorite salsa
- Salt to taste
- Tortilla chips

Directions :
1. Pour salsa into three ramekins and crack an egg into each one.
2. Season with salt.
3. Wrap ramekin tightly in foil.
4. Pour 1 cup water into your pressure cooker and insert steamer trivet.
5. Put the wrapped ramekin on top and seal the lid.
6. Hit "manual" and cook for 20 minutes on LOW pressure.
7. When the timer beeps, hit "cancel" and quick-release.
8. Serve in the ramekin, with chips for dipping.

Nutritional Info (½ recipe)
Total calories: 195 Protein: 12 Carbs: 14 Fat: 10 Fiber: 0

Honey-Chili Chicken Wings

Serves : 4
Time : 31 minutes (10 minutes prep time, 15 minutes cook time, 6 minutes broiler time)

Ingredients :
- 3 pounds chicken wings
- ½ cup honey
- 5 tablespoons butter
- 3 tablespoons sriracha chili sauce
- 1 tablespoon sweet chili sauce

Directions :

1. Melt butter in your pressure cooker on "sauté."
2. When hot, brown wings on both sides.
3. Remove wings and plate for now.
4. Mix honey and chili sauces together in the cooker.
5. When honey has melted and integrated with the sauce, add chicken wings, turning to coat.
6. Seal the lid.
7. Hit "manual" and adjust time to 15 minutes.
8. When time is up, hit "cancel" and quick-release.
9. For crispy wings, put wings on a foil-lined sheet and broil for 3 minutes on each side, slathering on more sauce.
10. Serve!

Nutritional Info (¼ recipe per serving):

Total calories: 911 Protein: 62 Carbs: 38 Fat: 59 Fiber: 0

Cranberry Chicken

Serves : 4

Time : 8 minutes

Ingredients :

- 4 boneless, skinless chicken breasts
- One 15-ounce can whole cranberry sauce
- 1 cup French dressing
- Chopped parsley to taste

Directions :

1. Mix cranberry sauce and dressing together.
2. Pour into cooker.
3. Add chicken breasts and turn to coat in the sauce.
4. Seal the lid.
5. Hit "manual" and adjust to 8 minutes.
6. When time is up, hit "cancel" and quick-release.
7. Serve with sauce and chopped parsley!

Nutritional Info (¼ recipe per serving):

Total calories: 535 Protein: 27 Carbs: 43 Fat: 29 Fiber: 0

BBQ Chicken Sandwiches

Serves : 4

Time : 25 minutes

Ingredients :

- 1 ½ pounds chicken breast
- ½ bottle of your favorite BBQ sauce
- Whole-wheat buns
- Pickles

Directions :
1. Add chicken and BBQ sauce into the pot.
2. Seal the lid.
3. Hit "manual" and adjust time to 25 minutes.
4. When time is up, quick-release.
5. Shred meat with two forks.
6. Serve with buns and pickles!

Nutritional Info (1 sandwich per serving):
Total calories: 431 Protein: 42 Carbs: 25 Fat: 6 Fiber: 4

Lemon-Coconut Chicken

Serves : 6
Time : 20 minutes (5 minutes prep time, 15 minutes cook time)

Ingredients :
- 1 can full-fat coconut milk
- 4 pounds chicken thighs
- ¼ cup lemon juice
- 1 tablespoon curry powder
- Salt to taste

Directions :
1. Mix coconut milk, curry powder, salt, and lemon juice into a cup.
2. Pour just enough into the pot to coat the bottom and add chicken on top.
3. Pour over the rest of the milk mixture.
4. Seal the lid.
5. Hit "manual" and adjust time to 15 minutes.
6. When time is up, hit "cancel" and quick-release. Chicken should be at 165-degrees.
7. Shred the chicken in the sauce before serving.

Nutritional Info (⅙ recipe per serving):
Total calories: 488 Protein: 70 Carbs: 3 Fat: 18 Fiber: 0

White Balsamic-Braised Game Hens

Serves : 4-6
Time : 22 minutes (7 minutes prep time, 15 minutes cook time)

Ingredients :
- Two halved 2-pound game hens, with necks and giblets removed
- One 6-ounce piece of diced pancetta
- ⅓ cup white balsamic vinegar
- ⅓ cup chicken broth
- 2 tablespoons ghee

Directions :
1. Turn your pot to "sauté" and add ghee.
2. Once melted, brown pancetta for 3 minutes and then plate.
3. Add hens, with the skin down, and brown for 4 minutes on one side.
4. Plate hens.
5. Pour broth and balsamic into the pot.
6. Return the pancetta and hens.
7. Seal the lid.
8. Hit "manual" and cook for 15 minutes.
9. When time is up, press "cancel" and quick-release.
10. Serve hens with pancetta and sauce.

Nutritional Info (¼ recipe per serving):
Total calories: 605 Protein: 32 Carbs: 5 Fat: 36 Fiber: 0

Cream-of-Mushroom Cheddar Chicken

Serves : 2
Time : 17 minutes (10 minutes prep time, 7 minutes cook time)

Ingredients :
- 2 large chicken breasts
- 1 family-sized can of cream of mushroom soup
- 1 cup cheddar cheese
- 1 chopped onion
- Water as needed

Directions :
1. Turn your pressure cooker to "sauté" and add onion.
2. Cook until beginning to turn clear. If they stick, add water.
3. Add chicken and cook until golden on both sides.
4. Pour in the cream of mushroom soup and seal the lid.
5. Hit "manual" and adjust time to 7 minutes.
6. When time is up, hit "cancel" and quick-release.
7. Chicken should be at 165-degrees. If not there yet, hit "sauté" again and finish cooking.
8. Sprinkle on cheese and allow to melt before serving.

Nutritional Info (½ recipe per serving):

Total calories: 518 Protein: 42 Carbs: 18 Fat: 27 Fiber: 1

Chicken + Cornbread Stuffing

Serves : 5-6
Time : 21 minutes (divided into thirds)

Ingredients :

- 4 big frozen, skinless + boneless chicken breasts
- 23-ounces of cream of chicken soup
- 14-ounce bag of cornbread stuffing
- 1 bag of frozen green beans
- 1 cup salted chicken broth

Directions :

1. Pour broth into your pressure cooker and add chicken.
2. Seal the lid.
3. Hit "manual" and adjust time to 15 minutes.
4. When time is up, hit "cancel" and quick-release the pressure. Chicken should be cooked to 165-degrees.
5. Open the lid and add green beans.
6. Seal lid, hit "manual," and adjust time to just 2 minutes.
7. When time is up, hit "cancel" and quick-release again.
8. Open the lid and add cornbread stuffing and pour over cream of chicken soup.
9. Seal the lid, hit "manual," and cook for 4 minutes.
10. When time is up, hit "cancel" and do a final quick-release of the pressure.
11. Stir everything together and serve!

Nutritional Info ($\frac{1}{5}$ recipe)
Total calories: 374 Protein: 34 Carbs: 36 Fat: 12 Fiber: 2

Honey-Balsamic Chicken Drumsticks

Serves : 4
Time : 15 minutes (10 minutes cook time, 5 minutes broil/simmer time)

Ingredients :

- 10 skin-on drumsticks
- ½ cup balsamic vinegar
- ¼ cup soy sauce
- ¼ cup honey
- 2 minced garlic cloves

Directions :
1. In a bowl, mix vinegar, soy sauce, honey, and garlic.
2. Pour into your pressure cooker.
3. Add drumsticks, turning to coat in the sauce.
4. Seal the lid.
5. Hit "manual" and adjust time to 10 minutes.
6. When the timer beeps, hit "cancel" and quick-release.
7. Open the lid and remove the drumsticks.
8. To get them crispy, broil for 2 minutes on a parchment-paper lined cookie sheet.
9. To get the sauce thicker, hit "sauté" and reduce until it reaches the consistency you like.
10. Serve chicken with sauce poured on top!

Nutritional Info (¼ recipe per serving):
Total calories: 362 Protein: 47 Carbs: 30 Fat: 8 Fiber: 0

French Onion Pork Chops

Serves : 4

Time : 27 minutes (12 minutes cook time, 10 minutes natural pressure release, 5 minutes broil time)

Ingredients :
- 4 boneless center-cut pork loin chops
- One 10.5-ounce French Onion soup
- One 10.5-ounce Campbell's chicken broth
- ½ cup sour cream

Directions :
1. Pour broth into the pressure cooker and lay in pork chops.
2. Seal the lid.
3. Hit "manual" and cook for 12 minutes.
4. When time is up, hit "cancel" and allow a natural pressure release.
5. Pork should be cooked to 145-degrees.
6. Mix sour cream and French Onion soup together.
7. Put pork chops in a baking dish and slather with mixture.
8. Broil in the oven for 3-5 minutes.
9. Serve!

Nutritional Info (¼ recipe per serving):
Total calories: 485 Protein: 37 Carbs: 11 Fat: 28 Fiber: 0

Easiest Southern Pork-Sausage Gravy

Serves : 8

Time: 30 minutes (15 minutes prep time, 5 minutes cook time, 10 minutes thickening time)

Ingredients:
- 1 pound pork sausage
- 2 cups whole milk
- 4 minced garlic cloves
- ¼ cup flour
- Water as needed

Directions:
1. Turn your pressure cooker to "sauté" and add garlic.
2. If they start to stick, pour in a little water.
3. When fragrant and golden, add the meat.
4. Cook until brown, breaking up with a spatula.
5. Add 1 ½ cups milk and seal the lid.
6. Hit "manual" and cook for 5 minutes.
7. When time is up, turn off the cooker and carefully quick-release the pressure. If it sprays too much, wait 5 minutes or so.
8. Mix flour and remaining milk in a bowl until smooth.
9. Hit "sauté" again on the open cooker, and slowly add into the gravy.
10. When it starts to bubble and thicken, it's ready to serve!

Nutritional Info (⅛ recipe):
Total calories: 247 Protein: 14 Carbs: 9 Fat: 18 Fiber: 0

Blueberry-Coconut Pork Roast

Serves: 4-6
Time: 1 hour, 12 minutes

Ingredients:
- 3-4 pounds pork shoulder roast
- 2 cups fresh blueberries
- 1 cup full-fat coconut milk
- 2 tablespoons balsamic vinegar
- 1 teaspoon salt

Directions:
1. Put all the ingredients in your pressure cooker and seal the lid.
2. Press "manual," and cook for 1 hour and 12 minutes.
3. When the timer beeps, press "cancel" and carefully quick-release the pressure.
4. Pork should be cooked to 145-degrees.
5. Serve meat with sauce.

Nutritional Info (¼ recipe per serving):

Total calories: 872 **Protein:** 71 **Carbs:** 13 **Fat:** 52 **Fiber:** 1.8

Shredded BBQ Pork

Serves : 5

Time : 1 hour, 45 minutes (90 minutes cook time, 10 minutes natural pressure release, 5 minutes simmer time)

Ingredients :

- 3 pounds pork roast
- 2 cups chicken broth
- Salt as needed
- Black pepper as needed
- BBQ sauce as desired

Directions:

1. Season pork generously with salt and pepper.
2. Pour broth in your pressure cooker and add pork. If the pork is unwieldy, cut in half.
3. Seal the lid.
4. Hit "manual" and adjust time to 90 minutes.
5. When time is up, hit "cancel" and wait 10 minutes before quick-releasing.
6. Shred.
7. Pour out all but ½ cup of the cooking liquid and add BBQ sauce.
8. Return pork to pot and mix with sauce.
9. Press "sauté."
10. After 5 minutes or so, serve!

Nutritional Info (¼ recipe per serving):

Total calories: 668 **Protein:** 53 **Carbs:** 0 **Fat:** 39 **Fiber:** 0

Pork Tenderloin with Apples + Onion

Serves : 5-6

Time : 1 hour, 38 minutes (10 minutes prep time, 58 minutes cook time, 30 minutes natural pressure release)

Ingredients :

- 4 pounds of pork rump roast
- 3 sliced apples
- 2 cups apple juice
- 1 cup chicken broth (with salt)
- 1 chopped onion

Directions:
1. Trim any excess fat from the pork.
2. Pour juice and broth into the cooker, and add apples and onion.
3. Put the pork in the pot and seal the lid.
4. Hit "manual" and adjust time to 58 minutes.
5. When the timer beeps, hit "cancel" and allow the pressure to decrease naturally.
6. Serve!

Nutritional Info (⅕ recipe per serving):
Total calories: 215 Protein: 23 Carbs: 15 Fat: 7 Fiber: 3

Brown-Sugar Baked Ham

Serves: 6
Time: 1 hour, 55 minutes (5 minutes prep time, 30 minutes cook time, 20 minutes natural pressure release, 1 hour oven time)

Ingredients:
- 3 pounds ham
- 1 cup brown sugar
- 1 ½ tablespoons ground mustard
- Water
- Distilled white vinegar

Directions:
1. Cut the ham into chunks and add to pressure cooker.
2. Measure out just enough water to cover the ham, without going over the max line, and then measure out ½ that amount of white vinegar.
3. Pour both into the cooker and seal the lid.
4. Hit "manual" and adjust time to 30 minutes.
5. When the timer beeps, turn off the cooker and allow the pressure to descend naturally.
6. Preheat your oven to 325-degrees.
7. Take out the ham and shred into smaller chunks.
8. In a bowl, mix mustard and brown sugar.
9. Layer half of the ham into a baking dish.
10. Sprinkle on brown sugar mixture, put rest of the ham in the dish, and sprinkle the rest of the brown sugar on top.
11. Wrap the whole dish in foil.
12. Bake in the oven for one hour.
13. Serve!

Nutritional Info (⅙ recipe per serving):
Total calories: 387 Protein: 40 Carbs: 41 Fat: 7 Fiber: 0

Jamaican-Jerk Pork Roast

Serves : 12

Time : 1 hour, 5 minutes (10 minutes prep time, 45 minutes cook time, 10 minutes natural pressure release)

Ingredients :

- 4 pounds pork shoulder
- ½ cup beef stock
- ¼ cup Jamaican Jerk spice blend
- 1 tablespoon olive oil

Directions :

1. Coat roast in oil and then rub on both sides with spice blend.
2. Hit "sauté" on your pressure cooker.
3. When warm, brown meat on both sides.
4. Pour in the stock and seal the lid.
5. Press "manual" and adjust time to 45 minutes.
6. When the timer beeps, hit "cancel" and wait 10 minutes before quick-releasing.
7. Shred the pork before serving.

Nutritional Info (4-ounce serving)
Total calories: 282 Protein: 23 Carbs: 0 Fat: 20 Fiber: 0

Sweet Sausage + Peppers

Serves : 4-8

Time : 30 minutes (5 minutes active time, 25 minutes cook time)

Ingredients :

- 2 pounds of sweet sausage
- 28-ounces crushed tomatoes with basil
- 8-ounces of tomato sauce
- 2 sliced sweet bell peppers
- 1 sliced Vidalia onion

Directions :

1. Divide the sausage into thirds.
2. Pour tomatoes and sauce into your pressure cooker.
3. Put sausage on top (don't stir it in) and top with peppers and sliced onion.
4. Seal the lid.
5. Hit "manual" and adjust cook time to 25 minutes.

6. When the timer beeps, hit "cancel" and quick-release the pressure.
7. Serve!

Nutritional Info (¼ recipe per serving)
Total calories: 420 Protein: 15 Carbs: 33.7 Fat: 24 Fiber: 5.3

Simple Pork Belly

Serves : 4

Time : 1 hour, 10 minutes (10 minutes prep time, 40 minutes cook time, 20 minutes natural pressure release)

Ingredients :
- 1 pound pork belly
- 1 cup white wine
- 3 garlic cloves
- Enough olive oil to coat the bottom
- One rosemary sprig

Directions :
1. Put just enough oil into the cooker to coat the bottom and heat on "sauté."
2. When hot, add pork and sear 3 minutes on each side, till golden.
3. Pour in wine.
4. Add garlic and rosemary sprig.
5. When the liquid is boiling, seal the lid.
6. Hit "manual" and adjust time to 40 minutes. For a more tender bite, cook for 30 minutes.
7. When the timer beeps, hit "cancel" and wait for a natural pressure release.
8. Pork should be at 145-degrees to be medium-rare.
9. When room temperature, slice and serve!

Nutritional Info (¼ recipe per serving):
Calories: 628 Protein: 11 Carbs: 1 Fat: 60 Fiber: 0

Basic Beef Picadillo

Serves : 4

Time : 17 minutes (10 minutes prep time, 7 minutes cook time)

Ingredients :
- 2 pounds diced Yukon Gold potatoes
- 1 pound of ground beef
- 1 can of diced tomatoes (with basil)
- ½ cup chopped onion
- Chili seasoning to taste

Directions :
1. Turn your cooker to "sauté".
2. When hot, add onion.
3. Cook until clear and beginning to turn golden.
4. Add meat and brown well, so there's just a little pink.
5. Dump in can of diced tomatoes and stir, scraping up any stuck-on food particles.
6. Add in potatoes and chili seasoning - you can always add more later, so don't go nuts.
7. Seal the lid.
8. Hit "manual" and adjust time to 7 minutes.
9. When time is up, hit "cancel" and quick-release.
10. Beef should be at 145-degrees.
11. Stir and season with more chili if needed before serving.

Nutritional Info (¼ recipe per serving):
Total calories: 369 Protein: 30 Carbs: 61 Fat: 8 Fiber: 1

Beef Ribs

Serves : 4
Time : 57 minutes (25 minutes cook time, 20 minutes natural pressure release, 12 minutes broil time)

Ingredients :
- 1 rack beef back ribs (totaling 2 pounds)
- 1 cup water
- 4 tablespoons favorite BBQ sauce
- Salt
- Black pepper

Directions :
1. Pull the membrane from the ribs and season with salt and black pepper.
2. Pour water into the pressure cooker.
3. Lower in trivet and put ribs on top.
4. Seal the lid.
5. Hit "manual" and adjust to 35 minutes for fall-off-the-bone ribs.
6. Hit "cancel" and wait for a natural pressure release.
7. While the pressure descends, preheat oven to 450-degrees.
8. Put ribs on a baking tray and brush with BBQ sauce.
9. Broil for 12 minutes.
10. Serve!

Nutritional Info (¼ recipe per serving):
Total calories: 835 Protein: 53 Carbs: 0 Fat: 173 Fiber: 0

Shredded Pepper Steak

Serves: 6

Time: 1 hour, 40 minutes (70 minutes cook time, 30 minutes natural pressure release)

Ingredients:
- 3-4 pounds beef
- 16-ounces of banana peppers
- ½ cup salted beef broth
- 1 tablespoon garlic powder
- Red chili flakes to taste

Directions:
1. Season beef with garlic powder and red chili flakes before adding to cooker.
2. Pour peppers and broth into cooker, too.
3. Seal the lid.
4. Hit "manual" and cook for 70 minutes.
5. When the timer beeps, hit "cancel" and wait for a natural pressure release.
6. When safe, open the cooker and shred the meat.
7. Serve!

Nutritional Info (⅙ recipe per serving)

Total calories: 442 Protein: 65 Carbs: 3 Fat: 18 Fiber: 0

Top Round Beef Roast with Bourbon Potatoes

Serves: 6

Time: 1 hour, 58 minutes (15 minutes prep time, 68 minutes cook time, 30 minutes natural pressure release, 5 minutes rest time)

Ingredients:
- 3 pounds beef top round
- 1 ½ pounds Yukon Gold potatoes
- 1 ½ cups salted beef broth
- ¼ cup bourbon
- 2 teaspoons black pepper

Directions:
1. Season your beef evenly with black pepper.
2. Turn your cooker to "sauté" and add meat.
3. Brown all over.
4. Pour broth and bourbon into the pot.
5. Seal the lid.
6. Hit "manual" and cook for 53 minutes.
7. When time is up, hit "cancel" and quick-release the pressure.

8. Add potatoes and seal the lid again.
9. Hit "manual" again and adjust time to 15 minutes.
10. When time is up, hit "cancel" and wait for the pressure to descend naturally.
11. Let the meat rest for 5 minutes before slicing.
12. Serve with potatoes and sauce.

Nutritional Info (⅙ recipe per serving):
Total calories: 593 Protein: 72 Carbs: 29 Fat: 19 Fiber: 3.6

Easiest Pot Roast

Serves : 6
Time : 1 hour, 20 minutes (10 minutes prep time, 40 minutes cook time, 15 minutes natural pressure release, 15 minutes simmer time)

Ingredients :
- 3 pounds chuck roast
- One 25-ounce jar of marinara sauce
- Garlic salt to taste
- Black pepper to taste
- Enough olive oil to coat the bottom of the pot

Directions :
1. Season meat evenly on both sides with garlic salt and pepper.
2. Add olive oil to pressure cooker and hit "sauté."
3. When hot, add meat and brown 3-4 minutes on each side.
4. Hit "cancel" and remove meat.
5. Cut into bite-sized cubes before returning to the pot.
6. Pour in the marinara sauce and seal the lid.
7. Hit "manual" and adjust time to 40 minutes.
8. When time is up, hit "cancel" and wait 15 minutes before quick-releasing.
9. If you want to thicken the sauce, remove meat and hit "sauté" again on the cooker.
10. Cook for 15 minutes until reduced.

Nutritional Info (⅙ recipe per serving):
Total calories: 820 Protein: 56 Carbs: 58 Fat: 38 Fiber: 0

Italian Beef

Serves : 4
Time : 1 hour, 5 minutes (10 minutes prep time, 45 minutes cook time, 10 minutes natural pressure release)

Ingredients :

- 2.5-pounds beef roast
- 2 cups beef broth
- 12-ounces pepperoncini
- 2 tablespoons minced garlic
- 2 tablespoons olive oil

Directions :

1. Turn your pressure cooker on and add oil.
2. When hot, brown the roast for 4 minutes on each side.
3. Cut off the stems from the pepperoncini and save half the liquid from the jar.
4. Hit "cancel" on the cooker and pour in broth, garlic, and the liquid from the pepperoncini jar, and the peppers.
5. Seal the lid.
6. Hit "manual" and adjust time to 45 minutes.
7. When time is up, wait 10 minutes before quick-releasing.
8. When safe, take out the peppers first, and then take out the beef to shred.
9. Serve on sandwiches!

Nutritional Info (¼ recipe per serving):
Total calories: 520 Protein: 64 Carbs: 4 Fat: 26 Fiber: 0

Easy Teriyaki Beef

Serves : 6
Time : 40 minutes

Ingredients :

- 2 pounds flank steak
- ½ cup + 3 tablespoons of good-quality teriyaki sauce
- 2-4 chopped garlic cloves
- 1 ½ teaspoons ground ginger
- Rice to serve

Directions :

1. Cut the steak into ½-inch strips.
2. Put all the ingredients in your pressure cooker and seal the lid.
3. Hit "manual" and cook for 40 minutes.
4. When time is up, hit "cancel" and quick-release.
5. Serve with rice!

Nutritional Info (¼ recipe per serving/not counting rice):
Total calories: 487 Protein: 51 Carbs: 23 Fat: 21 Fiber: 0

Sprouted Rice + Quinoa

Serves: 4
Time: 23 minutes (13 minutes cook time, 10 minutes natural pressure release)

Ingredients:
- 1 ½ cups sprouted rice and quinoa blend
- 3 cups chicken broth
- Lemon pepper seasoning to taste
- Salt to taste

Directions:
1. Rinse sprouted rice and quinoa.
2. Put into your pressure cooker with broth and salt.
3. Seal the lid and hit "manual," adjusting time to 13 minutes.
4. When time is up, hit "cancel" and wait 10 minutes.
5. Quick-release any remaining pressure.
6. Season to taste with lemon pepper and serve!

Nutritional Info (¼ recipe per serving):
Total calories: 263 Protein: 7 Carbs: 55 Fat: 3 Fiber: 4.5

Broccoli Cheese Rice

Serves: 4
Time: 20 minutes (15 minutes cook time, 5 minutes natural pressure release)

Ingredients:
- 2 ¼ cups vegetable broth
- 1 cup white rice
- 3 cups chopped broccoli
- 1 cup shredded Monterey cheese
- ¼ cup onion

Directions:
1. Put everything except cheese in your pressure cooker and seal the lid.
2. Hit "manual" and adjust time to 15 minutes.
3. When time is up, hit "cancel" and wait 5 minutes before quick-releasing.
4. Stir in cheese and when melted, serve.

Nutritional Info (¼ recipe per serving):
Total calories: 295 Protein: 12 Carbs: 40 Fat: 9 Fiber: 1.8

Pineapple Brown Rice

Serves: 4

Time : 9 minutes (7 minutes cook time, 2 minutes natural pressure release)

Ingredients :
- 1 cup brown rice
- 8-ounces crushed pineapple
- ¼ cup pineapple juice
- 1 tablespoon butter

Directions :
1. Put everything in your pressure cooker and seal the lid.
2. Hit "manual" and adjust time to 7 minutes.
3. When time is up, wait 1-2 minutes before quick-releasing.
4. Stir and serve!

Nutritional Info (¼ recipe per serving):
Total calories: 229 Protein: 5 Carbs: 46 Fat: 5 Fiber: 1.7

Turkey Verde Rice

Serves : 4
Time : 26 minutes (18 minutes cook time, 8 minutes natural release time)

Ingredients :
- 1 ½ pounds turkey tenderloins
- 1 ¼ cups long-grain brown rice
- ⅔ cup chicken broth
- 1 sliced yellow onion
- ½ cup salsa verde

Directions :
1. Pour chicken broth and rice into cooker.
2. Add onions, turkey, and salsa verde on top.
3. Seal the lid.
4. Hit "manual" and adjust time to 18 minutes.
5. When time is up, hit "cancel" and wait 8 minutes.
6. Open the lid, stir, and serve!

Nutritional Info (¼ recipe per serving):
Total calories: 269 Protein: 47 Carbs: 20 Fat: 2 Fiber: 1

Pasta with Meat Sauce

Serves : 4-6
Time : 11 minutes (6 minutes prep time, 5 minutes cook time)

Ingredients :
- 1 ½ pounds ground beef
- 8-ounces dried pasta
- 24-ounces pasta sauce
- 12-ounces water
- Italian seasoning to taste

Directions :
1. Turn your cooker to "sauté."
2. Add ground beef to brown, breaking it up with a spatula as it cooks.
3. When browned, hit "cancel" and pour in pasta, sauce, and water. You'll probably have to break the pasta in half.
4. Seal the lid and hit "manual," cooking for 5 minutes.
5. When time is up, hit "cancel" and quick-release.
6. Season with Italian seasoning to taste and serve!

Nutritional Info (¼ recipe per serving):
Total calories: 590 Protein: 47 Carbs: 58 Fat: 17 Fiber: 0

Chicken Alfredo Pasta

Serves : 2-3
Time : Under 5 minutes (3 minutes cook time)

Ingredients :
- 8-ounces fettuccine
- One 15-ounce jar of Alfredo sauce
- 2 cups water
- 1 cup cooked + diced chicken
- 2 teaspoons chicken seasoning

Directions :
1. Break your pasta in half so it fits in the cooker.
2. Add pasta, water, and chicken seasoning to the pressure cooker.
3. Seal the lid.
4. Hit "manual" and adjust time to 3 minutes.
5. When the timer beeps, hit "cancel" and quick-release.
6. Drain the pasta and add to serving bowl.
7. Mix in Alfredo sauce and chicken.
8. Serve!

Nutritional Info (⅓ recipe per serving):
Total calories: 491 Protein: 27 Carbs: 59 Fat: 16 Fiber: 0

Simple Salmon + Broccoli

Serves: 2
Time: 9 minutes (2 minutes prep time, 2 minutes cook time, 5 minutes natural pressure release)

Ingredients:
- 1 pound salmon fillet, cut in half
- 1 pound's worth of raw, fresh broccoli florets
- 1 cup water
- Lemon pepper seasoning to taste
- Garlic salt to taste

Directions:
1. Pour water into the pressure cooker.
2. Put fish and broccoli in your steamer basket.
3. Season generously with lemon pepper seasoning and garlic salt.
4. Lower basket into cooker and seal the lid.
5. Hit "Steam" and cook for just 2 minutes.
6. When time is up, hit "cancel" and wait for a natural pressure release.
7. Salmon should be cooked to 145-degrees.
8. Serve!

Nutritional Info (½ recipe per serving):
Total calories: 422 Protein: 57 Carbs: 27 Fat: 12 Fiber: 5.8

Lemon-Thyme Halibut

Serves: 2
Time: 9 minutes (4 minutes cook time, 5 minutes natural pressure release)

Ingredients:
- Two ½ pound halibut steaks
- 3 minced garlic cloves
- 2 cups water
- 1 juiced and zested lemon
- 1 teaspoon dried thyme

Directions:
1. Pour water into your pressure cooker.
2. Put halibut steaks in your steamer basket, and sprinkle with the dried thyme, lemon zest, and minced garlic.
3. Lower into cooker and seal the lid.
4. Hit "Steam" and cook for 4 minutes.

5. When time is up, hit "cancel" and wait 5 minutes before removing the lid.
6. Serve with lemon juice squeezed on top.

Nutritional Info (½ recipe per serving):
Total calories: 216 Protein: 43 Carbs: 2 Fat: 3 Fiber: 0

Halibut-Salsa Packets with Artichoke Hearts

Serves : 4
Time : 25 minutes (5 minutes prep time, 20 minutes cook time)

Ingredients :
- Four 6-ounce halibut fillets, 1-inch thick
- One 9-ounce package of thawed artichoke hearts
- 4 cups water
- 1 cup salsa
- 1 sliced shallot

Directions :
1. Cut four squares from parchment paper, about 15-inches by 15-inches.
2. Fold the square in half, and then open again, so you can fill them.
3. Lay down some shallot, fish fillet, 1 tablespoon of salsa, and artichoke hearts in each square.
4. Fold in half again, and fold down the edges, so the food doesn't fall out.
5. Pour 2 cups of water into the pressure cooker and lower in steamer basket.
6. You can cook two packets at a time. For your second batch, pour out water and add 2 cups of fresh liquid.
7. When the packets are in the basket, seal the lid.
8. Hit "manual" and adjust time to 10 minutes.
9. When time is up, hit "cancel" and quick-release. Fish should be at 145-degrees.
10. Serve with the rest of the salsa evenly topping each fillet.

Nutritional Info (¼ recipe per serving):
Total calories: 193 Protein: 34 Carbs: 8 Fat: 2 Fiber: 1.5

Easy Alaskan Cod with Cherry Tomatoes

Serves : 2-3
Time : 7 minutes (2 minutes prep time, 5 minutes cook time)

Ingredients :
- 1 large wild Alaskan cod fillet
- 1 cup cherry tomatoes
- 1 cup water
- 2 tablespoons cut salted butter

- Black pepper to taste

Directions :
1. Cut the fish into portions and season with black pepper.
2. Put tomatoes in a cooker-safe dish and lay fish on top.
3. Put butter on top of fish.
4. Pour water into your pressure cooker and lower in trivet.
5. Put the dish with fish on the trivet and seal the lid.
6. Hit "manual" and adjust time to just 5 minutes.
7. When the timer beeps, hit "cancel" and quick-release.
8. Serve hot.

Nutritional Info (½ recipe per serving)
Total calories: 174 Protein: 14 Carbs: 3 Fat: 12 Fiber: 0

Crab Legs with Garlic-Butter Sauce

Serves : 2-3
Time : 4 minutes

Ingredients :
- 1 cup water
- 2 pounds frozen crab legs
- 2 minced garlic cloves
- 4 tablespoons salted butter
- 1 halved lemon

Directions :
1. Pour water into the pressure cooker.
2. Put crab in the steamer basket and lower into cooker.
3. Seal the lid.
4. Hit the "steam" button and adjust time to 4 minutes.
5. While that cooks, sauté garlic in a hot skillet. If it starts to stick, add in a little water.
6. When the garlic is fragrant, melt in butter and squeeze in the cut lemon.
7. When the cooker beeps, hit "cancel" and quick-release.
8. Serve crab with the garlic butter.

Nutritional Info (½ recipe):
Total calories: 346 Protein: 44 Carbs: 2 Fat: 7 Fiber: 0

Spicy Sockeye Salmon

Serves : 4
Time : About 8 minutes (3 minutes prep time, 5 minutes cook time)

Ingredients :

- 4 wild sockeye salmon fillets
- 1 cup water
- 1 sliced lemon
- 1 juiced lemon
- 2 tablespoons assorted chili pepper seasoning

Directions :

1. Season salmon with juice from the juiced lemon and chili pepper seasoning.
2. Put fish in the steamer basket.
3. Pour 1 cup water into your pressure cooker and lower in the basket with the fish.
4. Seal the lid.
5. Hit "manual" and cook for 5 minutes.
6. When the timer beeps, hit "cancel" and quick-release.
7. Salmon should be cooked to 145-degrees.
8. Serve with sliced lemon.

Nutritional Information (¼ recipe):
Calories: 194 Protein: 24 Carbs: 1 Fat: 10 Fiber: 0

Lemon-Ginger Cod with Mixed Frozen Veggies

Serves : 4
Time : About 5 minutes (3 minutes prep time, 2 minutes cook time)

Ingredients :

- 1 pound, 1-inch thick frozen cod fillets
- 2 cups frozen veggies
- 1 cup water
- 2 teaspoons lemon pepper
- 2 teaspoons ground ginger

Directions :

1. Divide your fish into four servings.
2. Season evenly with lemon pepper and ginger.
3. Pour water into the pressure cooker.
4. Put fish and broccoli in the steamer basket, and lower into cooker.
5. Seal the lid.
6. Hit "manual" and adjust time to 2 minutes.
7. When the timer beeps, turn off the cooker and quick-release.
8. Cod should be cooked to 145-degrees while the broccoli should be tender.

9. Serve!

Nutritional Info (¼ recipe):

Calories: 113 Protein: 23 Carbs: 4 Fat: 1 Fiber: 1.2

Salmon Steaks

Serves : 4

Time : 11 minutes (6 minutes prep time, 5 minutes cook time)

Ingredients :

- 4 skin-on salmon steaks
- 1 cup water
- ¾ cup dry white wine
- 1 peeled and sliced onion
- 1 sliced lemon

Directions :

1. Pour water into your pressure cooker and insert trivet and steamer basket.
2. Lay down your onion slices first in the basket, and then add steaks.
3. Pour wine over the fish.
4. Lay down lemon slices.
5. Hit "sauté" and bring to a boil, boiling for 1 minute.
6. Seal the lid.
7. Hit "manual" and cook for 5 minutes.
8. When time is up, hit "cancel" and quick-release. Salmon should be cooked to 145-degrees.
9. Serve salmon with onions (if you like them) and tartar sauce!

Nutritional Info (¼ recipe per serving):

Total calories: 251 Protein: 24 Carbs: 4 Fat: 11 Fiber: 0

Lobster Tails

Serves : 4

Time : 14 minutes (10 minutes active time, 4 minutes cook time)

Ingredients :

- 4 lobster tails (1-pound each)
- 1 cup water
- ½ cup white wine
- ¼ cup melted butter
- Salt to taste

Directions :

1. If frozen, defrost tails in a bowl of cold water.
2. Cut tails tip-to-tip, to cut in half.
3. Pour water and wine in your pressure cooker and lower in steamer basket.
4. Put lobsters tails - the shell side down - in the basket.
5. Seal the lid.
6. Hit "manual" and cook for 4 minutes on LOW pressure.
7. When time is up, hit "cancel" and quick-release.
8. Lobster meat should be firm and solid white.
9. Serve with melted butter and salt!

Nutritional Info (¼ recipe)
Total calories: 190 Protein: 19 Carbs: 0 Fat: 12 Fiber: 0

Balsamic Mushrooms

Serves : 4
Time : About 7 minutes

Ingredients :
- 1 pound sliced mushrooms
- ⅓ cup olive oil
- 3 tablespoons balsamic vinegar
- Salt to taste
- Pepper to taste

Directions :
1. Hit "sauté" and add olive oil.
2. When hot, add mushrooms and stir to coat in the oil.
3. After 3 minutes, hit "cancel."
4. Pour in balsamic vinegar and stir, letting the residual heat cook for 1-2 minutes.
5. Sprinkle in salt and pepper.
6. Serve!

Nutritional Info (¼ recipe per serving):
Total calories: 191 Protein: 4 Carbs: 6 Fat: 19 Fiber: 1.2

Bacon Ranch Potatoes

Serves : 6
Time : 12 minutes (5 minutes prep time, 7 minutes cook time)

Ingredients :
- 2 pounds scrubbed red potatoes
- 3 bacon strips

- 4-ounces shredded cheddar cheese
- ⅓ cup good Ranch dressing
- 2 tablespoons water

Directions :

1. Chop potatoes into 1-inch pieces.
2. Put water, bacon, and potatoes in the cooker.
3. Seal the lid.
4. Hit "manual" and adjust time to 7 minutes.
5. When time is up, hit "cancel" and quick-release.
6. Stir in ranch and cheese.
7. Serve!

Nutritional Info (⅙ recipe per serving):
Total calories: 372 Protein: 7 Carbs: 34 Fat: 23 Fiber: 3.3

Smashed Sweet Potato with Ginger Butter

Serves : 8
Time : 21 minutes (11 minutes cook time, 10 minutes spice/smash time)

Ingredients :

- 4 pounds peeled and cubed sweet potatoes
- 3 cups water
- 3 tablespoons salted butter
- 2 tablespoons thawed + unsweetened pineapple juice concentrate
- 1 teaspoon ground ginger

Directions :

1. Pour water and sweet potatoes into your pressure cooker.
2. Seal the lid.
3. Hit "manual" and adjust cook time to 11 minutes.
4. When the timer beeps, hit "cancel" and quick-release the pressure.
5. Drain potatoes, and when cool enough to touch, peel off the skin with your fingers.
6. Hit "sauté" and add the butter in the pressure cooker to melt.
7. Stir in the ginger for a minute or so before adding pineapple juice.
8. Hit "cancel."
9. Return potatoes to the pot and smash with a wooden spoon.
10. When potatoes are incorporated with the ginger butter, serve!

Nutritional Info (⅛ of recipe):
Total calories: 241 Protein: 4 Carbs: 48 Fat: 5 Fiber: 6.8

Spaghetti Squash with Apple Juice Glaze

Serves : 4-6

Time : 38 minutes (8 minutes cook time, 30 minutes cool/glaze time)

Ingredients :
- One 3-lb spaghetti squash
- 1 cup water
- ¾ cup 100% apple juice
- 2 tablespoons olive oil
- Salt to taste

Directions :
1. Pour water in the pot and lower in steamer basket.
2. Put whole spaghetti squash into basket and seal the cooker lid.
3. Hit "manual" and adjust time to 8 minutes.
4. When time is up, hit "cancel" and quick-release.
5. Carefully remove the squash and let it cool before cutting it in half.
6. When halved, let it continue cooling while you **Make** the glaze.
7. Pour out the water from the pot and add apple juice.
8. Hit "sauté" and reduce until the juice becomes syrupy.
9. Stir in olive oil.
10. When the squash is cool, remove the seeds and scrape the squash strands into the cooker.
11. Stir to coat in the glaze.
12. Season with salt before serving.

Nutritional Info (¼ recipe per serving):

Total calories: 188 Protein: 1 Carbs: 29 Fat: 9 Fiber: 6

Butternut Squash with Sage-Infused Butter

Serves : 4

Time : 12 minutes (5 minutes prep time, 7 minutes cook time)

Ingredients :
- One medium-sized butternut squash
- 8 sliced sage leaves
- 1 cup water
- 4 tablespoons salted butter
- Black pepper to taste

Directions :
1. Peel, seed, and dice the butternut squash into 1-inch cubes.
2. Pour water into pressure cooker.
3. Put the squash cubes in the steamer basket and lower into cooker.

4. Seal the lid.
5. Hit "manual" and adjust time to 7 minutes.
6. While that cooks, melt butter in a skillet.
7. When hot, add sage and cook until it becomes crispy and fragrant.
8. When the pressure cooker beeps, hit "cancel" and quick-release.
9. Serve squash with infused butter and black pepper. You can eat the cooked sage leaves, too.

Nutritional Info (¼ recipe per serving):
Total calories: 267 Protein: 5 Carbs: 42 Fat: 12 Fiber: 6.7

Prosciutto-Wrapped Asparagus

Serves : 6
Time : 8 minutes (5 minutes prep time, 3 minutes cook time)

Ingredients :
- 1 pound of asparagus
- 8-ounces prosciutto
- 1 cup of water

Directions :
1. Pour water into the pressure cooker.
2. Wrap the asparagus spears in prosciutto.
3. If you have more asparagus than prosciutto, put unwrapped spears in the bottom of the steamer basket.
4. Lay the wrapped asparagus on top and lower basket into cooker.
5. Seal the lid.
6. Hit "manual" and adjust cook time to 3 minutes.
7. When time is up, turn off the cooker and quick-release the pressure.
8. Serve right away!

Nutritional Info (⅙ recipe per serving):
Total calories: 183 Protein: 12 Carbs: 3 Fat: 15 Fiber: 1.4

Carrots with Bacon + Butter

Serves : 4-6
Time : 16 minutes (10 minutes prep time, 6 minutes cook time)

Ingredients :
- 1 pound baby carrots
- 2 cups water
- 4-ounces diced bacon
- 2 tablespoons cut salted butter

- 1 leek

Directions :
1. Cook bacon on the "sauté" setting until crisp.
2. Add the green and white parts of the leek, cooking for one minute.
3. Stir in carrots to coat in the bacon fat, and then hit "cancel."
4. Move carrots, leeks, and bacon to a baking dish, about 1-quart.
5. Put butter pats on top.
6. Lay down a piece of parchment paper and then wrap the whole dish snugly in foil.
7. Wipe down the cooker before pouring in 2 cups of water.
8. Add trivet and set the baking dish on top.
9. Seal the pot lid.
10. Hit "manual" and adjust time to 6 minutes.
11. When time is up, hit "cancel" and quick-release the pressure.
12. Stir and serve!

Nutritional Info (¼ recipe per serving):
Total calories: 158 Protein: 5 Carbs: 11 Fat: 10 Fiber: 3.4

Corn with Cilantro Butter

Serves : 4
Time : 3 minutes

Ingredients :
- 4 ears of shucked corn
- 1 ⅕ cups of water
- 6 tablespoons salted butter, divided
- 2 tablespoons minced cilantro
- ½ teaspoon chili powder

Directions :
1. Mix water and chili powder into your pressure cooker.
2. Add shucked corn and 2 tablespoons butter.
3. Seal the cooker lid.
4. Press "manual" and adjust time to 3 minutes.
5. While that cooks, add the rest of the butter to a saucepan to melt.
6. When liquid, stir in cilantro.
7. When the pressure cooker cycle is done, hit "cancel" and quick-release the pressure.
8. Serve corn with the cilantro-infused butter.

Nutritional Info (1 ear of corn + butter per serving):
Total calories: 309 Protein: 5 Carbs: 32 Fat: 21 Fiber: 12

Sweet Potato Puree

Serves : 6
Time : 15 minutes (10 minutes cook time, 5 minutes blend time)

Ingredients :
- 2 pounds peeled and chopped white sweet potatoes
- 1 ½ cups bone broth
- ½ teaspoon salt
- Dash of black pepper

Directions :
1. Put the potatoes and broth into your pressure cooker and seal the lid.
2. Hit "manual" and adjust time to 10 minutes.
3. When time is up, hit "cancel" and quick-release the pressure.
4. The potatoes are done if they fall apart easily when you poke them with a fork.
5. Put in a blender with the liquid from the pressure cooker.
6. When very smooth, season with salt and black pepper, and serve!

Nutritional Info (⅙ recipe per serving):
Total calories: 176 Protein: 5 Carbs: 32 Fat: 2 Fiber: 4

Balsamic Brussels Sprouts with Bacon

Serves : 4
Time : 19 minutes (10 minutes prep time, 4 minutes cook time, 5 minutes dressing time)

Ingredients :
- 1 pound halved and trimmed Brussels sprouts
- 1 cup water
- 4 slices bacon
- 1 tablespoon olive oil
- 1 teaspoon balsamic vinegar

Directions :
1. Turn your pressure cooker to "sauté" and cook bacon until crispy.
2. Hit "cancel" on the cooker and plate bacon on a paper towel.
3. Pour 1 cup of water into your cooker.
4. Remove the rough outer leaves of the sprouts, and trim the stems down.
5. Cut in half with a sharp knife and put in the steamer basket.
6. Lower basket into the cooker and seal the lid.
7. Hit "manual" and adjust cook time to 4 minutes.
8. When time is up, turn off cooker and quick-release the pressure.
9. To **Make** the dressing, pour oil slowly into the balsamic vinegar, whisking, to emulsify them.
10. Pour dressing over sprouts and top with bacon before serving.

Nutritional Info (¼ recipe):
Total calories: 139 Protein: 6 Carbs: 9 Fat: 7 Fiber: 4.25

Whole White Beets + Beet Greens

Serves : 2
Time : 50 minutes (30 minutes soak time, 10 minutes cook time, 10 minutes additional time)

Ingredients :

- 3 whole white beets (with their greens saved + separated)
- 2 minced garlic cloves
- 1 tablespoon olive oil
- Half a lemon
- Water

Directions:

1. Begin by soaking the beets (not the greens) for a half hour.
2. When ready, put in the pressure cooker with just enough water to cover them.
3. Seal the lid.
4. Hit "manual" and cook for 10 minutes.
5. When the timer beeps, hit "cancel" and quick-release the pressure.
6. Poke with a fork. If they're still hard, return to pressure for another 2 minutes.
7. When done, add the greens and soak with the lid on the cooker - not sealed - for 5 minutes.
8. Pour beets and greens through a strainer, and wait until they're cool enough to touch.
9. Slice beets.
10. Heat oil in a skillet and let the beets sit in the hot oil for a minute.
11. Add garlic and greens.
12. When the greens have wilted and the garlic is aromatic, plate.
13. Squeeze on lemon juice and serve.

Nutritional Info (½ recipe per serving):
Total calories: 105 Protein: 3 Carbs: 15 Fat: 11 Fiber: 3

Zucchini-Ricotta Bites

Serves : 6
Time : 16 minutes (10 minutes prep time, 6 minutes cook time)

Ingredients :

- 3 large zucchinis
- 1 ¾ cups crushed tomatoes
- 1 cup whole-milk ricotta
- Italian seasoning to taste

- Salt to taste

Directions :
1. Mix Italian seasoning and ricotta.
2. Cut zucchinis into pieces, about 2 inches long, and carefully hollow out the middle, so the "shell" is ¼-inch thick on the sides, with a ½-inch bottom.
3. Fill with 2 tablespoons of ricotta.
4. Pour tomatoes into your pressure cooker.
5. Nestle in the zucchini bites and seal the lid.
6. Hit "manual" and adjust time to 6 minutes.
7. When time is up, hit "cancel" and quick-release.
8. Plate the zucchini bites and spoon over a bit of the tomatoes on each one.
9. Season with salt.

Nutritional Info (⅙ recipe per serving):
Total calories: 103 Protein: 6 Carbs: 8 Fat: 6 Fiber: 1.3

Cranapple (Cranberry + Apple) Sauce

Serves : 4

Time : 18 minutes + 1 hour chill time (5 minutes cook time, 10 minutes natural pressure release, 3 minutes simmer time, 1 hour chill time)

Ingredients :
- 12-ounces cranberries, fresh or frozen
- 1 peeled and chopped Honeycrisp apple
- ½ cup maple syrup
- ½ cup apple cider
- One large orange

Directions:
1. Zest the orange and squeeze its juice into a cup.
2. Add all the ingredients into your pressure cooker and stir well.
3. Seal the lid.
4. Hit "manual" and adjust time to 5 minutes.
5. When the timer beeps, turn off the cooker and wait 10 minutes.
6. Manually release any remaining pressure.
7. Hit "sauté" and simmer for 2-3 minutes.
8. When thickened, store in the fridge until chill.

Nutritional Info (¼ recipe):
Total calories: 173 Protein: 1 Carbs: 43 Fat: 0 Fiber: 4.5

Garlic Roasted Potatoes

Serves: 4

Time: 27 minutes (10 minutes prep time, 7 minutes cook time, 10 minutes natural release)

Ingredients:
- 2 pounds baby red potatoes
- 4 tablespoons salted butter
- 3 garlic cloves
- ½ cup veggie stock
- 1 rosemary sprig

Directions:
1. Turn your cooker to "sauté" and add butter.
2. When hot and melted, add garlic, potatoes, and rosemary sprig.
3. When the potatoes are golden and coated in butter, poke each one with a fork.
4. Pour in the stock and seal the lid.
5. Press "manual" and cook for 7 minutes.
6. When the timer beeps, turn off the cooker and wait 10 minutes for a natural pressure release.
7. Pick out the rosemary sprig before serving.

Nutritional Info (¼ recipe):

Total calories: 304 Protein: 5 Carbs: 45 Fat: 11 Fiber: 3.8

2-Minute Steamed Asparagus

Serves: 3-4

Time: 2 minutes

Ingredients :
- 1 lb. trimmed asparagus
- 1 cup of water
- 2 tablespoons olive oil
- Salt to taste
- Squeeze of fresh lemon juice

Directions :
1. Pour water into the pressure cooker.
2. Put asparagus in your steamer basket, and drizzle on olive oil.
3. Lower basket into cooker and seal the lid.
4. Hit "steam" and adjust time to just 2 minutes.
5. When the timer beeps, turn off the cooker and quick-release.
6. Season with salt and lemon juice.

Nutritional Info (¼ recipe):

Total calories: 84 Protein: 3 Carbs: 5 Fat: 0 Fiber: 4

Stewed Tomatoes + Green Beans

Serves : 4-6
Time : 10 minutes (5 minutes prep time, 5 minutes cook time)

Ingredients :
- 1 pound trimmed green beans
- 2 cups fresh chopped tomatoes
- 3 crushed garlic cloves
- Water as needed
- Salt to taste

Directions :
1. Turn your cooker to "sauté" and add garlic.
2. Cook until golden. If it starts to stick, pour in a little water.
3. Stir in tomatoes.
4. If the tomatoes aren't super juicy, pour in ½ cup of water.
5. Add green beans to the steamer basket and salt.
6. Lower basket into cooker on top of tomatoes, and seal the lid.
7. Hit "manual" and adjust time to 5 minutes.
8. When time is up, hit "cancel" and quick-release.
9. Pour green beans into tomatoes and stir.
10. Serve!

Nutritional Info (⅙ recipe):
Total calories: 55.3 Protein: 1.6 Carbs: 6.3 Fat: 3.2 Fiber: 2.6

Cheesy Stone-Ground Grits

Serves : 4
Time : 25 minutes (5 minutes prep time, 10 minutes cook time, 10 minutes natural pressure release)

Ingredients :
- 3 cups water
- 1 ¾ cups cream
- 1 cup stone-ground grits
- 4-ounces cheddar cheese
- 3 tablespoons salted butter

Directions :
1. Turn your cooker to "sauté" and add butter.
2. When hot and melted, add grits and stir to toast for 3 minutes.
3. Hit "cancel" and stir in the other ingredients (except cheese) and seal the lid.

4. Hit "manual" and cook for 10 minutes.
5. When the timer beeps, hit "cancel" and wait 1o minutes before releasing any leftover pressure.
6. Stir in cheese and serve!

Nutritional Info (¼ recipe):
Total calories: 694 Protein: 17 Carbs: 71 Fat: 38 Fiber: 2

Green Beans + Mushrooms

Serves : 4
Time : 12 minutes

Ingredients :

- 1 ½ pounds fresh green beans
- 4-5 sliced mushrooms
- 1 cup chicken stock
- 1 teaspoon minced garlic
- Salt to taste

Directions :

1. Add all the ingredients into your pressure cooker and stir.
2. Lock the lid.
3. Press "manual" and cook for 12 minutes.
4. When time is up, hit "cancel" and quick-release.
5. Serve with more salt if needed.

Nutritional Info (¼ recipe per serving):
Total calories: 38 Protein: 3 Carbs: 4 Fat: 0 Fiber: 6

Vegan Apple Spice Oats

Serves : 2
Time : 9 minutes (4 minutes cook time, 5 minutes natural pressure release)

Ingredients :

- 1 ½ cups almond milk
- 1 peeled and chopped apple
- ½ cup steel-cut oats
- 1 teaspoon ground cinnamon
- Dash of nutmeg

Directions :

1. Put everything in your pressure cooker and seal the lid.
2. Hit "manual" and cook for just 4 minutes.

3. When time is up, hit "cancel" and wait for a natural pressure release.
4. Stir and serve!

Nutritional Info (½ recipe per serving):
Total calories: 198 Protein: 5 Carbs: 39 Fat: 4 Fiber: 5

Blueberry-Buckwheat Porridge

Serves : 3-4
Time : 15 minutes (5 minutes cook time, 10 minutes natural release)

Ingredients :
- 3 cups almond milk
- 1 cup buckwheat groats
- 1 cup fresh blueberries
- 1 teaspoon cinnamon
- Maple syrup to taste

Directions :
1. Rinse buckwheat before putting into your pressure cooker.
2. Pour in milk and blueberries.
3. Seal the lid.
4. Hit "manual" and adjust time to just 5 minutes.
5. When the timer beeps, hit "cancel" and wait for a natural pressure release.
6. Stir in maple syrup and cinnamon before serving.

Nutritional Info (¼ recipe per serving):
Total calories: 185 Protein: 6 Carbs: 37 Fat: 3 Fiber: 5

Vegan Italian Tofu Scramble

Serves : 4
Time : 4 minutes

Ingredients :
- 1 block of extra firm tofu
- 1 can Italian-style diced tomatoes
- ¼ cup veggie broth
- 2 tablespoons jarred banana pepper rings
- 1 tablespoon Italian seasoning

Directions :
1. Crumble the tofu in your pressure cooker, and pour over broth, banana peppers, can of diced tomatoes, and Italian seasoning.

2. Mix well and seal the lid.
3. Hit "manual" and adjust cook time to 4 minutes.
4. When the timer beeps, hit "cancel" and quick-release the pressure.
5. Stir and serve!

Nutritional Info (¼ recipe per serving):
Total calories: 137 Protein: 11 Carbs: 9 Fat: 6 Fiber: 3.7

Lentil + Potato Soup

Serves : 8

Time : 30 minutes (10 minutes prep time, 20 minutes cook time)

Ingredients :
- 8 cups of veggie broth
- 2 cups uncooked brown lentils
- 2 big Yukon gold potatoes
- 2 carrots
- 2 tablespoons garam masala

Directions :
1. Rinse the lentils, throwing out any hard shriveled ones.
2. Pour broth into your pressure cooker and hit "sauté"
3. Prepare your veggies by slicing and peeling the carrots, and cubing the potatoes.
4. By now, the broth should be hot.
5. Add lentils, carrots, and potatoes.
6. Seal the lid.
7. Hit "manual" and adjust time to 10 minutes.
8. When time is up, hit "cancel" and wait 5 minutes before quick-releasing the pressure.
9. The potatoes and lentils should be fork-tender. If not, hit "sauté" again and simmer till finished.
10. Sprinkle in your garam masala and serve.

Nutritional Info (⅛ recipe per serving):
Total calories: 126 Protein: 8 Carbs: 32 Fat: 0 Fiber: 14.7

Spiced-Carrot Chilled Soup

Serves : 4-6

Time : 1 hour, 40 minutes (30 minutes cook time, 10 minutes blend time, 1 hour chill time)

Ingredients:
- 2 pounds trimmed, peeled, and chopped carrots
- 3 tablespoons olive oil
- Salt to taste

- Dukkah to taste
- Water as needed

Directions:
1. Put carrots in your pressure cooker with ½ cup of water.
2. Seal the lid.
3. Hit "manual" and adjust time to 30 minutes.
4. When time is up, hit "cancel" and quick-release.
5. Remove carrots and blend with olive oil until smooth.
6. Pour soup through a sieve to get a really smooth texture.
7. Add water if necessary to get the right consistency.
8. Add salt to taste before storing in the fridge until chill.
9. Before serving, whisk and sprinkle on dukkah.

Nutritional Info (¼ soup per serving):
Total calories: 159 Protein: 2 Fat: 12 Carbs: 15 Fiber: 4

Spiced Cauliflower Rice

Serves : 4

Time : 12 minutes (5 minutes prep time, 2 minutes cook time, 5 minutes toast time)

Ingredients :
- 1 large head of cauliflower
- 1 cup water
- 1 lime
- 2 tablespoons olive oil
- ½ teaspoon turmeric

Directions :
1. Wash and chop the cauliflower into small pieces, throwing out the leaves.
2. Pour 1 cup of water into the pressure cooker.
3. Put cauliflower into the steamer basket and put into pot.
4. Seal the lid.
5. Hit "manual" and cook for just 2 minutes.
6. When the timer beeps, hit "cancel" and quick-release the pressure.
7. Remove the cauliflower and discard the water.
8. Pour 2 tablespoons of oil into the cooker and press "sautè."
9. When the oil is hot, add cauliflower and smash with a potato masher, turning in the oil.
10. When toasty, you can move to a food processor to get a real rice texture if you want.
11. Before serving, season with turmeric and a squeeze of lime.

Nutritional Info (¼ recipe per serving):
Total calories: 115 Protein: 4 Carbs: 12 Fat: 7 Fiber: 3

Vegan Alfredo Sauce

Serves : 2-4
Time : 18 minutes (5 minutes prep time, 3 minutes cook time, 5 minutes natural pressure release, 5 minutes blend time)

Ingredients :

- 12-ounces cauliflower florets
- ½ cup water
- Almond milk if needed
- Garlic salt to taste
- Black pepper to taste

Directions :

1. Pour water into your pressure cooker.
2. Put cauliflower florets into your steamer basket and lower into cooker.
3. Seal the lid.
4. Hit "manual" and cook for 3 minutes.
5. When the timer beeps, hit "cancel" and wait for a natural pressure release.
6. Remove steamer basket and cool cauliflower for a few minutes.
7. Pulse cauliflower with pot liquid in a blender until very smooth.
8. If it isn't quite creamy enough, add a splash of almond milk.
9. Season with garlic salt and black pepper.

Nutritional Info (¼ recipe per serving):
Total calories: 39 Protein: 3 Carbs: 5 Fat: 0 Fiber: 1.7

Vegan Holiday Roast

Serves : 8
Time : 18 minutes (10 minutes prep time, 8 minutes cook time)

Ingredients :

- One Field Roast (like the Celebration Roast)
- 1 cup + 1 tablespoon veggie broth
- 4 garlic cloves
- 1 chopped onion
- Salt

Directions :

1. Hit "sauté" on your pressure cooker.
2. When hot, add the onion and cook until softened. If it starts to stick, pour in a tablespoon of broth.
3. Add garlic, and continue cooking until fragrant.

4. Add roast and pour in the broth.
5. Season with salt and seal the lid.
6. Hit "manual" and cook on LOW pressure for 8 minutes.
7. When the timer beeps, hit "cancel" and quick-release the pressure.
8. Serve hot!

Nutritional Info (⅛ recipe per serving):
Total calories: 147 Protein: 16 Carbs: 10 Fat: 4 Fiber: 1

Vegan Mashed Potatoes

Serves : 6

Time : 25 minutes (10 minutes prep time, 15 minutes cook time)

Ingredients :
- 4 pounds peeled and rinsed potatoes
- 1 ½ cups water
- ¼ cup almond milk (add as needed)
- 2 tablespoons Earth Balance olive oil
- 1 teaspoon salt

Directions :
1. Pour water in your pressure cooker and lower in the steamer basket with potatoes.
2. Seal the lid.
3. Hit "steam" and adjust time to 15 minutes.
4. When time is up, hit "cancel" and quick-release the pressure.
5. Blend potatoes with ¼ cup almond milk, olive oil, and salt.
6. As needed, add milk ¼ cup at a time.

Nutritional Info (⅙ recipe):
Total calories: 82 Protein: 2 Carbs: 12 Fat: 3 Fiber: 6.6

Mexican Casserole

Serves : 4

Time : 33 minutes (28 minutes cook time, 5 minutes warm time)

Ingredients :
- 5 cups water
- 2 cups uncooked brown rice
- 1 cup canned + drained black beans
- 6-ounces tomato paste
- Chili seasoning to taste

Directions :
1. Add all the ingredients (except beans) to your pressure cooker and seal the lid.
2. Hit "manual" and adjust time to 28 minutes.
3. When the timer beeps, hit "cancel" and quick-release.
4. Stir in beans to warm them through.
5. Serve!

Nutritional Info (¼ recipe):
Total calories: 322 Protein: 6 Carbs: 63 Fat: 2 Fiber: 9

Easy Seitan (Vegan Meat Substitute)

Makes : 1 pound
Time : 26 minutes (10 minutes prep time, 16 minutes cook time)

Ingredients :
- 1 ¾ cup vegan veggie broth
- 1 cup vital wheat gluten
- 3 tablespoons nutritional yeast
- 1 tablespoon smoked paprika
- 3 teaspoons seasoning of choice (Italian seasoning, Herbes de Provence, Jamaican jerk seasoning, etc.)

Directions :
1. Pour 1 cup of broth into the pressure cooker.
2. Mix the remaining ingredients together in a big bowl, forming a sticky ball.
3. Knead for two minutes or so.
4. Form into a sausage-shaped loaf and cut into slices with a sharp, wet knife.
5. Put seitan loaf in the pot, making sure it's just covered by broth.
6. Seal the lid.
7. Hit "manual" and adjust cook time to 16 minutes.
8. When the timer beeps, hit "cancel" and quick-release.
9. Serve as the meat substitute in any dish!

Nutritional Info (⅓ recipe)
Total calories: 195 Protein: 26 Carbs: 15 Fat: 2 Fiber: 1.6

Tapioca with Fresh Berries

Serves : 4
Time : 14 minutes (4 minutes cook time, 10 minutes natural pressure release)

Ingredients :
- 2 cups almond milk

- 2 cups fresh berries
- ½ cup small pearl tapioca
- ¼ cup organic sugar
- 1 teaspoon pure vanilla

Directions :
1. Rinse tapioca under cold water for half a minute.
2. Pour milk into the pressure cooker, and then add the tapioca.
3. Stir and seal the lid.
4. Hit "manual" and cook for 4 minutes.
5. When time is up, hit "cancel" and wait 10 minutes before quick-releasing leftover pressure.
6. Mix in sugar and vanilla.
7. To **Make** it a parfait, spoon 2 tablespoons of berries in a glass, followed by tapioca, and then berries, and so on.

Nutritional Info (¼ recipe)
Total calories: 180 Protein: 2 Carbs: 39 Fat: 2 Fiber: 1

Cranberry-Almond Quinoa

Serves : 4
Time : 10 minutes

Ingredients :
- 2 cups water
- 1 cup quinoa
- 1 cup dried cranberries
- ½ cup slivered almonds
- ¼ cup salted sunflower seeds

Directions :
1. Rinse quinoa before putting it in the pot with water.
2. Seal the lid.
3. Hit "manual" and adjust time to 10 minutes.
4. When time is up, turn off the cooker and quick-release.
5. Mix in sunflower seeds, almonds, and dried cranberries.

Nutritional Info (¼ recipe):
Total calories: 383 Protein: 8 Carbs: 66 Fat: 9 Fiber: 7.5

Sweet Thai Coconut Rice

Serves : 4
Time : About 23 minutes (3 minutes cook time, 10 minutes natural release, 5-10 minutes rest time)

Ingredients :

- 1 ½ cups water
- 1 cup Thai sweet rice
- ½ can full-fat coconut milk
- 2 tablespoons sugar
- Dash of salt

Directions :

1. Add water and rice into the cooker and seal the lid.
2. Hit "manual" and adjust time to 3 minutes.
3. When the timer beeps, hit "cancel" and wait 10 minutes before quick-releasing leftover pressure.
4. While the pressure descends, heat coconut milk, salt, and sugar in a saucepan.
5. When the sugar has dissolved, remove from heat.
6. Mix coconut milk mixture into your finished rice.
7. Put the pressure cooker lid back on and let the rice sit for 5-10 minutes.
8. Serve!

Nutritional Info (¼ recipe):

Total calories: 269 Protein: 4 Carbs: 47 Fat: 8 Fiber: 0

Coconut-Cream Chocolate Fondue

Serves : 2-4

Time : Less than 5 minutes

Ingredients :

- 2 cups water
- 3.5-ounces coconut cream
- 3.5-ounces chopped 70% dark bittersweet chocolate
- 1 teaspoon cane sugar

Directions :

1. Pour water into your pressure cooker and insert trivet.
2. In a pressure-cooker safe bowl, add chocolate, coconut cream, and sugar.
3. Put bowl on the trivet in the cooker and seal the lid.
4. Hit "manual" and cook for just 2 minutes.
5. When the timer beeps, hit "cancel" and quick-release.
6. Remove bowl, wearing oven mitts, and quickly whisk mixture until it becomes smooth.
7. Serve right away!

Nutritional Info (¼ recipe):

Total calories: 216 Protein: 1.8 Carbs: 11.7 Fat: 20.3 Fiber: 2.6

Potato Soup

Serves: 5-7

Time: 35 minutes (10 minutes prep time, 20 minutes cook time, 5 minutes blend time)

Ingredients:
- 5 pounds Yukon Gold potatoes
- 2 cups chicken broth (with salt)
- 2 cups water
- 1 cup chopped cooked bacon
- ½ cup cheddar cheese

Directions:
1. Scrub and dice potatoes, leaving the skin on.
2. Put potatoes in the pot with water and chicken broth.
3. Seal the lid.
4. Hit "manual" and adjust time to 20 minutes.
5. When time is up, hit "cancel" and quick-release the pressure.
6. Add ¾ cup of the bacon and mash or blend until you get the consistency you want.
7. Serve with cheese and the rest of the bacon on top!

Nutritional Info (⅕ recipe per serving):

Total calories: 453 Protein: 16 Carbs: 117 Fat: 7 Fiber: 10

White Chicken Chili

Serves: 8

Time: 1 hour, 33 minutes (58 minutes cook time, 30 minutes natural pressure release, 5 minutes simmer time)

Ingredients:
- 8 cups chicken broth
- 1 pound rinsed and dried Great Northern beans
- 4 cups cooked shredded chicken
- 2 cups salsa verde
- 2 tablespoons cumin

Directions:
1. Pour broth and beans into the pressure cooker.
2. Hit "manual" and adjust to 58 minutes.
3. When the timer beeps, hit "cancel" and wait for the pressure to come down naturally.
4. Open the lid and mix in chicken, salsa verde, and cumin.
5. Hit "sauté" and simmer for 5 minutes to blend the flavors.
6. Serve!

Nutritional Info (⅛ recipe per serving):

Total calories: 206 Protein: 17 Carbs: 41 Fat: 2 Fiber: 5.8

Chicken Congee

Serves : 7
Time : 1 hour, 5 minutes (5 minutes prep time, 30 minutes cook time, 20 minutes natural pressure release, 10 minutes simmer time)

Ingredients :
- 6 chicken drumsticks
- 7 cups water
- 1 cup Jasmine rice
- 1 tablespoon fresh ginger
- Salt to taste

Directions :
1. Rinse rice under cool water for a few minutes.
2. Pour rice, water, ginger, and drumsticks into the pressure cooker.
3. Seal the lid.
4. Hit "manual" and adjust time to 30 minutes.
5. When time is up, hit "cancel" and wait for a natural pressure release.
6. When safe, open the lid and hit "sauté."
7. Keep stirring while the congee thickens.
8. Season with salt.
9. Pull off the chicken with tongs, and throw away the bones.
10. Serve right away!

Nutritional Info (1/7 recipe per serving):
Total calories: 248 Protein: 20 Carbs: 21 Fat: 9 Fiber: 0

Hearty Chicken Stew

Serves : 6
Time : 25 minutes

Ingredients :
- 4 pounds chicken thighs
- 4 large peeled and chopped Yukon Gold potatoes
- 3 cups chopped beefsteak tomatoes
- 1 sliced onion
- Salt to taste

Directions :

1. Add all the ingredients into your pressure cooker and seal the lid.
2. Hit "manual" and cook for 25 minutes.
3. When the timer beeps, hit "cancel" and quick-release the pressure.
4. Stir, salt, and serve!

Nutritional Info (⅙ per serving):
Total calories: 773 Protein: 49 Carbs: 24 Fat: 53 Fiber: 1

Beef + Broccoli Soup

Serves : 6-8
Time : 29 minutes (5 minutes prep time, 24 minutes cook time)

Ingredients :
- 4 ¾ cups beef stock with salt
- 2 pounds frozen broccoli florets
- 2 pounds tri-tip beef
- 4 garlic cloves
- 1 cup cheddar cheese

Directions :
1. Turn your cooker to "sauté."
2. Add garlic and cook for a few minutes until golden and fragrant.
3. Scrape out the garlic, so it doesn't burn.
4. Put the beef in the cooker and brown for 5 minutes on each side.
5. Return garlic to the pot and pour in broth.
6. Seal the lid and hit "manual," cooking for 20 minutes.
7. When the timer beeps, hit "cancel" and quick-release the pressure.
8. Add broccoli and stir.
9. Seal the lid again.
10. Hit "manual" and adjust time to just 4 minutes.
11. When time is up, hit "cancel" and quick-release again.
12. Stir in cheese and serve!

Nutritional Info (⅙ recipe)
Total calories: 270 Protein: 37 Carbs: 13 Fat: 7.5 Fiber: 3

Split Asparagus Soup

Serves : 5
Time : 21-22 minutes (7 minutes prep time, 4-5 minutes cook time, 10 minutes cool time)

Ingredients :
- 2 pounds split (cut in half) asparagus

- 4 cups salted chicken broth
- 1 cup diced cooked ham
- 5 pressed garlic cloves
- 1 diced onion

Directions :

1. Turn your pressure cooker to "sauté."
2. Add onion and cook for 5 minutes until translucent and becoming golden.
3. Add chicken broth, ham, and garlic.
4. Simmer for 2-3 minutes.
5. Add asparagus and seal the lid.
6. Hit "Soup/Stew" and cook for 4-5 minutes.
7. When time is up, hit "cancel" and quick-release the pressure.
8. When safe to open the cooker, let it cool for 10 minutes or so before pureeing in a blender.
9. Serve!

Nutritional Info (⅕ recipe):
Total calories: 196 Protein: 17 Carbs: 18 Fat: 7 Fiber: 4

Apple Dumpling Cobbler

Serves : 5
Time : 12 minutes (5 minutes prep time, 7 minutes cook time)

Ingredients :

- 5 chopped + peeled medium-sized sweet apples
- 1 can of crescent rolls
- ½ cup + 2 tablespoons water
- 4 tablespoons chopped butter
- 1 teaspoon cinnamon

Directions :

1. Turn your pressure cooker to "sauté" and add apples.
2. If the apples aren't super juicy, pour in 2 tablespoons of water.
3. Cook and stir for 5 minutes or so until the apples have softened.
4. Hit "cancel" and pour in ½ cup of water.
5. Take your crescent rolls and cut into pieces, rolling them into balls.
6. Put crescent balls and pats of butter on top of the apples.
7. Seal the lid.
8. Hit "manual" and adjust time to 7 minutes.
9. When time is up, hit "cancel" and quick-release the pressure.
10. The crescent balls should be cooked through.
11. Serve hot with cinnamon on top!

Nutritional Info (⅕ recipe per serving):

Total calories: 321 Protein: 3 Carbs: 40 Fat: 17 Fiber: 3.5

Tapioca Pudding

Serves : 4-6

Time : 31 minutes + 3 hours chill time (3 minutes prep time, 8 minutes cook time, 15 minutes natural release time, 5 minutes rest time)

Ingredients :

- 1 ¼ cups vanilla almond milk
- 1 ½ cups water
- ⅓ cup cane sugar
- ⅓ cup seed tapioca pearls
- Sprinkle of cinnamon

Note: For a consistency more like porridge, add another ½ cup of almond milk.

Directions :

1. Pour 1 cup of water into the pressure cooker.
2. Rinse tapioca pearls and mix in a cooker-safe bowl with ½ cup water, sugar, milk, and the vanilla bean.
3. When the sugar is dissolved, put into the steamer basket and lower into cooker.
4. Seal the lid.
5. Hit "manual" and adjust time to 8 minutes.
6. When the timer beeps, hit "cancel" and wait for a natural pressure release.
7. Turn the valve, and if there's no pressure left, wait another 5 minutes before opening the lid.
8. Stir before either serving warm with cinnamon, or chilling in the fridge covered with saran wrap for at least 3 hours.

Nutritional Info (¼ recipe):

Total calories: 187 Protein: 2.5 Carbs: 39.6 Fat: 2.5 Fiber: .1

Peach Simple Syrup

Makes : About 1 cup

Time : 55 minutes (5 minutes cook time, 10 minutes natural release time, 30-4o minutes boil time)

Ingredients :

- 4 cups fresh chopped peaches
- 2 cups water
- 2 cups sugar

Directions :

1. Pour water and peaches into the pressure cooker.

2. Seal the lid.
3. Press "manual" and adjust time to 5 minutes.
4. When the timer beeps, turn off the cooker and wait for a natural pressure release.
5. When safe to open the lid, mash the peaches really well with a wooden spoon to get out all the sweet juices.
6. Strain pot contents into a bowl, and then pour bowl back into the cooker.
7. Hit "sauté" on the cooker and bring the pot to a boil.
8. Add sugar and keep boiling until the sugar is dissolved and liquid has reduced by ½ into a syrup.
9. Let the syrup cool to room-temperature before moving to glass jars, and storing for up to 2 weeks in the fridge.

Nutritional Info (1 tablespoon):
Total calories: 97 Protein: 0 Carbs: 28 Fat: 0 Fiber: 0

Lemon-Ruby Pears

Serves : 4

Time : 36 minutes + overnight (10 minutes prep time, 11 minutes cook time, 15 minutes cool time)

Ingredients :
- 4 ripe Bosc pears
- 3 cups grape juice
- 1 cup currant jelly
- 1 lemon
- ½ split vanilla bean

Directions :
1. Remove the core from the pears, but leave the top of the pear and stem intact.
2. Pour grape juice and jelly into the pressure cooker.
3. Hit "sauté" and heat until jelly melts.
4. Grate the lemon into the pot, and then squeeze in the juice, as well.
5. Toss in vanilla bean.
6. Cut out four squares of foil, to wrap your pears in.
7. Before wrapping, turn the pears in the cooker sauce.
8. Wrap pears in foil tightly and put in your steamer basket.
9. Insert basket into cooker.
10. Seal the lid.
11. Hit "manual" and adjust to 11 minutes.
12. When the timer beeps, hit "cancel" and quick-release the pressure.
13. Unwrap the pears, put in a baking dish, and pour over sauce.
14. Wait till pears are room temperature before storing them in the fridge overnight and then serve!

Nutritional Info (¼ recipe per serving):
Total calories: 414 Protein: 1 Carbs: 109 Fat: 0 Fiber: 5.5

Pear Sauce

Makes: 4-5 pints
Time: 19 minutes (5 minutes prep time, 4 minutes cook time, 10 minutes natural pressure release)

Ingredients:
- 10 cored skin-on pears
- 1 cup apple juice
- 2 teaspoons cinnamon
- 2 teaspoons lemon juice
- ½ teaspoon nutmeg

Directions:
1. Pour the pears, apple juice, lemon juice, and spices in the cooker.
2. Seal the lid.
3. Hit "manual" and cook for 4 minutes.
4. When the timer beeps, hit "cancel" and wait for a natural pressure release.
5. When the cooker is safe to open, puree pears till smooth.
6. Cool to room temperature before storing in glass jars and keeping in the fridge up to 5 days.

Nutritional Info (1 cup per recipe):
Total calories: 98 Protein: 1 Carbs: 26 Fat: 0 Fiber: 6

Fresh Raspberry Jam

Makes: 2 pints (64 tablespoons)
Time: About 25 minutes (3 minutes prep time, 2 minutes cook time, 10 minutes natural pressure release, 10 minutes 'gel' time)

Ingredients:
- 2 pounds fresh raspberries
- 1 ½ pounds light honey

Directions:
1. Put raspberries and honey into the pressure cooker.
2. Turn your pot to the "keep warm" setting and stir for just 3 minutes, so the honey can melt and become a smooth liquid.
3. Hit "sauté" and let the mixture come to a boil.
4. Seal the lid right away once it's boiling.
5. Press "manual" and adjust time to just 2 minutes.
6. When time is up, hit "cancel" and wait 10 minutes for a natural pressure release.
7. Remove the lid and hit "sauté" so the jam boils. You want it to come to 220-degrees. This should take about 10 minutes.
8. When that temperature has been reached, hit "cancel."

9. Pour jam into clean half-pint jars and tighten the lids.
10. Jam lasts in the fridge for 4-6 weeks.

Nutritional Info (1 tablespoon per serving):
Total calories: 181 Protein: 1 Carbs: 44 Fat: 0 Fiber: 0

Granola-Stuffed Peaches

Serves : 5
Time : 8 minutes (5 minutes prep time, 3 minutes cook time)

Ingredients :
- 5 large ripe peaches
- 1 cup soft granola (like Bear Naked)
- 1 cup water
- 2 tablespoons salted butter
- 2 tablespoons brown sugar

Directions :
1. Slice ¼ inch from the top of the peaches.
2. With a sharp knife, carefully remove the pits, creating a hollow, so the peaches still have a ½-inch "shell."
3. In a bowl, melt the butter and mix with granola.
4. Fill peaches with buttery granola.
5. Sprinkle brown sugar evenly on peaches.
6. Put stuffed peaches in your steamer basket.
7. Pour 1 cup of water into your pressure cooker, then lower in the basket.
8. Seal the lid.
9. Hit "manual" and cook for just 3 minutes.
10. When time is up, hit "cancel" and quick-release. Peaches should be soft, with the brown sugar caramelized.
11. Serve!

Nutritional Info (1 stuffed peach per serving):
Total calories: 219 Protein: 6 Carbs: 30 Fat: 9 Fiber: 1

Apple Cider

Makes : 6 quarts
Time : 25 minutes (15 minutes cook time, 10 minutes natural pressure release)

Ingredients :
- 10 apples (a mixture of a few green ones with sweet)
- 2 cinnamon sticks
- 1 orange

- 2 teaspoons cloves
- Water

Directions :

1. Chop apples and orange.
2. Put in the pressure cooker with spices.
3. Pour in just enough water to cover everything and seal the lid.
4. Hit "manual" and adjust time to 10 minutes.
5. When time is up, hit "cancel" and quick-release.
6. Mash up the fruit a little to release the juices.
7. Seal the lid again and cook for another 5 minutes on high pressure.
8. When time is up, hit "cancel" and wait for a natural pressure release.
9. Strain the cider. If you want, you can add some of the apples back into the pot.
10. Cool before refrigerating, if you aren't drinking it right away, or serve hot!

Nutritional Info (½ quart per serving):

Total calories: 49 Protein: 1 Carbs: 20 Fat: 0 Fiber: 0

Orange-Glazed Poached Pears

Serves : 4

Time : 23 minutes (5 minutes prep time, 7 minutes cook time, 5 minutes natural pressure release, 6 minutes sauce time)

Ingredients :

- 4 ripe pears
- 1 cup orange juice
- ⅓ cup sugar
- 1 cinnamon stick
- 5 teaspoons apple pie spice

Directions :

1. Peel the pears, leaving the stem intact.
2. Pour orange juice, apple pie spice, and cinnamon stick into the pressure cooker.
3. Put pears in the steamer basket and insert into cooker.
4. Seal the lid.
5. Hit "manual" and cook for 7 minutes.
6. When the timer beeps, hit "cancel" and wait 5 minutes, then quick-release the pressure.
7. Remove the steamer basket with pears, and the cinnamon stick.
8. Hit "sauté" on your cooker and add ⅓ cup sugar into the cooking liquid.
9. Stir until sugar has dissolved and liquid has thickened into a sauce.
10. Pour sauce over pears.

Nutritional Info (¼ recipe):

Total calories: 188 Protein: 1 Carbs: 49 Fat: 0 Fiber: 6

Pumpkin Butter

Serves : 8

Time : 3 hours, 3 minutes (3 minutes cook time, 3 hours cool time)

Ingredients :

- Two cans of pure pumpkin
- 1 cup apple juice
- ½ cup white sugar
- 4 teaspoons pumpkin pie spice
- 1 teaspoon ground ginger

Directions :

1. Put all the ingredients in your pressure cooker and seal the lid.
2. Hit "manual" and cook for 3 minutes.
3. When time is up, hit "cancel" and quick-release.
4. Cool for 3 hours before storing in jars in the fridge.

Nutritional Info (⅛ recipe per serving):
Total calories: 95 Protein: 7 Carbs: 24 Fat: 1 Fiber: 2.6

Chai Rice Pudding

Serves : 5

Time : 36 minutes (10 minutes prep time, 16 minutes cook time, 10 minutes natural pressure release)

Ingredients :

- 6 cups whole milk
- 1 cup Arborio rice
- ⅔ cup sugar
- ¼ cup chopped crystallized ginger
- 3 teaspoons chai spice blend

Directions :

1. Mix milk, rice, and sugar in your pressure cooker.
2. Hit "sauté" and stir until boiling.
3. Seal the lid.
4. Hit "manual" and adjust time to 16 minutes on LOW pressure.
5. When the timer beeps, turn off the cooker and wait 10 minutes, then quick-release.
6. Stir in ginger and chai spice.
7. Serve warm or store in the fridge until cold.

Nutritional Info (⅕ recipe per serving):

Peach Cobbler

Serves : 8
Time : 35 minutes (5 minutes prep time, 20 minutes cook time, 10 minutes natural pressure release)

Ingredients :
- One 16.5-ounce white cake mix
- 6 peeled and sliced peaches
- 1 cup water
- ½ cup softened butter

Directions :
1. Lay peaches in the bottom of a pressure-safe baking dish.
2. In a bowl, cut butter into cake mix with a fork, so it has a crumbly texture.
3. Sprinkle this mix over peaches.
4. Put a paper towel on top of the dish.
5. Pour water into your pressure cooker and lower in trivet.
6. Put the dish on trivet and seal the lid.
7. Hit "manual" and adjust time to 20 minutes.
8. When time is up, hit "cancel" and wait for a natural pressure release.
9. Serve hot!

Nutritional Info (⅛ recipe per serving):
Total calories: 426 Protein: 12 Carbs: 80 Fat: 10 Fiber: 1.2

Almond Fudge Drop Candy

Makes : 30 pieces
Time : 25 minutes (5 minutes cook time, 20 minutes freeze time)

Ingredients :
- One 14-ounce can of sweetened condensed milk
- 12-ounces semi-sweet chocolate chips
- 2 cups water
- 1 cup chopped almonds
- 1 teaspoon vanilla

Directions :
1. Add milk and chocolate chips into a cooker-safe bowl and wrap in foil.
2. Pour water into your pressure cooker and add the trivet.
3. Put bowl on top of trivet and seal the lid.
4. Hit "manual" and adjust time to 5 minutes.

202

Homemade Vanilla Yogurt

Makes: 2-3 quarts
Time: About 12 hours

Ingredients:
- 1 gallon 2% milk
- ½ cup yogurt starter (plain yogurt) with active cultures
- 3 tablespoons powdered milk
- 2 tablespoons pure vanilla extract
- 1 vanilla bean

Directions:
1. Pour all the milk into your pressure cooker.
2. Add the powdered milk and stir well.
3. Secure the lid on the pressure cooker and plug it in.
4. Select the "yogurt" setting.
5. Keep pressing "adjust" until you reach "boil."
6. The boil takes about an hour, after which you unplug the cooker and carefully remove the lid to let the milk cool to 115-degrees F.
7. When that temperature is reached, add the yogurt starter and vanilla extract.
8. Lock the lid and select "yogurt."
9. After 8 hours, pour the yogurt into nut milk bags (which you can find on Amazon) and strain for ½-1 hour.
10. When time is up, put the yogurt back into the cooker and add the seeds from the vanilla bean. Mix thoroughly.
11. Put the yogurt into Mason jars and refrigerate overnight.
12. When you're ready to enjoy, add any sweeteners, fruit, granola, or whatever else you like with your yogurt!

Nutritional Info (1/10 of recipe): Total calories - 218 Protein - 14 Carbs - 20 Fiber - 0 Fat - 8

Steel-Cut Oats

Serves: 3-4
Time: 6-7 minutes

Ingredients:
- 2 cups of water

203

Easy Soft-Boiled Egg Breakfast

Serves: 4
Time: 4 minutes

Ingredients:
- 4 eggs
- Two toasted English muffins
- Salt and pepper to taste

Directions:
1. Pour 1 cup of water into the pressure cooker and insert the steamer basket.
2. Put four canning lids into the basket before placing the eggs on top of them, so they stay separated.
3. Secure the lid.
4. Press the "steam" setting and choose 4 minutes.
5. When ready, quick-release the steam valve.
6. Take out the eggs using tongs and dunk them into a bowl of cold water.
7. Wait 1-2 minutes.
8. Peel and serve with one egg per half of a toasted English muffin. Season with salt and pepper.

Nutritional Info (1 egg + ½ English muffin): Total calories - 139 Protein - 9 Carbs - 14 Fiber - 2 Fat - 6

Maple-Syrup Quinoa

Serves: 4-5
Time: 11 minutes

Ingredients:
- 2 ¼ cups water
- 1 ½ cups uncooked, rinsed quinoa
- 2 tablespoons maple syrup
- ½ teaspoon vanilla

204

French Toast Bake

Serves: 4
Time: 35 minutes

Ingredients:

- 3 big, beaten eggs
- 3 cups stale cinnamon-raisin bread, cut into cubes
- 1 ½ cups water
- 1 cup whole milk
- 2 tablespoons maple syrup
- 1 teaspoon butter
- 1 teaspoon sugar
- 1 teaspoon pure vanilla extract

Directions:

1. Pour the water into your pressure cooker and lower in the steam rack.
2. Grease a 6-7 inch soufflé pan.
3. In a bowl, mix milk, vanilla, maple syrup, and eggs.
4. Add the bread cubes and let them soak for 5 minutes.
5. Pour into the pan, making sure the bread is totally submerged.
6. Set in the pressure cooker.
7. Hit "Manual" and adjust the time to 15 minutes on "high pressure."
8. Quick-release the pressure when time is up.
9. Sprinkle the top with sugar and broil in the oven for 3 minutes.

Nutritional Info (¼ of recipe): Total calories - 183 Protein - 8 Carbs - 21 Fiber - 0 Fat - 3

Cheesy Sausage Frittata

Serves: 2-4
Time: 40 minutes

Ingredients:

- 1 ½ cups water
- 4 beaten eggs
- ½ cup cooked ground sausage
- ¼ cup grated sharp cheddar
- 2 tablespoons sour cream
- 1 tablespoon butter
- Salt to taste
- Black pepper to taste

Directions:
1. Pour water into the pressure cooker and lower in the steamer rack.
2. Grease a 6-7 inch soufflé dish.
3. In a bowl, whisk the eggs and sour cream together.
4. Add cheese, sausage, salt, and pepper. Stir.
5. Pour into the dish and wrap tightly with foil all over.
6. Lower into the steam rack and close the pot lid.
7. Hit "Manual," and then 17 minutes on "low pressure."
8. Quick-release the pressure.
9. Serve hot!

Nutritional Info: Total calories - 282 Protein - 16 Carbs - 1 Fiber - 0 Fat - 12

Creamy Strawberry Oatmeal

Serves: 1
Time: 20 minutes

Ingredients:
- ⅔ cup whole milk
- ⅓ cup rolled oats
- 2 tablespoons strawberries
- ½ teaspoon sugar
- 1 pinch of salt

Directions:
1. Pour 2 cups of water into the pressure cooker and lower in the steamer basket.
2. Mix the milk, strawberries, oats, and salt in a small bowl.
3. Put the bowl into the pressure cooker and lock the lid.
4. Hit "Manual" and then 10 minutes on "high pressure."
5. When the timer goes off, hit "Cancel" and wait for the pressure to go down.
6. When the pressure is gone, open the lid and stir.
7. Serve with sugar and a sprinkle of cinnamon, if desired.

Nutritional Info: Total calories - 207 Protein - 8.6 Carbs - 28.3 Fiber - 2.8 Fat - 7.3

Creamy Banana Oatmeal

Serves: 4

Time: 18 minutes

Ingredients:
- 2 ¼ cups water
- ½ cup steel-cut oats
- 2 very ripe, chopped bananas
- ½ cup packed light brown sugar
- ¼ cup half-and-half
- 2 teaspoons vanilla extract
- ½ teaspoon ground cinnamon
- ¼ teaspoon salt

Directions:
1. Mix oats, bananas, brown sugar, vanilla, salt, and cinnamon with 2 ¼ cups and pour into the pressure cooker.
2. When the brown sugar dissolves, close the lid.
3. Select "Manual" and then 18 minutes at "high pressure."
4. When time is up, hit "Cancel" and wait for the pressure to come down on its own.
5. When time is up, carefully open the cooker.
6. Stir in the half-and-half, and enjoy!

Nutritional Info (¼ recipe): Total calories - 130 Protein - 3 Carbs - 26 Fiber - 2 Fat - 3

Ham, Apple, and Grits Casserole

Serves: 4-6
Time: 22 minutes

Ingredients:
- 8 ounces of chopped Canadian bacon
- 4 sliced scallions
- 2 big, beaten eggs
- ¾ cups instant grits
- ½ cup shredded cheddar cheese
- 1 peeled and chopped green apple
- 2 tablespoons butter
- 1 teaspoon dried thyme

Directions:
1. Turn your pressure cooker to "Sauté" to melt the butter.
2. Add the ham, stirring, and cook for 1 minute.
3. Toss in the scallions, thyme, and apples.
4. Stir and cook for another minute.
5. Move everything to a bowl and set aside.
6. Hit "Cancel" on the cooker.
7. Wipe down the inside of the pot with a paper towel.
8. Turn "Sauté" back on and pour in 3 cups of water.

Savory Breakfast Porridge

Serves: 4
Time: 1 hour

Ingredients

- 2 cups chicken broth
- 2 cups water
- 4 eggs
- 4 chopped scallions
- ½ cup rinsed and drained white rice
- 1 tablespoon sugar
- 1 tablespoon olive oil
- 2 teaspoons soy sauce
- ½ teaspoon salt
- Black pepper

Directions:

1. Pour water, broth, sugar, salt, and rice into the pressure cooker.
2. Close the lid.
3. Hit "Porridge" and 30 minutes on "high pressure."
4. While that cooks, heat oil in a saucepan.
5. Crack in the eggs one at a time, so they aren't touching each other.
6. Cook until the whites become crispy on the edges, but the yolks are still runny.
7. Sprinkle on salt and pepper.
8. When the pressure cooker timer goes off, hit "Cancel" and wait for the pressure to go down on its own.
9. If the porridge isn't thick enough, hit "Sauté" and cook uncovered for 5-10 minutes.
10. Serve with scallions, soy sauce, and an egg per bowl.

Nutritional Info (¼ recipe): Total calories - 214 Protein - 10 Carbs - 24 Fiber - 1 Fat - 2

Sticky Sesame Chicken

Serves: 4
Time: About 30 minutes

Ingredients:
- 6 boneless chicken thigh fillets
- 4 peeled and crushed garlic cloves
- 5 tablespoons hoisin sauce
- 5 tablespoons sweet chili sauce
- ½ cup chicken stock
- 1 chunk of peeled, grated fresh ginger
- 1 ½ tablespoons sesame seeds
- 1 tablespoon rice vinegar
- 1 tablespoon soy sauce

Directions:
1. Spread chicken thighs flat and place them into the pressure cooker.
2. Whisk garlic, ginger, chili sauce, hoisin, vinegar, sesame seeds, broth, and soy sauce into a sauce.
3. Pour over chicken and stir.

Blueberry Croissant Pudding

Serves: 7
Time: 40 minutes

Ingredients:
- 3 big, cut-up croissants
- One 8-ounce package softened cream cheese
- 2 eggs
- 1 cup blueberries
- 1 cup milk
- ⅔ cup sugar
- 1 teaspoon vanilla

Directions:
1. Put the croissants and blueberries in a heat-safe bowl you know fits in the pressure cooker.
2. In a separate bowl, mix cream cheese, eggs, sugar, and vanilla.
3. Add milk and mix again.
4. Pour over the croissants and rest for 20 minutes.
5. When ready, put the bowl in the cooker and lock the lid.
6. Press "Manual," and then "high pressure" for 20 minutes.
7. When time is up, hit "Cancel" and then quick-release.
8. Serve!

Nutritional Info (1/7 recipe): Total calories - 263 Protein - 8 Carbs - 40 Fiber - 2 Fat - 18

4. Select "Manual," and then 15 minutes on "high pressure."
5. When time is up, hit "Cancel" and wait for a natural pressure release.
6. When all the pressure is gone, open up the cooker and serve the chicken with rice.

Nutritional Info (¼ serving): Total calories - 428 Protein - 30 Carbs - 52.9 Fiber - 1 Fat - 9

Printed in Great Britain
by Amazon